W9-CMS-692

Like Lin Carter's other splendid "look behind" volumes (on J. R. R. Tolkien and H. P. Lovecraft), this book examines the background and creation of the imaginary worlds of some of the most famous writers to appear in the field of Adult Fantasy, of which Ballantine Books is the leading publisher.

IMAGINARY WORLDS is a book about fantasy, about the men who write it, and how it is written. It is a joyful excursion by a man who himself loves fantasy, into the origins and the magicks of such writers as Dunsany, Eddison, Cabell: it examines the rise of fantasy in the American pulp magazines and delights in the sturdy health of "sword and sorcery": it looks with pleasure on the works of some modern masters and knowledgeably explores the techniques of world-making.

It is, in short, a happy exploration of worlds, and men, and writers, and writings, by an author whose enthusiasm for his subject is boundless— and is thus a joyous guide for fantasy lovers everywhere.

IMAGINARY WORLDS

The Art of Fantasy

Lin Carter

BALLANTINE BOOKS • NEW YORK

SBN 345-03309-4-125

First Printing: June, 1973

Printed in the United States of America

Cover art by Gervasio Gallardo

BALLANTINE BOOKS, INC.
201 E. 50th Street, New York, N. Y. 10022

Dedication

I enjoy dedicating my books to my friends and fellow-writers, and I usually strive to match the book to the man. Since this book is a history of fantasy, it seems to me fitting that I dedicate it to the fantasy writers of tomorrow, to those men and women not yet born, whom I shall never know, whose books I shall not live to read, but whose dreams I have shared and whose visions would not be strange or alien to me.

—*Lin Carter*

Contents

Introduction

The Empire of Imagination

Each change of many-colour'd life he drew,
Exhausted worlds, and then imagin'd new.
—Samuel Johnson: "Prologue . . ."[1]

WHY do we who love fantasy read it with such delight and gusto, returning to it again and again over the years as to a source of entertainment that is inexhaustible?

Our mania—and it is virtually that—is shared by few. Most people, an overwhelming majority of the populace in fact, read nothing at all beyond their newspapers, a few glossy magazines, and an occasional fat best seller. Even those who do read books seldom pursue one genre with the devotion and intensity of our passion. I cannot believe that devotees of the whodunit, the western, or the "ladies' Gothic romance" read and collect books in their chosen province of literature as assiduously as do we.

Frankly, I have no answer to this question; nor am I even going to attempt to answer it. In fact, I can hardly understand the sort of mind that would require an answer to such a question. We read fantasy because we love it; we love it because we find it a source of the marvel and mystery and wonder and joy that we can find nowhere else.

We return again and again to our favorite writers, (and to individual books,) because the magic of their imagination is ever fresh and new and exciting to us. Some of us may prefer Lord Dunsany or James Branch Cabell, T. H. White or J. R. R. Tolkien; others may like H. P. Lovecraft or A. Merritt, Robert E. Howard

1

or Clark Ashton Smith, C. S. Lewis or Edgar Rice Burroughs. But never mind slight differences in taste; we understand each other: our common enthusiasm is —*fantasy*. Many of us do not even differentiate between adult and juvenile fantasy—indeed, a very thin line divides the two.

Are we incurable romantics—idle dreamers, bored by the everyday world around us—seeking escape from the sordid realities we find repellent? Or are we men and women whose esthetic or intellectual development was somehow arrested in childhood, so that we still yearn for the stuff of dreams, the sort of thing we found in fairy-tales and children's books when we were young? The charge of "escapist reading" is most often leveled against fantasy and science fiction, by those who have forgotten or overlooked the simple fact that virtually *all* reading—all music and poetry and art and drama and philosophy, for that matter—is a temporary escape from what is around us.

Why do I read fantasy? I really don't know; I really don't care. All I know is that something within me wakes and thrills and responds to phrases like "the splendid city of Celephais, in the Valley of Ooth-Nargai, beyond the Tanarian Hills," where galleys "sail up the river Oukranos past the gilded spires of Thran," and "elephant caravans tramp through perfumed jungles in Kled," where "forgotten palaces with veined ivory columns sleep lovely and unbroken under the moon."[2]

Such phrases, such sequences of gorgeous imagery, touch something that is within most of us, really. I believe that a hunger for the fabulous is common to the human condition. To be a human being is to possess the capacity to dream; and few of us are so degraded or brutalized that we have no thirst for miracles. But try the experiment yourself—does something stir within you when you read of "Ilek-Vad, that fabulous town of turrets atop the hollow cliffs of glass that overlook the twilight sea wherein the finned and bearded Gnorri build their singular labyrinths," or of "Zamora, with its dark-haired women and towers of spider-haunted mystery," or "Stygia, with its shadow-guarded tombs"?[3]

If so, then you already understand what I am talking about; if not, then this book is probably not for you. But whatever it is that sings within me to such imagery, I am happy that it is there.

THIS is a book about fantasy, about the men who write it and how it is written. Oddly enough, no one has ever written a book on fantasy before. The neighboring provinces of imaginative literature have not suffered the same neglect, for excellent surveys of science fiction and supernatural literature continue to appear. It is fantasy alone—the source from which both sister genres originally sprang—which has so curiously and so persistently been ignored by the historians of literature.

This is not to say that books have not been written about the more important authors of fantasy. There are critical studies of Cabell and Tolkien, bibliographies of Merritt and Smith, formal biographies of Burroughs and White, informal memoirs of Dunsany and Lovecraft. (For a listing of such, see *Bibliography I: General References,* at the end of this book.) But these books do not cover sufficient ground: of necessity, such works limit their scope to the achievements and the career of one writer—and where they do touch upon the genre to which the writer contributed, it is generally to discuss only those authors who influenced him, and those whom he in turn influenced. What is needed, obviously, is a book that focuses not merely upon this or that writer in the genre, but upon the genre itself: the tradition from which evolved writers such as those I have already mentioned and to which they contributed so much.

This neglect of what is, after all, a major province of narrative literature seems to me inexplicable. I can only assume that the historians of literature have neglected fantasy because it does not seem "serious" enough to be worthy of study by the academic mind. When serious scholars think of fantasy they think of mythol-

ogy, of fairy tales—the sort of thing long since rel-
egated to the nursery. Fantasy, they seem to believe,
does not come to grips with the human condition, as
does the modern psychological novel; it very often tends
to "merely" entertain, rather than probing into in-
justice as does the novel of social realism.

Of course, as you and I know, this is nonsense.
Fantasy is a very large and rich and important province
of fiction, and a very ancient one. If I wished, I could
cite a considerable body of evidence which suggests that
fantasy is no less than *the original form of narrative
literature* itself. I will go into this theme a bit further
on, so I will not pause to develop it here. But it is
certain that those academicians who neglect fantastic
literature to analyze the more "serious" schools of fiction, such as the novel of realism—those who win their
reputations as serious scholars by learned dissertations
on the sources of Hemingway or Dos Passos—are
passing over a distinguished and venerable province of
letters for a comparatively recent, and perhaps transient,
innovation.

After all, the realist school looks to Gustave Flaubert
as its first master, and to *Madame Bovary* as the first
successful attempt at a scrupulously accurate portraiture
of everyday life. And *Madame Bovary* was only published in 1856. Thus, the novel of social realism is a
very modern development; but then, so is the novel
itself, which only emerged as a distinctly individual art
form about two hundred years ago, with Daniel Defoe,
Samuel Richardson, and Henry Fielding. It amuses me
to recall that the very earliest beginnings of the European novel—with Rabelais' *Gargantua and Pantagruel*
(1535), say, or with Cervantes' *Don Quixote* (1605,
1615)—were a revolt against fantasy, which then
dominated literature in the form of the romance. Both
Gargantua and the great *Quixote* are literary lampoons,
caricaturing the ridiculous excesses of the fantastic
extravaganzas written in imitation of *Amadis of Gaul*
and *Palmerin of England* and the like, which are prime
examples of the heroic fantasy. Yes, fantasy was going

strong centuries before this emergence of the novel, and fantasy was the theme of the old prose romances which the novel rose to replace, even as it was, still earlier, with the literature of epic, saga and myth which flourished before the birth of romance.

Considering the antiquity of the genre, its neglect by the scholars and literary historians becomes all the more lamentable. It is a neglect which I hope, however modestly, to correct.

Now—what exactly do I mean by "fantasy"? Webster defines it as "imagination or fancy; a product of imagination, specifically, an image; mood, especially a whimsical or capricious one." Well, so much for the boys who write the dictionaries! We shall let them remain in blissful ignorance of an entire genre of fiction.

Aficionados will agree that the term "fantasy" covers a wide variety of different kinds of stories. Careless reviewers of books and movies use the term so loosely as to include everything from *Dracula* to *2001: A Space Odyssey,* and oddly enough, they are not too far off. In the broadest possible sense, fantasy is any kind of fiction that is fantastic, that is, fiction that is not realistic. Since neither ghost stories nor space operas are true to everyday life, they come under the term "fantasy."

What actually happened is that, way back when, both the tale of supernatural horror and what then passed as science fiction were part of the broad field of fantastic literature. Both, however, managed to isolate and concentrate their individual natures and became polarized, breaking away from the central fantasy tradition and evolving into sub-genre all their own. The supernatural tale did this quite early, about 1765 or so, with the publication of Horace Walpole's *The Castle of Otranto,* which founded and was the first great success of the school of the Gothic novel. As for science fiction, it began to emerge as a separate genre of fantastic literature about a century ago—say, sometime after

1862, the year in which Jules Verne made his first great popular success with a novel called *Cinq semaines en ballon* (*Five Weeks in a Balloon*, that is). This novel was the first of a genre originally called, *à la* Verne, *voyages imaginaires*—a genre which became known as "the scientific romance" during the *floruit* of H. G. Wells, and which evolved with time into what Hugo Gernsback called "science fiction."[4]

But what I mean by the word "fantasy" is a narrative of marvels that belong to neither the scientific nor the supernatural. The essence of this sort of story can be summed up in one word: *magic*. A fantasy is a book or story, then, in which magic really works—not a fairy-tale, not a story written for children, like *Peter Pan* or *The Wizard of Oz*, but a work of fiction written for adults—a story which challenges the mind, which sets it *working*.

Now there are all kinds of stories in this broad category. Before the Victorian romancer William Morris entered the picture, there were oodles of books written that might be described as fantasy—novels that were mythological, or Arthurian, or theosophical, or Rosicrucian, or occult, or alchemical, or mystical, or whatever. To widen our discussion to include all of these varieties would lengthen this book into several volumes, so let us narrow our scope a bit.

In the real world in which we live, magic does not work. A fantasy, by the above definition, is a story set in a milieu that includes magic as an integral part of the natural world. Since we have yet to find a place among the laws of physics for magic powers, such tales imply —in fact, such tales actually require—the construction of an *invented* milieu. To compose a fantasy, an author must construct a literary universe in which magic works; hence the title of this study, *Imaginary Worlds*—for that is precisely what fantasy is all about.

The invented milieu, of course, can be used for things other than fantasy. *The Prisoner of Zenda,* although set in an imaginary country called "Graustark," is *not* a fantasy (although it could be, if there were any Graustarkian magicians in the story). The difference lies in the fact that *The Prisoner of Zenda* is not a narrative of marvels but an adventure story. There are many similar examples in literature of the invented milieu used for purposes other than fantasy, such as Gilbert and Sullivan's imaginary country "Barataria" in *The Gondoliers*, and William Faulkner's "Yoknapatawpha County" in Mississippi, which was introduced in the novel *Sartoris* (1929), but I trust that you understand the difference between such usages and fantasy itself—magic works neither in Faulkner's invented Mississippi county, nor in the imaginary setting of the comic opera.

So we focus upon one particular kind of fantasy, which might be called the *mainstream,* the central tradition, of fantasy as a whole. Some critics prefer the term "pure fantasy" or "heroic fantasy" to my term, "the imaginary world" story, but we are all talking about the same thing: the story laid in settings completely made up by the author, whether such settings consist of a single country or an entire world, or even an imaginary period of the remote past or the distant future.

To further complicate this problem of defining our terms, there are those stories set in imaginary settings *not* invented by their author, but borrowed by him or her from another source—T. H. White, for example, who lifted the milieu for *The Once and Future King* from Arthurian literature; or Fletcher Pratt and L. Sprague de Camp, who borrowed the scenery of *The Castle of Iron* from Ariosto; or Evangeline Walton, who set *The Island of the Mighty* in the world of Welsh mythology. Many another national mythos has been ransacked by fantasy writers, including the Irish, Norse, Finnish, and Roman; even American Indian folklore has not gone untouched.[5]

We do not generally include these stories in the central fantasy tradition, although of course they border closely upon it. The deciding factor is, I suppose, tradition: William Morris invented the imaginary-world novel, and the central tradition derives from his pioneering romances, which are laid in Medieval worldscapes completely his own invention, although quite similar to those in Malory and in *Sintram,* generally considered to be his sources. Stories that are firmly part of the tradition Morris founded are stories set in worldscapes invented by their author, just as Morris did it. That may sound mighty arbitrary, but there it is. Every literary genre is an arbitrary system of classification which can be debated endlessly (is *Macbeth* a play or a poem? Is *Hamlet* a ghost-story or a murder-mystery? Is *A Midsummer Night's Dream* a comedy or a fairy-tale?). You have to establish your criteria first, before you can discuss anything in depth.

So, those of us who are interested in the imaginary-world tale have set up our system of definition and hew to it, letting the quibbles fall where they may. And while stories such as those mentioned above are still imaginary-world fictions of a kind—in a certain limited sense—they are not pure examples of the genre. That is, their settings were not completely invented by their authors, even though these settings are still largely imaginary and have no valid claim to genuine historical existence. No Arthur Pendragon, tutored by Merlyn, armed with Excalibur, ever kinged it in many-spired Camelot while his knights rode around the countryside hunting for the Holy Grail; neither did any such sorcerer as Atlantes ever stable a hippogriff in a magic iron castle atop the Pyrenees; and while the high gods of Wales might have had their origin in a bunch of prehistoric chieftains, I doubt if they were the sort of giants and magicians the *Mabinogion* describes.

In other words, these are imaginary worlds, all right, but second-hand ones at best, and only peripheral to what I am defining as the central tradition of fantasy, which stretches in unbroken sequence from the Victorian novelist, William Morris, to the Tolkiens of today. Thus, I must relegate such peripheral works to merely cursory attention. Obviously, in a book of this length I do not have room enough to talk about every variety of fantasy, and if something has to go it might as well be atypical works of only marginal importance to the main tradition. That goes for children's books, too. I would love to talk about the imaginary-world tradition in juvenile literature, a subject which interests me greatly, but that is another book. The Marvelous Land of Oz and the equally delightful Narnia of C. S. Lewis will come in for some mention here, but only where relevant.

The main focus of this book will be a critical, even a technical, analysis of the imaginary-world tradition as embodied in the work of the major fantasy writers of the past three quarters of a century. I hope to be your guide as we explore this Empire of Imagination. We are going to look at fantasy *not* as allegory or symbolism or mythopoeia, but as literature. I want to show you how fantasy is made, how the best writers in the genre create the illusion of a genuine historical reality, how they construct a viable worldscape on paper and in the minds of their readers. No book has ever come to grips with this subject before; I think it will be exciting, and I think it will be fun.

I'm afraid we'll have to begin with some sort of summary of the life and work of the major writers who built this tradition. I would really rather not do it this way—I would prefer to plunge right into the central discussion, taking it for granted that you know all about Lord Dunsany and E. R. Eddison and Clark Ashton Smith and the others—but I think some historical exposition is required at the beginning. Since I have talked about most of these writers in my introductions to those of their books we have already published in the Adult Fantasy Series, to discuss them again will seem to some like a mere rehash of what I have already written. I'm afraid this can't be helped. Not everyone who picks up this book will be a faithful follower of the fifty-or-so volumes we have published thus far under the Sign of the Unicorn's Head. And to enter into a detailed analysis of fantasy literature without giving some expository background information on the authors whose work we will scrutinize would seem cultish and in-groupy, and would certainly make my argument incomprehensible to the newcomer. So I must ask those of you who have followed the Series faithfully from *The Blue Star* to this month's release to bear with me, please.

—LIN CARTER

Hollis, Long Island, New York

IMAGINARY WORLDS

The Art of Fantasy

. . . Some of us awake in the night with strange phantasms of enchanted hills and gardens, of fountains that sing in the sun, of golden cliffs overhanging murmuring seas, of plains that stretch down to sleeping cities of bronze and stone, and of shadowy companies of heroes that ride caparisoned white horses along the edges of thick forests; and then we know that we have looked back through the ivory gates into that world of wonder which was ours before we were wise and unhappy.

—H. P Lovecraft: *Celephais*

1

From Uruk to Utterbol:

William Morris and the First Fantasy Novels

Dreamer of dreams, born out of my due time,
Why should I strive to set the crooked
  straight?
—William Morris: "The Earthly Paradise"

To term fantasy a major province of literature is, perhaps, to be guilty of understatement. "Province," indeed! It is not a province at all, but a great kingdom. To stretch this play on words a bit farther, you could say that fantasy is in fact an empire, a once-mighty empire, now shrunken and impoverished, hoary with age but having a history that glitters with glorious names; an empire long since divided into newer realms, which centuries ago lost its unchallenged dominance of the world of literature, but whose heartland remains intact and still guards its precious history and splendid tradition.

As I remarked earlier, you could make quite a case for fantasy as the original form of narrative literature. In fact, the very oldest great work of literature known—the first of the world's great books—is an heroic fantasy laid in an imaginary world. I refer, of course, to the famous epic *Gilgamesh,* which some unknown genius of old Sumeria set down in cuneiform on baked-clay tablets 4000 years ago.[1] It is a thousand years older than any other great literary work—a thousand years older than the *Odyssey* or the Vedic hymns, the *Mahabharata* or Akhnaten's *Hymn to the Sun,* or the earliest parts of the Bible.[2] "The first story ever told"—or ever written, at least. And it is as much an heroic fantasy as any of Robert E. Howard's yarns

13

of Conan of Cimmeria, or the old Greek myths of Hercules of Tiryns, for that matter. The *Gilgamesh* is a quest story about a gigantic warrior king of Uruk who goes beyond the world of men in search of the secret of immortality, which he hopes to earn from Ut-napishtim, who was a king of Shurrupak before the Flood. This Sumerian Noah was the protégé of the god Ea, one of the creators of mankind. En route to his abode, the king of Uruk battles his way past the Hunwawa monster and other ferocious obstacles; he finds the immortal Ut-napishtim in Dilmun, the Sumerian paradise, "the country where the sun rises." The tale has epic grandeur and nobility; even in translation it is beautiful and moving, which is why it is the world's first literary masterpiece and not just a curiosity like the old Mayan *Popol Vuh* or the very much older *Instruction* of Ptah-hotep.[3]

We don't know what rank the Gilgamesh epic held in Sumerian or Babylonian literature, but a surprising number of the world's great literatures accumulated around a central epic or mythological book of hero-tales that are nothing else but fantasy. The national epic of Greece is the *Odyssey,* which, with its wandering hero and imaginary islands, its scheming sorceresses and interfering gods and one-eyed cannibal giants, is a fantasy. And so, of course, is the national epic of Rome, the *Aeneid* of Virgil, with its wandering hero-king of divine lineage, its winged harpies and magical apparitions, its prophetic foretellings of the future and (again) interfering gods. So, too, are the national epics of India, the *Ramayana* and the *Mahabharata,* with their demons and enchanted weapons and horrible monsters and magnificent warrior-princes. The national epic of Persia, the *Shah Namah,* is a tremendous compilation of superb fantastic tales, with flying thrones and undying heroes, evil genies and the wicked usurper, Zohak, who is cursed by having snakes grow out of his body. And, of course, much of the story concerns itself with the mighty hero, Zal, who was raised from boyhood by a magic talking bird called the Simourgh, and with Rustum, his son, who encounters a dragon or two en route to the enchanted kingdom of Mazinderan.

The greatest epic of Finland, the central classic of the Finnish national literature, is that famous poem, the *Kalevala,* with its mighty warriors and wise magicians who battle to save the Land of Heroes from the clutches of the evil witch, Louhi, who has stolen the sun and locked it in a cave. The epic is filled with marvels, such as the scene in which the great wizard, Wainamoinen, climbs down in the gullet of a sleeping giant and forces him to disgorge—literally!—the Lost Words of Power, magical spells of enormous potency. And the closest thing there is to a national epic of Wales is a collection of prose tales called the *Mabinogion,* which is filled with gods and heroes, monsters and magicians. *Beowulf,* the mighty Anglo-Saxon epic that stands at the beginning of English literature, is certainly a fantasy, what with its warrior-prince who slays ogres and fights a fire-breathing dragon with his magic sword.* The German national epic, the *Nibelungenlied,* is also rich in spectacular fantasy, as it includes in its cast the hero Siegfried, the dragon Fafnir, the king of the dwarves, and a former Valkyrie, to say nothing of the famous enchanted sword Gram, or Balmung.[4] I could carry this list further, but I guess you see my point.

THAT a great fantasy epic like *Beowulf* should appear at the very beginning of the history of English literature is significant: it is even prophetic.

---

*By a most contrived coincidence, my fantasy anthology *Dragons, Elves, and Heroes* (New York, Ballantine, 1965) contains selections from the more fantastic pages of most of these works: to be precise, from the *Shah Namah,* the *Kalevala,* the *Mabinogion, Beowulf,* and from fourteen other works, including the Russian *Kiev Cycle,* the romance *Palmerin of England,* and the *Gesta Romanorum.* Another anthology, *Golden Cities, Far,* which was published the following year, contained still more goodies: fantasy scenes or stories from the *Arabian Nights,* the romances of Voltaire, the *Orlando Furioso,* the French romance *Huon of Bordeaux, Amadis of Gaul,* and one of the more fantastic of the Sumerian epics.

I say this because a surprising number of the great novels and book-length poems in English literature are fantasies, and among the world's greatest. The list starts with Sir John de Mandeville's *Travels,* written in 1355, which has been called the first book written in the history of English literature that did not happen to be a religious work.* Next followed Sir Thomas Malory's *Le Morte d'Arthur* (1485), which was the last great English book to be written before the introduction of printing, and when it was printed, it was the first great English printer, William Caxton, who did the job. The next one to come along was More's *Utopia* (1516), which has the distinction of being the only science fiction novel ever written by a canonized saint of the Roman Catholic Church. Then came Edmund Spenser's romantic epic, *The Faerie Queene* (1590–1595), which has the distinction, in my opinion, of being the second longest and the second dullest poem in the language. Honors for being first in both categories belongs to Charles Doughty's *The Dawn in Britain* (1906)—also a fantasy, by the way, and so excruciatingly atrocious you wouldn't believe. Look it up sometime, if you feel in a masochistic mood.

Milton's *Paradise Lost* (1667), although drawn from Jewish mythology, must be ranked as a fantasy from the most cursory look at its plot and characters; so must John Bunyan's *The Pilgrim's Progress* (1684), a religious allegory, this one from the Christian mythology, but a fantasy for the same reasons. Swift's *Gulliver's Travels* (1726–1727), is the biting satire of a consummate cynic, but considering its Lilliputians and Brobdingnagians, talking horses, and especially the flying island of Laputa, it is certainly a fantasy. So also is Samuel Johnson's *Rasselas* (1759), hardly in a class

---

*But it really wasn't the first; *Beowulf,* written shortly before 750 A.D., most likely in Northumbria, certainly qualifies for that honor. However, the only known manuscript of *Beowulf* got lost quite early on, and it stayed lost for the better part of a thousand years, until it turned up in the 17th century, bound with nine other old parchments in a volume called the Codex Vitellius.

with most of these famous masterpieces, but note-
worthy if only in that it is perhaps the best novel
anyone ever wrote in only seven days. James Mac-
Pherson's *Ossian* (1762–1763) is a literary hoax, but
a hoax of genius, and as fantastic as the *Iliad* or the
Aeneid, both of which it resembles in certain ways.
Alfred Lord Tennyson's *Idylls of the King* (1859–1885)
translates the Arthurian legends into exquisite Victorian poetry which rises, at times, to astounding heights
of nigh-Shakespearean power and beauty,[5] making it
the last work that came anywhere near to being *the*
great national epic of English literature (*i.e.*, the epic
of King Arthur), which no one ever wrote but someone
should have. (Milton considered it for a while, but
passed it up in favor of his first love, the above-
mentioned Jewish myths of the Satanic rebellion, the
war in heaven, and the temptation and fall of man;
ah, well.)

Lewis Carroll's *Alice in Wonderland* (1865, 1872)
is probably as immortal as any classic in the language,
and certainly as much a fantasy. H. Rider Haggard's
She (1887) is the most successful and beloved fantastic
romance in the history of the English novel, and W. H.
Hudson's *Green Mansions* (1904) is a charming and
dream-like idyll . . . but here we are already in the
20th century, the age of *The Worm Ouroboros, Titus
Groan, Perelandra, The Once and Future King,* and
The Lord of the Rings—and if I don't stop here I will
soon get way ahead of my story!*

*I hope you won't think I am being needlessly pedantic in
mentioning the names of the authors of the books listed above.
Of course, you know that Milton wrote *Paradise Lost* and that
Swift is the author of *Gulliver's Travels*, and so on, and it
probably looks as if I am talking down to most of my readers.
But in one of my books I dropped a casual reference to the
Arabian Nights, not thinking I needed to identify the book in
any sort of detail. Well, when the fan-mail started to come in, one
reader utterly astounded me by asking about "this book, *Arabean*
(*sic*) *Nights*," and where he might get a copy of it! I suppose
some authors would merely smirk cynically and toss such a
letter out in the garbage without reply, but I am great of heart
and generous of soul, and dropped the fellow a note informing

THE modern history of the fantasy novel begins with
the pioneering Victorian romances of William Morris
(1834–1896), but, of course, an example or two can
be found even earlier. My favorite of these, and about
the earliest of them all, was William Beckford's delicious *Arabian Nights* fantasy, *Vathek* (1786).* Beckford (1760–1844) was a fabulously wealthy young
man, descended from every Magna Carta baron except
those who died without issue, who inherited £300,000
from his grandfather, becoming, at the tender age of
eleven, the wealthiest commoner in England. He toured
Europe like a prince, lived like a duke, and built a fantastic country estate worthy of a caliph; and—which is
the only really important thing about him—at twenty-
two he sat down and composed, in a mere three days
and two nights, the immortal *Vathek*. The tale is intense
with Oriental color, delicately erotic, even perverse, and
teeming with rich imaginative incident. It does not,
however, qualify as a valid imaginary-world novel, as
Beckford chose for his hero an actual historic personage, Harun al-Wathik, ninth caliph of the Abbasid
dynasty; his settings are equally authentic, and even
when he strays off the map of *terra cognita* and into
the weird mountain of Kaf and the subterranean palace
of Eblis, he is merely borrowing his locale from Islamic
legend. The book is written with great dash and aplomb,
though, and the style is nimble and charming.

---

him that the *Arabian Nights* was a world-famous classic available
in every public library in America. When I began thinking about
the above list, I shuddered at the possibility of a landslide of
such letters asking me about various world-famous literary works.
To nip such inquiries in the bud, I have given author, title, and
date of each work to help interested readers search out a copy.

*Most of the classic fantasies we shall be discussing in this book
have recently been reprinted by Ballantine Books in the Adult
Fantasy Series. I receive many letters from readers asking for a
complete list of the Series so they can be certain they have
all of the books we have published under the Sign of the
Unicorn's Head. However, for your information, I have included
at the back of this book a *complete* list of all the books published
in the Series through the end of 1973. See Bibliography II: The
Adult Fantasy Series.

Then there was George Macdonald (1824–1905), the gifted Scots preacher-turned-poet. He was a crony of Lewis Carroll's, read *Alice* in manuscript, and turned out an amazing *oeuvre* of strange, symbolist narratives— half nightmares, half fairy-tales—the greatest of which are the two celebrated "faerie-romances," *Phantastes* (1858) and *Lilith* (1895), which won high praise from C. S. Lewis and which, in various ways, anticipate both Freud and Kafka. While the geography of the two romances is not of this world, the books do not quite make it as progenitors of the central imaginary-world tradition; they are vivid dreams, not stories, and the weird countries through which their characters move do not constitute serious, detailed attempts to construct an invented milieu that gives the illusion of genuine reality, which is a prerequisite of the genre. Still, they are profound and beautiful and strange: they make the mind to work, and they are indubitably fantastic.

Another author who, like Beckford, tried his hand only once at the fantasy novel was George Meredith (1828–1909), who produced, in *The Shaving of Shagpat* (1855), an astounding Oriental phantasmagoria more than one hundred thousand words long, told in a gorgeous and magical prose, sprinkled with brilliant poetic images, and obviously modeled on the *Arabian Nights*. Written at twenty-five, this was Meredith's first try at the novel. He was a raw newlywed with a baby yowling in the crib and bill-collectors hammering on the door when he wrote it, and it must have been a labor of love, the work of a youthful poet drunk on the intoxicating magic of the *Arabian Nights,* for a less commercial novel could hardly be imagined. Even fantasy-buffs find it stiff going in places, and the novel-readers of Meredith's day were quite bewildered by its heady, quirky prose, and stayed away from their booksellers in droves. There was, however, the flash and dazzle of genius in it, which caught the appreciative eye of a discerning few—among them, William Morris' lifelong friend, the poet Dante Gabriel Rossetti. Undaunted by his initial failure, Meredith shrugged off

his meager royalties, consoling himself with the knowledge that he had succeeded in doing what he had set
out to do—that is, to capture the flavor and substance
of the Oriental fable—and turned confidently to a second attempt. His next novel was something called
Farina (1857), in which he strove manfully to catch
the gloom and grotesquerie of the old German romantics. This time he failed to duplicate the miracle:
nobody liked *Farina,* which drew a blank even with
the discerning few. At that point Meredith turned his
back on fantasy and settled down to a long, successful
career turning out "serious" novels like *The Ordeal of
Richard Feverel.*

None of these early tries succeeded in stimulating
wide enough enthusiasm to encourage imitation, which
is the usual manner in which literary traditions are
born. That honor was reserved for that astounding man
of protean talents, William Morris. But I wonder if
Morris did not—just possibly—get the idea from *The
Shaving of Shagpat,* which, while Oriental in scene, is
set in the Orient of no world yet mapped by Rand
McNally. It is possible: the link between Meredith and
Morris would have been Rossetti, who was impressed
with *Shagpat* to the point of making friends with its
author. Surely, in his new enthusiasm Rossetti would
have urged *Shagpat* on Morris. Being one of those
writers—like C. S. Lewis or Poul Anderson—who was
obsessed with "the Northern thing," Morris would have
found the book's Eastern setting alien to his interests
and its gaudy, florid style not to his taste; but he might
well have been struck by the idea of a romance laid in
an invented milieu, and realized the potentials of the
concept. Who knows? It could just be; if so, he waited
forty years before using the idea.

THE father of modern fantasy was a Welshman whose
family came from the upper Severn Valley of the Welsh
Marches to Worcester, and later to London, in the
closing years of the 18th century. It was Morris' grandfather who led the exodus, and he was probably the

first to drop the Welsh "ap Morris" in favor of the less ethnic "Morris." His son got a partnership in a brokerage, married the daughter of a prosperous Worcestershire merchant-landowner, and moved to the quiet country village of Walthamstow in Essex near Epping Forest. It was there that William Morris was born on March 24, 1834.

Until recently, biographies of Morris, such as Mackail's *Life,* have avoided any candid appraisal of Morris' tragic married life, veiling the details of his bitter unhappiness with bland Victorian restraint. The result has been a picture of Morris as a serene Medievalist, a cloistered dreamer, rousing himself at times from his hand-illuminated poetry manuscripts to tilt at windmills with the genteel fervor of a Utopian idealist.

Nothing could possibly be further from the truth about the man. No ineffectual aesthete wistfully yearning for golden ages that never really were, he was an intense, violent, emotionally complex man with the vigor of a bull and the vision of a prophet. His wife, Jane, seems to have been a shallow, sickly, moody girl. She was also a young woman of incredible, almost supernatural beauty, with whom Morris was passionately in love. It was his tragedy that she loved his best friend, Dante Rossetti; Morris hopelessly adored her, and this rather sticky *ménage-à-trois* made his personal life utterly miserable. It also, perhaps, gave certain of his poems, such as the famous "Defense of Guinevere," a fire and intensity which lifts them above the level of most of his facile, empty verse. Some of us use the symbols of art and the images of poetry to build a private iconography wherewith to interpret the events and personages in our life: Morris did it the other way around. But I am getting ahead of my story here.

He came down to London from Oxford in 1855 with a sheaf of early poems in his pocket, a love of the Medieval in his heart, and a passion for Gothic architecture got from Ruskin. His first friends were sensitive aspiring young poets and painters, and into this circle of lisping exquisites he fell like a thunderbolt. Morris was a burly, thick-bearded, barrel-chested man; he must have stood out among the bored, languid, artistically-inclined undergraduates like a Zulu war chief in full regalia at the Vicar's garden-party. They were fascinated by this Welsh wildman who dominated every conversation with his bellowing voice and vehement gestures.

A group formed around him—the painter Burne-Jones, the poet Rossetti, the young Ford Maddox Brown. While they drifted idly with every current, Morris had sighted his true direction early on, and drove straight for his goal with stubborn determination and an enormous capacity for sheer labor. He swept them into his orbit, dominated them with the intensity of his own convictions, and turned a delicate, wispy group of Pre-Raphaelites into a powerful movement that altered the history of design in Europe.

Morris & Company was established in 1861. The firm took England by storm. Its display was the surprise hit of the International Exposition of 1862. Spectators flocked in droves to gape at stained-glass windows and hand-painted furniture which so authentically captured the Medieval spirit that some exhibitors attempted to have the work disqualified as forgeries, genuine museum-pieces merely touched up. The firm walked off with two medals and an armful of commissions to decorate churches at Brighton, Scarborough, Selsley, and Cambridge. Such painstaking craftsmanship had not been seen in Europe for centuries. Before the firm was five years old it was world-famous, with commissions to decorate entire rooms at St. James's Palace and the South Kensington Museum. At first it was stained-glass, furniture, and embroidered fabrics; soon the firm began producing tile, jewelry, church ornaments, carpets, hand-woven tapestries, hand-printed wallpaper. William Morris' wallpaper seized the public fancy, conquered its taste. Before long the walls of every living-room in England were adorned with the exquisite designs. Printed by hand in subtle colors, hand-cut in pearwood blocks, his designs revolutionized the Victorian decor and ushered in the era of *art nouveau*. Morris & Company was a commercial triumph, with works at Merton Abbey and a plush showroom on Oxford Street.

William Morris was a success in every endeavor he attempted—every endeavor, that is, except the closest of human relationships, that of man and wife. From Ruskin he learned to adore Gothic architecture, and he tirelessly championed the preservation of ancient buildings and their loving, careful restoration. From Thorpe's *Northern Mythology* he caught a passion for the Icelandic sagas, traveled to Iceland to explore on foot the very ground the saga-heroes had walked, and from his enormously successful translations a generation of readers learned to love a great literature—a generation that included E. R. Eddison, Fletcher Pratt, and C. S. Lewis. Revolted by the shoddy wares, the inhuman slums, the ugly factories, the ruthless exploitation of labor, and the ferocity of *laissez-faire* capitalism, he fired his generation with his own passionate hatred of the Industrial Revolution and brought Socialism into England. He was a man of many passions.

He was also a man of protean talents, tremendous vigor, dogged determination, and fanatic vision. But he was right about most things, and artists as far apart as Toulouse-Lautrec and Frank Lloyd Wright have hailed him.[6] In the last six years of his life he founded the Kelmscott Press and printed the most perfect and beautiful books of his age, hand-printed books set in hand-cut type he had himself designed, books so exquisitely illustrated, printed, and bound that they are among the finest works of the bookwrights' art produced since the Middle Ages.

Almost as an afterthought, he invented the fantasy novel. It came about in this way: in 1888 he had finished an historical romance called *The House of the Wolfings,* a novel about noble and enlightened Saxons battling against the invading legions of Rome. This was the first of a series of prose romances that were to occupy his last years. He followed it at once with a second, *The Roots of the Mountain;* both were published the following year, 1889.

Now, *The House of the Wolfings* was a good, rousing adventure story, but it was nothing particularly new. It was, after all, just another historical novel, the sort of thing Sir Walter Scott was writing twenty years before William Morris was born.[7] Morris looked around for something new, something that would be all his own. It may be that he found working within a known historical/geographical context uncomfortably confining; or perhaps something excitingly original and different was needed to crown a long career. Morris was fifty-five when *The House of the Wolfings* appeared— he had only seven years left. Almost as if he knew his time was running out, he began writing at a furious rate, producing romance after romance, some of such prodigious length they required printing in two volumes (one of the last romances ran to over a quarter of a million words, the longest written in the genre until *The Lord of the Rings*). In the last nine years of his life he produced a body of fiction equal to the lifelong output of many novelists.

He turned immediately to the composition of *News from Nowhere,* a Utopian romance serialized in *Commonweal,* the Socialist magazine he had founded and first edited years before. Its first book version appeared in America in a pirated edition taken directly from the magazine serialization. Morris was too busy to bother about it; he was launched upon the last phase of a magnificent artistic career: he would, in all, create seven great romances; and upon the greatest of them the central tradition of modern fantasy would be founded.

News from Nowhere was completed in 1890, when he was fifty-six. He immediately began another romance, this time a novella called *The Story of the Glittering Plain.* This story told of Hallblithe and his quest for the country of eternal youth, and it is oddly reminiscent of *Gilgamesh*. It was published the following year, the first book issued from the Kelmscott Press.

Morris was finding his way to something no one else had done before him to any extent. The romantic quest story laid in an imaginary Medieval worldscape offered exciting possibilities: he was the first to explore them.

He began planning a major romance. It would be a long, adventurous quest like the Grail romances, told in a limpid prose style of lyric simplicity, studded with quaint archaisms—a narrative style borrowed from Malory. He would set the scene in a fresh, scrubbed, morning world, painted in the clear primary colors of a Medieval tapestry. The romance would open in the ordinary, bustling, workaday world, symbolized by the city of Langton; then it would follow the wanderings of a knightly young hero out into a hazy landscape of dewy meadows and green hills where old magics linger yet from forgotten, elder days; and at length it would stray beyond the world of men into the gloom of shadowy and mysterious forests where strange creatures lurk, a timeless realm of enchantment dominated by a veiled woman of queenly and magnificent beauty.

And so he wrote *The Wood Beyond the World*, the first great masterpiece of the imaginary-world tradition, the fountainhead from which imaginative literature springs. It was published in 1894,[8] a century after *Vathek*.

His end was almost upon him. He labored prodigiously, with that grim determination and tremendous capacity for sheer work that always amazed weaker men. Great romances poured from his pen. By the end of April 1895 he had finished *The Water of the Wondrous Isles*. Tennyson died, and, passing over Swinburne, the laureateship was offered to Morris. He declined the honor: time was running out. He strove no more in the arena of politics for social reform; his work in the labor movement was ended: there was no time left. In 1896 he published that astounding masterpiece, *The Well at the World's End*. It was the noblest of all the quests, that search for Utterbol at the world's edge, where one may drink of the waters of the Well and find peace. He had composed this enormous work, two hundred and twenty-eight thousand words long, in less than four years. It was followed almost immediately by another story, *The Sundering Flood*. But that was the last romance.

These last years he spent at Kelmscott, a little village on the Thames shore near Hammersmith, in the house where George Macdonald had written *The Princess and the Goblin* and *At the Back of the Northwind;* but it was William Morris who made it famous. It was there, in 1896, that he reached the Utterbol of his life. I hope that he, too, drank peace at last.

William Morris died on October 3, at the age of sixty-two, and was buried in the churchyard of Kelmscott village.

He was not forgotten.

The World's Edge, and Beyond:

The Fiction of Dunsany, Eddison and Cabell

One man with a dream, at pleasure,
  Shall go forth and conquer a crown;
And three with a new song's measure
  Can trample an empire down.
              —Arthur O'Shaughnessy: "Ode"

WHEN William Morris died in 1896, the first great writer to follow him in the fantasy tradition had just had his first piece published in a professional journal. The piece was a poem called "Rhymes from a Suburb," the journal in question was the *Pall Mall Magazine,* and the author was an eighteen-year-old boy, then the Hon. Edward John Moreton Drax Plunkett, later to succeed to the family title and be known as Lord Dunsany.

Dunsany was at this time just out of Eton and being privately tutored in preparation for Sandhurst. His father was the seventeenth baron in a line whose domains, titles and castles stretch back to the 12th century and form the oldest baronial possessions in the British Isles. In fact, Lord Dunsany belonged to one of the half-dozen families in the British peerage today who are of actual Norman descent.[1]

Dunsany's ancestors were swaggering Norse-French adventurers who came a-conquering into England on the heels of William the Bastard, settled in England after the Conquest, and anglicized their family name to Plunkett. In the 12th century, during the reign of the first Plantagenet, Henry II, they lent their swords to the conquest of Ireland, and one of these conquistadors in particular, who called himself John Plunkett, stayed to found two lordships north of Dublin in County Meath. This was the richest part of Ireland, the land most steeped in song and fable: of old it had been the domain of the *Ard-ri* himself, the High King; here was Tara of the Kings on the Rock of Cashell, which was so sacred and venerable that the king who held it was deemed the king of all other kings. The two lordships John Plunkett founded were those of Dunsany and Fingall; his descendants became robber barons—indeed, the old Irish historian who wrote the *Annals of the Four Masters* says of them: "There be two great robber barons on the road to Drogheda, Dunsany and Fingall; and if you save yourself from the hands of Fingall, you will assuredly fall into the hands of Dunsany."

If you're going to be a writer of heroic fantasy, let me point out, it certainly doesn't hurt to be born into a family like Dunsany's, with its rich history of adventure and romance!

Shortly after succeeding to the family title as eighteenth baron, Dunsany joined the first battalion of the Coldstream Guards at Chelsea Barracks and sailed for Gibraltar as a young officer. He fought in the Boer War, and later in World War I, receiving a wound in action. But the military life was no career for him, with his restless, vivid, romantic imagination. He lived a singularly exciting life—hunting lions on safari in Africa, teaching English in Athens and escaping one jump ahead of the Nazis, sailing up the Nile in a steam-launch as far as Aswan—a life so filled with variety of experience that without half trying I could fill this chapter with anecdotes about him. As senior peer for Ireland, for example, he stood swathed in ermine, a glittering coronet on his brows, as three of his sovereigns in succession were crowned at Westminster. A playwright during the glorious renaissance of the Irish drama, he hobnobbed with Yeats and Synge and Lady Gregory at Dublin's famous Abbey Theatre. Everything he did was done with dash and style—as a dramatist, for example, he had his works performed not only in Dublin and London, but in New York and even in Moscow (of all places). He once had *five* plays being performed simultaneously at different theatres on Broadway![2]

He was soldier, peer, and poet rolled into one—a globe-trotting adventurer, a devoted sportsman and hunter, a notable cricketer. In his time he was famous for being "the worst-dressed man in Ireland," and he was once chess champion of Scotland, Wales and Ireland as well. When I met him during his last trip to America—the evening of February 24, 1954, when he talked and read from his works at the Theresa L. Kaufmann Auditorium of the YM-YWHA Poetry Center in Manhattan—he was a lively, vigorous man in his sixty-seventh year. He stood three or four inches over six feet, straight as a soldier, and had ruddy apple-cheeks, frosty eyes, and a trim little spike of white goatee. He wore a loose, sloppy suit of grey tweed, his baggy pockets stuffed with scraps of verse, and a soft-collared white shirt with flowing, old-fashioned foulard instead of a tie. He spoke in a deep, rich, resonant orator's voice in whose tones the lilt of Ireland vied with the crisp accents of Eton.

Lord Dunsany lived to a hale and hearty eighty years, dividing his time between the family seat in Meath, the 13th-century Norman keep known as Castle Dunsany, and Dunstall Priory, a handsome old house near Shoreham in Kent that had belonged to his mother. At his death the title passed to his son Randall, a bluff, unbookish, outdoorsy sort of man who had soldiered in India. The line seems in no danger of extinction, happily, for the present nineteenth baron took a Brazilian wife in 1939, by whom he has a son. When our author died in 1958 he had published at least sixty-six books; and it is with these books, and not his long and colorful life, that we must concern ourselves here.

Dunsany's initial claim to our attention is as an innovator. He was the first writer to adapt William Morris' invention, the imaginary-world romance, to the short story; he was also the first to introduce an Oriental flavor and milieu into the genre. But his real importance to us rests on far more interesting grounds than mere technical innovation. He was, simply, a writer of incomparable style—in the opinion of many, including myself, the greatest of all fantasy writers.

While many of his poems, a few of his novels, and several of his better-known plays are fantasy, it is for his short stories that we remember him, and chiefly his very earliest short stories, at that. His first collection of short works was a slender volume of prose poems or brief sketches, *The Gods of Pegāna,* which Elkin Mathews published in London in 1905, with the author footing the bill. Between this date and 1919, eight slim volumes of short stories were published, containing many of the finest fantasy tales anyone has ever written.

Dunsany's work displays so many excellences that it is difficult to choose among them. First of all, he was a magnificent stylist, a great master of language who combined an exquisite lyricism with verbal richness in a crystalline prose of superb clarity and unmatched beauty. His plots and settings enormously broadened the scope of the genre, going far beyond the simple Malorean medievalism of William Morris' worldscapes to introduce exotic Eastern lands to the tradition. Many of his tales are set in "the little kingdoms at the Edge of the World" or in "the Third Hemisphere"—almost always "beyond the Fields we Know." In these tales he was the first to explore the potential spectrum of the fantastic tale in its widest possible variety, from the Oriental fable to the "grown-up fairy tale," from the heroic legend to the weird fantasy, anticipating the work of almost everyone who was to come after him, especially H. P. Lovecraft, Clark Ashton Smith, and Robert E. Howard.

The secret of his power, perhaps, lies in the fact that at heart he was really a poet. He possessed the poet's unique gift of stating a thing perfectly, succinctly. He demonstrates his mastery of this power again and again, in passages that linger in the memory: "Without saying a word, or even smiling, they neatly hanged him on the outer wall—and the tale is one of those that have not a happy ending," he said at the conclusion of one story. Ending another, which told of the proud kings of Zaccarath and how in their splendor and arrogance they ignored the babbling of ragged prophets crying doom, he wrote: "Only the other day I found a stone that had undoubtedly been a part of Zaccarath; it was three inches long and an inch broad; I saw the edge of it uncovered by the sand. I believe that only three other pieces have been found like it."

Tale after tale teems with brilliant and memorable images. When three adventurers came to a waste place in the midst of the Dubious Land, he tells us: "Something so huge that it seemed unfair to man that it should move so softly, stalked splendidly by them." In another story, he quietly informs us: "The Gibbelins eat, as is well known, nothing less good than man," demonstrating a gift for understatement; but he had also a gift for hyperbole, as when, in the same tale, he wrote: "Their hoard is beyond reason; avarice has no use for it; they have a separate cellar for emeralds and a separate cellar for sapphires; they have filled a hole with gold and dig it up when they need it." He had, in particular, a gift for choosing words that crystallize a scene of fantasy and magic; his novel *The King of Elfland's Daughter* tells of the witch Ziroonderel, who lived "on high lands near the thunder, which used to roll in Summer among the hills." When Prince Alveric visits her, seeking help to forge an enchanted sword, she sends him out hunting for thunderbolts which lie cooling among her cabbages. Elsewhere, he tells of the archers of Tor and how they shoot their ivory arrows at strangers, lest any foreigner should come to change their laws, which are bad laws, but not to be altered by mere foreigners.

He had also a remarkable gift for titles that intrigue and delight the imagination and that stick in the memory. Every reader will have his own favorites, but

I in particular have always relished "The Distressing Tale of Thangobrind the Jeweller and of the Doom that Befell him," and "The Fortress Unvanquishable, Save For Sacnoth," and "The Injudicious Prayers of Pombo the Idolater."

Above and beyond all of these qualities, he had supremely the gift of coining magical and evocative names. As will be discussed in the second half of this book, the coining of names is an art unique to fantasy writing and of transcendent importance to sustaining an illusion of reality in a story set in imaginary lands or worlds. No one has *ever* excelled Lord Dunsany in this unusual and difficult art: the tale that opens *The Book of Wonder* tells of "Zretazoola, the city of Sombelenë the centauress"; elsewhere we read of "Linlunlarna, the river that rises at the Edge of the World," and of "Sardathrion, that marble city of which the gods dream when they slumber," and of the great jewel named "Ong Zwarba," wherewith the King of Babbulkund adorns his daughter, and of the long-dead heroes of Merimna, who leave Paradise when their city is in peril to go among the dreams of the youth of that city and rouse them against the stealthy approach of the foe—of "Welleran, Soorenard, Mommolek, Rollory, Akanax, and young Iraine."

IN the year William Morris died, when the future Lord Dunsany was a youth of eighteen, Eric Rücker Eddison was a fourteen-year-old boy. He was born at Adel in Yorkshire in 1882, received a public schooling, and entered the civil service, serving on the Board of Trade. From 1930 until 1937 he was deputy comptroller-general for the Department of Overseas Trade, from which post he retired, at the age of fifty-five, to devote the rest of his life to the crafting of some of the most marvelous and remarkable romances in the English language.

Eddison's life remains an obscure subject and little has ever been written about him. Unlike Morris, who became the subject of several biographies, his life remains unwritten; and unlike Dunsany or Cabell, he never ventured into autobiography. At the age of forty, however, he came suddenly to the attention of the world through an amazing and spectacular fantasy epic which stands today as one of the great masterpieces of the genre, quite possibly the finest fantasy novel of all time and certainly one of the four or five supreme masterpieces in imaginative literature.

I refer, of course, to that incredible book, *The Worm Ouroboros,* which E. P. Dutton & Company first published in London in 1922. Although he had been dabbling away at the writing of "strange stories" from the age of ten, this was Eddison's first major book to be published and it took five years of steady work to complete it. He began *The Worm Ouroboros* rather clumsily, and in an unnecessarily complicated fashion, with a modern-day Englishman named Lessingham who ventures to the planet Mercury in a dream and who observes there, in a state of invisibility, the flow and sequence of actions that form the story of the novel. The use of this viewpoint character is an artificial device which both the reader, and the author himself, quickly forget all about, for the tale is the thing. And what a glorious tale it is!

The World of the Worm—for nobody ever thinks of it as being Mercury, and Eddison himself quickly stopped using the name—is divided into the powerful kingdoms of Witchland and Demonland, and the war that breaks out between these rival nations is the theme of this modern prose-*Iliad*. As Orville Prescott remarked in his essay on this book, such a war was never chronicled before, although "suggestions of it may be found in Homer, in the Icelandic sagas and in the Morte D'Arthur." These allusions are not far-fetched at all, but very apt. The novel begins in precisely the language wherewith the Norse scalds began their adventure-filled prose epics: "There was a man named Lessingham dwelt in an old low house in Wastdale, set in a gray old garden where yew-trees flourished that had seen Vikings in Copeland in their seeding-time;"[3] as for the Homeric parallel, both the villains and the heroes of the romance are larger than life and are seen, not as villains *vs.* heroes, but as two groups of heroic and magnificent warriors unfortunately pitted against each other by Fate in an almost-equal contest; and there is a strong flavor of Malorean medievalism in background and setting. This is not true, however, of the language in which the book was written, which in no way resembles the simple, lucid prose of Malory or Morris. Instead, Eddison hearkened back to the 17th century and the ornate, elaborate style of Sir Thomas Browne. However, his prose is more richly colorful than that of the great 17th-century masters, having an Elizabethan, almost a Chaucerian, gusto and verve that must be read with delight and relish, if at all. (For not every reader can make his way through this old-fashioned kind of writing, alas.)

It quickly becomes obvious that Eddison was a great admirer of William Morris, although in his romances he is very much his own man. But his second book, for example, was exactly the sort of thing that Morris himself wrote and would certainly have loved, had he been alive to read it. This was a novel called *Styrbiorn the Strong* (1926), which is not at all a fantasy but an historical romance based on matter from the Norse sagas, which are, as you probably know, generally historical or biographical rather than fictional and fantastic. Morris himself translated many of them into English—including the *Eyrbyggja Saga,* by the way, which dealt in part with the history of Styrbiorn, a fact that did not escape Eddison's attention, since he quotes from it in his foreword and singles out the Morris translation by name.

Eddison followed *Styrbiorn* four years later with something even closer to the sort of thing Morris did, a book called *Egil's Saga,* published in London in 1930. This was an actual prose translation of one of the longer, book-length sagas—one of the ones Morris never got around to doing. Both in his preface and in his notes to the *Egil,* Eddison mentions William Morris with affection, praising his work in this area.

In *The Worm Ouroboros,* Eddison exhausted the story possibilities of this particular world by inventing a circular plot-form, that is, by having the story end with the same scene with which it began. (The worm ouroboros is, of course, the worm which eats its tail.) For some years after finishing it he worked at other tasks such as those mentioned above, not returning to the imaginary-world romance until 1935 when he published *Mistress of Mistresses,* which had taken him four years to write. Since he had used up the possibilities of the World of the Worm in his first novel, he struck upon the unique concept of setting his second novel in the *Heaven* of that world—a most extraordinary and original idea, indeed! Perhaps, during the thirteen years between the publishing of *The Worm Ouroboros* and *Mistress of Mistresses,* Eddison struggled to think of a way of getting back to his invented world without violating the time-loop introduced at the ending of the former novel. On the other hand, for all we know, he had his solution in mind even before completing work on *The Worm.* For in Chapter XII of that romance, in the scene in which his heroes are scaling the great mountain of Koshtra Pivrarcha en route to the splendid palace of Queen Sophonisba, "the fosterling of the gods," from whom they hope to discover the whereabouts of their lost brother, the Lord Goldry Bluzco, who had earlier been carried off by a fearsome act of sorcery, the heroes catch a glimpse of the legendary realm of Zimiamvia, far off amidst dim peaks:

Juss looked southward where the blue land stretched in fold on fold of rolling country, soft and misty, till it melted in the sky. "Thou and I," said he, "first of the children of men, now behold with living eyes the fabled land of Zimiamvia. Is that true, thinkest thou, which philosophers tell us of that fortunate land: that no mortal foot may tread it, but the blessed souls do inhabit it of the dead that be departed, even they that were great upon earth* and did great deeds when they were living, that scorned not earth and the delights and the glories thereof, and yet did justly and were not dastards not yet oppressors?"

"Who knoweth?" said Brandoch Daha, resting his chin in his hand and gazing south as in a dream. "Who shall say he knoweth?"

They were silent awhile. Then Juss spake, saying, "If thou and I come thither at last, O my friend, shall we remember Demonland?" And when he answered him not, Juss said, "I had rather row on Moonmere under the stars of a summer's night, than be a King of all the land of Zimiamvia."

At any rate, Eddison subtitled *Mistress of Mistresses* "A Vision of Zimiamvia," and the scene of this second novel is set in the enchanted country glimpsed by the far-traveling heroes in the first of his stories. *Mistress,* however, is the less excellent of the two and represents a falling-off from the heights he attained in *The Worm Ouroboros.* The first novel teems with superb and spectacular set-pieces: the hand-to-hand battle with the dreadful Mantichore while crossing the glacier; the sensational scene in Chapter IV where the sorcerous King Gorice employs necromancy to conjure up a powerful spirit to do battle against his foes. The second book lacks anything comparable to these scenes, although the "Night-Piece on Ambremerine" in Chapter IV is a lovely bit of mood and atmosphere which lingers long in the memory, and the magician Dr. Vandermast remains an extremely interesting character, almost as good as the ones in the first novel.

But where *The Worm Ouroboros* is one magnificent epic filled with swordplay and adventure—"battles on sea and land, perilous journeys, base treacheries and mighty deeds, performed by authentic heroes and ma-

---

Sic. An example of what I meant when I said that before he was many pages into his book Eddison forgot all about the fact that he had set the story on the planet Mercury. He also had an avenue lined with "Irish yews" in one scene, and several of his characters quote from Sappho and some of the Elizabethan poets.

jestic villains"[4]—*Mistress of Mistresses* is a dull, talky novel of political intrigue. Very gorgeously written political intrigue, I confess, but still, just intrigue, not adventure on the heroic scale and in the grand manner.

Eddison followed *Mistress* with a sequel (of sorts) called *A Fish Dinner in Memison,* which was published in 1941, and he was at work on another sequel when he died in 1945. This concluding volume, consisting of notes and fragments and some complete scenes, was eventually published under the title *The Mezentian Gate* in a privately-printed edition which did not appear until 1958. All of these works, including *The Mezentian Gate,* are now available in Ballantine editions.

Considered as a whole, this Zimiamvian trilogy is less fun to read than that first, glorious romance. If I may indulge in the liberty of quoting myself on this point, I summed up the difference thusly in my book, *Tolkien: A Look Behind "The Lord of the Rings":*

> The Zimiamvian books are less successful than the mighty *Worm,* or at least they are less interesting to read. *The Worm* has a swift, direct appeal to the primary emotions: it is concerned with nothing but glorious, stirring adventure. But the Zimiamvian books have a dual theme: they are about adventure but are equally involved in the symbolic presentation of a complex and abstruse philosophy. *The Worm* is a richly-colored, thundering tale of battle and quest and heroic derring-do. The trilogy is about political intrigue and politics, plot and counterplot. *The Worm* is Homeric; the trilogy is Machiavellian: and most people enjoy reading Homer more than Machiavelli.

EDDISON did not achieve anything like the international popularity won by Dunsany, but he found his admirers. Among them were many of his fellow-writers, such as James Stephens, the author of a remarkable fantasy novel called *The Crock of Gold,* and the first of the great American fantasy writers, James Branch Cabell, who praised *The Worm* as "a rather majestic example of romance which purchases, through its own unadulterated magic, and for no utilitarian ends what-

ever, the momentary 'suspension of disbelief' in many
very beautiful impossibilities." Somewhat later, the publication of *Mistress of Mistresses* elicited from him the
opinion that Eddison was "the finest living writer of
pure romance."

Cabell was of an old, rather distinguished Virginia
family; his great-grandfather had served as governor of
the state; his grandfather had known Robert E. Lee
and had been a boyhood friend and schoolmate of
Edgar Allan Poe. Cabell himself, born in Richmond on
April 14, 1879, was related to most of the better
families among the local gentry, whose proprieties he
must have offended to some extent, since as a young
man he taught French and Greek briefly at William
and Mary, worked as a newspaperman, labored briefly
in the coal mines of West Virginia, performed genealogical research for hire—in other words, he actually
earned his living by the sweat of his brow for some
years before settling down to an equally dubious but
somewhat more genteel career as a gentleman of letters.

His earliest poems were published in the college
monthly in 1895, while he was still an undergraduate.
His short stories began appearing in national magazines
as early as 1902, and his first book, *The Eagle's
Shadow,* was published two years later. While this early
work displayed subtlety, polish and sophistication, it
hardly indicated his extraordinary imaginative power;
it was not until the eighth of his books, called *Domnei,*
came into print in 1913 that any suggestion of his
talent for fantasy was observed. By 1917, when the
first of his great fantasy novels, *The Cream of the Jest,*
appeared, those critics and connoisseurs who appreci-
ated fine prose recognized the emergence of an artist
of unique skill. Cabell's first dozen books sold poorly,
attracted little attention, and were generally ignored by
the critics—although they had their admirers, among
them nationally prominent figures as diverse as Mark
Twain and Theodore Roosevelt. But with the appearance of *The Cream of the Jest* Cabell began finding
his audience and started winning to his cause the first

of a number of very important and highly respected champions, such as Burton Rascoe, Vincent Starrett, H. L. Mencken, and Carl Van Doren.

Perceptive critics of cosmopolitan taste observed with surprise the appearance of a novelist with the sort of wit and irony we generally associate with Voltaire or Pope, the exquisite style and beautiful prose of Anatole France, and the gusto of Rabelais. What was so surprising about this was that an artist of such sophistication should arise south of the Mason-Dixon line, and in an era of rather barbarous taste, when the literary accolades were being handed out to such negligible nitwits as General Lew Wallace, the author of *Ben-Hur: A Tale of the Christ,* and the acclaim of the reading populace was generally reserved for hack-work of the level of *The Cardinal's Snuff-Box* and *The Prisoner of Zenda.*

Cabell might never have amounted to anything more than an obscure curiosity of literature—a minor stylist to be mentioned in the same breath with Edgar Saltus, let us say—had it not been for one of those peculiar accidents that sometimes occur. In his case, it happened with the publication of his fifteenth book, a novel called *Jurgen,* in 1919. Some readers professed to find highly erotic scenes therein, rather thinly veiled behind ancient mythological symbolism. On January 14 of the following year, that tireless champion of Puritanical morals, the self-appointed (or anointed) watchdog of literary lechery, Mr. John S. Sumner, executive secretary for the New York Society for the Suppression of Vice, came thundering into the offices of the Robert M. McBride Company, Cabell's publishers, armed with a warrant and clothed in the stern and wrathful self-righteousness of the fiery Christian crusader he doubtless thought himself to be.

Sumner made off with the plates and all copies of *Jurgen* on the premises and summoned the company and its department manager, Guy Holt, to appear in court the following day to answer charges of having violated Section 1141 of the Penal Code of the State

of New York. Neither Cabell nor his publisher nor
his circle of influential colleagues seems to have been
thrust into abysmal gloom by this seeming misfortune,
for the incident was a fairly common one in the United
States during this benighted era. Many a book had
been worried into the courts by howling witch-hunters
eager to sniff out lewd and lascivious *littérateurs,* works
as different as Joyce's *Ulysses* and Dreiser's *The Genius*
having already been so honored. Some of the most
distinguished authors and critics in the country rallied
to Cabell's defense; it became a *cause célèbre,* argued
all over the front pages of the newspapers; the courts
squashed the indictment in one of those landmark
decisions that were happily turning the tide of popular
opinion against this sort of Puritanical censorship—and,
of course, everyone flocked to the bookstores to snatch
up *Jurgen* and see what all the shouting had been about.
Overnight, Cabell found himself transformed from a
little-known, obscure gentleman of letters into a perse-
cuted martyr, a native American genius at bay before
the wolf-packs of ignorance and superstition, and, of
course, the author of a best-seller.

Sales boomed—*Jurgen* has never been out of print
from that day to this—and his next few books enjoyed
a healthy sale as well. The notoriety, or fame, has
never quite faded from his name since, and with an
ironic distaste he resigned himself to being known thereafter as "the author of *Jurgen.*"

In books like *Jurgen* and *The Cream of the Jest,* and
in later works like *Figures of Earth* and *Something
About Eve* and *The Silver Stallion,* Cabell elaborated
an invented milieu that went far beyond anything done
up to his time. Morris had invented a worldscape as
medieval as those in Malory or in *Sintram,*[5] but not
markedly different from those models; Dunsany had
created dozens of fabulous Oriental kingdoms "at the
Edge of the World," and had devoted the whole of his
first book to the gods worshipped in those kingdoms,
to their myths, their liturgies, even the writings of their
prophets; Eddison had brought an entire world to

robust, vigorous life, and had gone on to create the heaven of that world in even greater depth and detail. But Cabell invented an entire universe: not only this world of living men, but the amazing variety of heavens, hells, limbos and Valhallas and Faëries beyond that world—an entire cosmogony.

He began by inventing an imaginary province of Medieval France called Poictesme, which he made the seat of the redoubtable Dom Manuel, pig-tender turned prince. He went on to elaborate the pseudo-geography of that realm and of the lands adjacent thereto, combing obscure mythologies and neglected books for legendry and lore. For instance, the son of the magician Miramon Lluagor—the magician who plays the Merlin to Dom Manuel's Arthurus Rex—is one Demetrios, "lord of the lands between Quesiton and Nacumera." The casual or inattentive reader will assume those dominions to be imaginary, as they cannot be found on the admirable maps prepared by the estimable Messrs. Rand McNally; the knowing Cabellist, however, can never quite be sure of this. And, in fact, if he searches diligently enough he will find, in that very old and delightful book called *The Voyages and Travels of Sir John de Mandeville,* first written in 1355, both realms listed among the catalogue of strange and curious countries visited by Sir John in his travels.

Cabell's characters, moreover, have the disconcerting habit of frequently wandering, not only off the map, but out of this world, as well—as when the pawnbroker-hero of *Jurgen,* searching for his lost shrew of a wife, seeks for her, not without good reason, in the sulphurous region of Hades. His journeys also take him to the court of Guenevere's father, Gogyrvan Gawr, king of Glathion and the Red Islands—realms known only to the authors of the Welsh mythological prose epic, the *Mabinogion*—and, in the guise of a certain Pope John XX, he visits heaven and has a lengthy interview with God. Heaven he finds a depressingly gaudy sort of Oriental capital, decorated in the sleazy bad taste ascribed to it by the rather pixilated author of *Revela-*

tions, while God himself is an amiable but pompous bore, unable, like most authors who made a big hit with their first book, to talk about anything else but Literature, especially in the company of a suave young poet like Jurgen.

This brief précis cannot convey a fraction of the wit and charm of *Jurgen,* but it gives you a notion of Cabell's playful use of lore and learning. Pope John the Twentieth, of course, never reigned, as he was an anti-Pope. But Jurgen talks his way glibly past the befuddled old Fisherman who guards the Pearly Gates into Heaven, arguing that if there had been no Pope John the Twentieth, how could there have been a Pope John the Twenty-first, and that if a Supreme Pontiff is willing to admit having made such a simple error in everyday arithmetic, what does that do to the doctrine of papal infallibility? Cabell must also be noted for his originality: no one before Cabell had ever depicted God, the presumed source of inspiration who, as it were, dictated the text of the Bible to the various prophets, as a talkative amateur whose first book was a big best-seller *à la* Margaret Mitchell and *Gone with the Wind,* and few could have handled the scene with such subtlety and droll humor as to avoid giving offense to all but the most hypersensitive.

Jurgen is an amusing, glib-tongued con-man who has a trick of talking his way out of tight spots (and, on occasion, into the bedrooms of handsome women) by citing such authorities as Sabellius, Artemidorus Minor, Sornatius, and so on. "Besides, what does all this flimsy sophistry avail against Nicanor's fine chapter on this very subject? Crushing, I consider it. His logic is final and irrefutable," Jurgen argues at one point, talking to a capricious goddess. "What can anyone say against Saevius Nicanor?" he insists.

Ah—what indeed! Cabell, at this point, is having fun with the pompous style of argument employed by learned academicians; and since those he talks to in this manner invariably hasten to agree with him (having obviously never heard of these Classical authorities, much less actually read them), he is also having a joke at the expense of those easily intimidated by such displays of erudition. But in Cabell the jokes usually have yet a third dimension to them; in this case, the authorities cited by Jurgen are scholars whose works are entirely lost, so that no one he talks to could *possibly* have read them. It is this extra scintilla of wit that makes Cabell what he is; any other author would simply have made up Classical-sounding phony names, but Cabell searches them out, finding Saevius Nicanor mentioned, for example, in Suetonius, and Sornatius referred to in Pliny.

The goddess Jurgen is talking to in the passage above is named Mother Sereda. Cabell did not invent her, either; he found her in the more obscure pages of Russian folklore.

The Cabellian cosmos is so enormously complicated and ingenious that I have room to do little more than merely suggest it here. Jurgen goes beyond the cheap, flashy Semitic paradise to find the *real* ruler of the universe, a busy little bureaucrat named Koshchei, toiling away in a back room behind a cluttered desk. Elsewhere, in *The Silver Stallion,* Donander, one of the lords of Poictesme, falls in battle with the Northmen, slaying his pseudo-Viking even as he himself is slain; the pseudo-Valkyrie and the angel who come simultaneously to bear the souls of the slain off to their respective Rewards get mixed up, and the Viking goes to Heaven while Donander gets carried off to something rather like Valhalla. An enterprising and practical-minded Christian gentleman, Donander makes the best of a bad bargain, attracts the roving eye of a susceptible young goddess of the local pantheon, and marries into the family. A family of gods, I must add, wherein the above-mentioned Koshchei is only a playful infant divinity, still toying with the juvenile pleasure of world-making.

Most of Cabell's novels fit together into a complicated mosaic which he calls *The Biography of Manuel.* Cabell admired Eddison, had read Dunsany, and goes each of them one better. Eddison equipped his books with maps and chronological lists of significant dates; Dunsany composed the "Bible" of his Pegāna pantheon before telling hero-legends of the lands wherein the Gods of Pegāna are worshipped. But Cabell has all of his characters—whether in modern-day Lichfield, a Southern city that sounds very like Richmond, Virginia, or in Medieval Poictesme, and the equally imaginary realms that border upon it—related to each other, and he published a work of formal, scientific genealogy to prove it!

The first great American master of fantasy, who died on May 5, 1958, holds up well in comparison with the great British masters of the genre. Among the more than fifty books he published are some of the most witty, ingenious, and sheerly imaginative fantasies ever crafted, and they demonstrate a sophisticated prose style second to no other.

WITH the appearance of James Branch Cabell, the history of fantasy diverts from Britain to America. In the main, the American masters of the genre wrote for the popular fiction magazines of their day. One of the few who did not was Austin Tappan Wright; like Cabell, he was primarily an author of books rather than a writer of magazine stories. Unlike Cabell, however, it is as the author of a single novel that he is remembered.

That book is *Islandia,* which was first published in April of 1942, eleven years after the death of its author, and which Norman Cousins has hailed as a work "unique in the history of all literature." "Unique" is certainly the *mot juste,* for here we have a fantasy that is completely devoid of the slightest element of fantasy, and a romance from which romance itself has been eliminated.

Austin Tappan Wright was born in Hanover, New Hampshire, in 1883. His father was a professor of Latin and Greek and went on in later years to become Dean of the Harvard Graduate School; his mother

was the author of several novels which take place in
an imaginary college town called Great Dulwich. Wright
himself emulated the accomplishments of both parents,
in his own peculiar way. Like his father, he was a
college man, studying at the Harvard Law School and
later at Oxford, returning after practicing law for some
years with a firm in Boston to accept a professorship
in law at Berkeley, and later, at the University of
Pennsylvania. Like his mother, Wright's venture into
fiction was concerned with an imaginary milieu of his
own concoction. He was killed in an automobile accident in Las Vegas, New Mexico, in 1931. At the time
of his death, no one had any idea that he had secretly
devoted most of his adult life to writing fiction except
for his immediate family, and especially his four children, who had been in on the game virtually from the
beginning.

And a game it certainly was: in the spirit of a
British contemporary and colleague, whose initials are
J. R. R. T., the writing of the novel was only incidental
to the game itself, which consisted of the careful and
meticulous invention of an entire continent, its history,
its geography, its language, and its own peculiar and
unique way of life. Wright did not publish any of
Islandia during his own lifetime, probably for the same
reason that Tolkien has yet to publish anything of *The
Silmarillion:* because he was not yet through with it.
The creation of *Islandia,* the book and the nation, was
a task at which he still busied himself up to the time
of his death.

His daughter, Sylvia Wright, has left us a fascinating
description of the Islandia papers.[6] The original manuscript of the novel itself was close to six hundred
thousand words long, which makes it one of the longest
novels ever attempted in the entire history of prose
literature; it is about one hundred thousand words
longer than the published text of *The Lord of the
Rings,* for example, and more than twice the length of
The Well at the World's End. But beyond the actual
novel itself, the Islandia papers include yet unpublished

works of history, geography, and genealogy, a gazetteer of the several provinces of Islandia, a glossary of the Islandian language, a complete historical peerage, specimens of native Islandian literature, and something like nineteen cartographic works, one of which is a scholarly geological map of the continent.

Do not make the mistake of thinking that these peripheral works are mere monographs or brief articles, like the several appendices to the Tolkien trilogy. One of the unpublished volumes of Islandian non-fiction is a formal work of historical scholarship, the *Islandia: History and Description,* by M. Jean Perier, the first French consul to Islandia. That particular book is about one hundred and thirty-five thousand words long.

A decade before the first printing of *The Lord of the Rings,* then, Wright had uncannily anticipated the coming of Professor Tolkien, and had already transcended his accomplishment in advance, at least in so far as the construction of appendices goes.

Islandia is a large nation in the southern part of the continent of Karain. Unique in the entire body of fantastic literature known to me, this imaginary-world novel takes place in the here and now—for Karain is a continent somewhere on earth today. As I have remarked above, it is also unique in that the only element of the fantastic in the entire book is the presumed existence of the Karain continent itself, for there are no magicians in Islandia, no elves or dwarves or dragons. In the pages of the novel *Islandia,* we are not dealing with heroic or romantic matters—with the high and noble wars of Faërie or the doings of the Gods—but with a simple, quiet, deeply-moving story of a young American's visit to Islandia in 1908 and his travels through that country. The essence of the novel is the simple, rural lifestyle of the Islandian people themselves, and how the young American, John Lang, falls in love with the beauty of their country and their way of life. It is not, however, that the book contains nothing of the heroic or the adventurous, but rather that the heart of the story does not center about the heroic or the adventurous. In this way, too, *Islandia* is unique. The secret of its fascination for its readers does not lie so much in the presence of drama and derring-do, but in the manner in which these elements are subordinated to the true matter of the book: the detailed creation on paper of a slow, quiet, lovely, and ancient civilization. It is beautifully done.

The actual book was created out of Wright's immense volume of papers by his widow and her children. It was largely Mrs. Wright herself who transcribed the twenty-three hundred pages of the manuscript from her husband's longhand, teaching herself how to type in order to assemble the material for the publisher. It was Wright's daughter and a sympathetic and interested editor at Farrar & Rinehart who trimmed the manuscript down to publishable length. Appearing in print at the height of the Second World War, the novel attracted the attention of influential critics like Orville Prescott, Norman Cousins, and Lewis Gannett, and it quickly became the object of a cult composed of literary people like Basil Davenport and news commentator Elmer Davis—both of whom were eventually to write minor additions to the Islandian corpus. The little brochure by Davis took the form of an entry for Islandia that should have been included in the *Britannica Year Book* for 1943, if the editors of encyclopedias were not a dour and humorless lot.

Really good books have a way of lingering on—and on. Thus, in 1958 *Islandia* was reissued by Rinehart with a new introduction by Sylvia Wright. And in 1969 Mark Saxton, the sympathetic editor who had helped get the original edition into print, wrote a modern sequel called *The Islar, or Islandia Today—A Narrative of Lang III,*[7] published by Houghton Mifflin in Boston. And a bit later, Paperback Library brought out both *Islandia* and *The Islar* in their first paperback editions.

Neither *Islandia* nor its modern sequel are for every

reader. Some will find them boring and interminable because of their length and their lack of color, excitement, and drama. But they constitute a remarkable and very unusual form of the imaginary-world romance and are, in their genre, truly unique.

Lost Cities, Forgotten Ages:

The Rise of Fantasy in the American Pulp Magazines

Know, O Prince, that between the years when the oceans drank Atlantis and the gleaming cities, and the years of the rise of the Sons of Aryas, there was an Age undreamed of, when shining kingdoms lay spread across the world like blue mantles beneath the stars.

—Robert E. Howard:
"The Phoenix on the Sword"

FROM their inception the popular pulp fiction magazines in America specialized in swiftly-moving, action-filled, easy-reading stories with a primary emphasis on entertainment value to the exclusion of literary quality. Outgrowths of the "penny dreadfuls" and "dime novels" that enthralled our grandfathers with their hair-raising yarns of Buffalo Bill and Nick Carter the detective, they quickly became enormously popular and shaped the reading-habits of the nation for thirty years.

The earliest of them were generally unspecialized. They published a little of everything, from murder mysteries and pirate stories and historical adventures down the spectrum to society romances and love stories. Weird and fantastic fiction and the more primitive varieties of science fiction were also popular, especially after 1912. For in its February issue of that year a leading pulp called *All-Story*, published by the Frank A. Munsey Company, had introduced a new author, Norman Bean, and his first serial, *Under the Moons of Mars.*

The world was never quite the same again, because behind that pen-name was concealed the greatest adventure-story writer of all time, Edgar Rice Burroughs, and beneath that title, later changed for the book edition, was the first installment of the immortal *A Princess of Mars,* the first of eleven books Burroughs was to write about John Carter of Mars, the greatest swordsman of two worlds, and his heroic adventures on the Red Planet.

Burroughs had been born in Chicago on September 1, 1875. He had done a little prospecting, tried to run a stationery store, bluffed his way into a job with Sears, Roebuck as an accountant, and in general had flopped at about everything until turning his hand, at 36, to writing adventure fiction—the one profession in the world, it seems, for which he was spectacularly suited. *All-Story* had been publishing since January 1905, but Burroughs was something unique to their experience— a hard-headed businessman who quibbled over copyrights and royalties, reserving television rights long before the glass-fronted box was even off the drawing-boards, as well as an extremely popular writer who could produce amazingly good fiction at a fantastic rate. They serialized his first novel in six parts, beginning with the February and ending with the July issue; and only three months after the end of this first, tremendously successful serial they began printing his second, which was even more of a sensation with the readers. It was a jungle adventure thing, something called *Tarzan of the Apes.*

Tarzan, of course, remains Burroughs' most famous literary creation, and twenty-six books of his adventures have been published, twenty-five written by the master, the twenty-sixth by Fritz Leiber. To a considerable extent, however, Burroughs' Tarzan books derived from the kind of fantastic romances about lost cities in Africa that H. Rider Haggard had begun writing in 1885, twenty-seven years before the first appearance of Tarzan. Such books as *She* and *King Solomon's Mines* and *Allan Quatermain* had been enormously successful, coming as they did during what I call "the heroic age of archaeology." Alcubierre had already excavated the buried city of Pompeii before Haggard began publishing; Grotefend had stumbled on the secret of Babylonian cuneiform; Champollion had conquered the mystery of the Rosetta Stone; Botta was digging up Nineveh and Layard was at work on the tomb of Nimrod, while Schliemann had opened the lost city of Troy and Brugsch was laying bare the age-forgotten secrets of the Valley of Kings—and Europe was electric with excitement. Haggard cleverly realized that the only thing more sensational than the discovery of a dead, ruined city of the ancient past would be the discovery of *a living city,* still inhabited by the descendants of the lost civilization that had established it ages before.

To a large extent, Burroughs simply appropriated this idea, and in his twenty-five Tarzan books the ape man discovers a lost colony of Atlanteans, twin cities inhabited by Amazons, another pair of cities inhabited by Crusaders, yet another pair of ancient Roman colonies, and so on—and on. By the tail end of the series, running low on antique civilizations, Burroughs took Tarzan out of Africa to a lost city of Mayans in the Pacific.

ONLY five years after bringing the first of Burroughs' novels into print, *All-Story* discovered yet a second talent, equally important and far superior as a craftsman to the creator of John Carter of Mars and Tarzan of the Apes. This was Abraham Merritt, the son of Quaker parents, who was born in Beverly, New Jersey, nearly a decade after Burroughs, on January 20, 1884. Like Burroughs, who had served in the U. S. Cavalry, gold-mined in Idaho, and worked as a railway cop in Salt Lake City, A. Merritt was of an adventurous disposition. Bored with high school, he dropped out after his first year and left home to go treasure-hunting in the jungles of Yucatan, where he became one of the first white men in a hundred years to enter the ancient Mayan city of Tuluum. Returning home, he attended lectures in law at the University of Pennsylvania; again formal schooling bored him, and at nineteen he became a cub reporter on a Philadelphia newspaper, rose to be night editor, moved over to the Hearst empire, and ended up in 1937 as top man on the prestigious *American Weekly,* a position he held until his sudden death from a heart attack on August 30, 1943, at his summer home in Florida.

Merritt's first story—under his own name, at least[1]—was a short, beautifully written gem of fantasy called "Through the Dragon Glass," which *All-Story* published on November 24, 1917. Seven months later the same magazine published the first part of a stunning novel called *The Moon Pool,* which was followed by a brilliant succession of imaginative masterpieces that took the fantasy-reading public by storm—*The Face in the Abyss, Dwellers in the Mirage, The Ship of Ishtar,* and others. While Burroughs published something like sixty-six books, Merritt only produced twelve: eight novels, a posthumous collection of short stories, a volume of articles from *The American Weekly,* and two fragments which were completed by the fantasy artist and long-time Merritt fan, Hannes Bok, as full-length novels, via a posthumous collaboration like those August Derleth was later to perform on the notes left by H. P. Lovecraft.

This was a great loss to fantasy literature, for Merritt was an absolute master of the adventure fantasy, a writer of clearly superior skills. His stories had strong dramatic plots, vivid and memorable characters, a wealth of highly original imaginative invention, and they were told in a gorgeously-colored prose by a man who could create mood and atmosphere second to none. His stories left his readers gasping and begging for more, and it is a pity that he wrote so few of them. The trouble with Merritt, of course, was that he held a responsible editorial position at which he earned a good salary, while Burroughs wrote for a living.

There is a lesson here: no first-rate fantasy writer should *ever* be tempted with a good job!

MANY competitors arose to challenge *All-Story* for the large market the magazine had created. Competition grew fierce, and eventually the magazines began to specialize in order to survive. This was eventually carried to the point of absurdity; at various times there were entire pulp magazines devoted to every conceivable reading taste—not just westerns and murder-mystery magazines, for there were dozens of those, but magazines like *Pirate Stories, Jungle Stories, Oriental Stories, War Stories, Baseball Stories, Railroad Stories, Sea Stories, Navy Stories,* and even something called *Zeppelin Stories!*

Now, this was specialization with a vengeance, and naturally the market for most of these magazines was far too small to support them for long.[2] But, with specialization the order of the day, the time was ripe for some enterprising publisher to venture into the field of fantasy. There were a few false starts in this direction, but finally a small Chicago firm, the Rural Publishing Corporation, decided to give it a try. The head of the firm, J. C. Henneberger, had successfully launched a popular magazine called *College Humor* in 1920, and had followed it with the *Magazine of Fun* somewhat later. Deciding to add new titles to his line, Henneberger hired a mystery writer named Edwin Baird to edit a new magazine called *Detective Tales*. It seems Henneberger was a great admirer of Poe and an enthusiast of macabre literature in general, so Baird was also assigned to edit a periodical in that line. Thus it was that *Weird Tales* was born.

The first issue of "The Unique Magazine," as it was subtitled, appeared on newsstands of America in March 1923. It ran to 192 pages, sold for 25¢, and contained twenty-four stories, most of them having crude, overobvious titles like "The Ghoul and the Corpse," "The Grave," and "The Place of Madness." The first issue hardly looked promising; none of the authors represented in it were exactly names to conjure with—in fact, they were largely unknown. The whole thing had a rather shaky look to it, and this shakiness became quite apparent before the magazine had lasted a full year. In fact, its first-anniversary issue was very nearly its last issue, for by that point Henneberger has lost $51,000, and any publisher in business to make money would have seriously considered scuttling so unsuccessful a venture.

What saved *Weird Tales* from extinction after its thirteenth issue was, quite simply, Henneberger's own liking for the kind of fiction it printed, and his faith in the future of the magazine. Baird, after some initial fumbling, had begun finding his way to some remarkably talented writers; then again, the readership, while small, was actively enthusiastic; finally, it is easier to keep a magazine going with new funding or extended credit in the hope that it will begin to pay its own way than to discontinue it and thus take a dead loss. What Henneberger did was to turn the magazine over to its printers with the understanding that they were to keep it going on their own until the magazine's sales had paid off his debt to them.[3] And thus the fourteenth issue of *Weird Tales* finally came out, under the aegis of the new Popular Fiction Publishing Company of Indianapolis. Henneberger continued as nominal publisher but he had really lost control of the magazine for the foreseeable future, and his original editor, Edwin Baird, was replaced by a mediocre Chicago author named Farnsworth Wright on orders from the new owners.

To the surprise of almost everyone concerned, the magazine kept going for the next thirty years and published two hundred and seventy-nine consecutive issues before it succumbed at last to old age. By the time the final issue of *Weird Tales* was published, the magazine had outlived every other pulp magazine that had been in existence when it was originally launched. The last issue was dated September 1954, and with it the immortal *Weird Tales* passed into oblivion—or into legend, I should say—and its passing marked the end of an epoch.

Although the lifespan of *Weird Tales* covered thirty-one years, the greatest decade of the magazine was its first, the glorious span between 1923 and 1933. It is, in a way, unfair that Farnsworth Wright's name is the one most closely identified with *Weird Tales*. Great editor though he unquestionably was, the fame of the magazine, and thus his own, rests on those early years and the first three great talents who won for the magazine the eminence and enormous prestige that clung to it all its long life. And those three writers who made *Weird Tales* immortal were, every one of them, the discoveries of Edwin Baird.

THE first writer of this remarkable triumvirate was, of course, Howard Phillips Lovecraft, celebrated today as undoubtedly the greatest author of supernatural fiction in American literature since Edgar Allan Poe. Lovecraft's first story to appear in *Weird Tales* was called "Dagon," published in the issue for October 1923.

While it was Baird who first bought him, Lovecraft was really the personal discovery of J. C. Henneberger, who had found a couple of his early stories in a short-lived, quasi-professional magazine called *Home Brew,* published by a Brooklyn couple, Mr. and Mrs. George Julian Houtain. Henneberger was impressed with the "style and craft" of the stories, and he felt that Lovecraft was "the equal of Edgar Allan Poe." The Houtains obligingly put him in touch with the eccentric Providence author, who was happy to send his stories to *Weird Tales,* especially since *Home Brew* soon suspended publication. Henneberger was perhaps the first to recognize Lovecraft's darkling genius, and he formed a great liking and admiration for the erudite recluse. In fact, Lovecraft was Henneberger's choice of a replacement for Edwin Baird, although the new publishers overruled him in this. At times during those early years, Henneberger forced the reluctant Baird to accept a Lovecraft story that, for one reason or another, he had rejected—"The Rats in the Walls," for example. Henneberger remained a friend of Lovecraft long after his association with *Weird Tales* terminated; he was, in fact, the last person to visit Lovecraft in 1937 as he lay dying in the Jane Brown Memorial Hospital in Providence from a combination of Bright's disease and intestinal cancer.

Lovecraft was born in Providence, Rhode Island, on August 20, 1890, and spent almost his entire life in that city save for a brief stay in Brooklyn, New York, during an unsuccessful fling at marital life.

I have already discussed his life and career at great length in a book called *Lovecraft: A Look Behind the "Cthulhu Mythos,"* which Ballantine Books published in February, 1972, so I will only briefly treat of such matters here. However, it may be said that Lovecraft was descended from old English stock, a fact in which he took much pride. As a sickly, coddled, extraordinarily precocious child, smothered by a neurotically over-protective mother, Lovecraft quit school early, seldom mixed with children his own age, and turned to books, as precocious youngsters generally do under such circumstances, for the companionship he missed in everyday life. His lengthy, fascinating, and quite revealing letters—of which three volumes have thus far been published—record his early literary infatuations: the *Arabian Nights,* Jules Verne, Poe. He also developed at an early age a deep and inquisitive interest in astronomy, archaeology, and antarctic exploration, three scientific topics that he would later put to excellent use in his stories.

Lovecraft did not live what most of us would consider a very happy or healthy life, although he seems to have resigned himself to the fact and to have found contentment along the way. For his entire life, Lovecraft was haunted by the spectres of poor health, isolation from personal friendships, failure to achieve any success in his chosen career (success came after his death), shabby and genteel but extreme poverty, and an unhappy family heritage of madness.[4] With this in mind, it is no wonder that Lovecraft's tastes inclined him to the literature of the macabre and the supernatural, although he was in no way drawn to the woozy speculations of modern occultists and remained a confirmed and lifelong atheist.

His later, much more famous weird fiction need not concern us here. It is the vivid pastel fantasies he produced in his early period that bring him within the compass of our study. Lovecraft began writing such tales early in 1918, beginning with "Polaris," a dream-like fable about the doom of an imaginary, prehistoric polar civilization called Lomar. The following year Lovecraft first encountered the work of Lord Dunsany, which made an intense impression on him as he was already drifting in precisely the same direction; that same year, 1919, he made the journey to Boston to hear the celebrated baron speak at the Copley-Plaza. Dunsany, then a robust forty-one and at the height of his fame, could hardly have guessed that the lantern-jawed young man in the shabby, old-fashioned but immaculately laundered suit, seated only ten feet from the podium in the first row of the auditorium, would become his foremost literary disciple over the next decade.

Lovecraft returned to Providence afire with enthusiasm and plunged immediately into a phase of writing Dunsanian fantasies. The tales poured from his pen with a productivity remarkable for Lovecraft, who in later years produced as few as one story per year. During the remainder of that year and the year following, Lovecraft wrote no fewer than sixteen stories and prose poems, most of them in a direct and precise imitation of the style and manner of Dunsany—"The Doom That Came to Sarnath," "The White Ship," "The Cats of Ulthar," "Celephais," "The Tree," and so on. These were dreamy, gorgeous, image-filled legends set in vaguely Oriental countries situated in a *terra incognita* of Lovecraft's own invention.

During the next several years, Lovecraft developed and extended the horizons of his imaginary world in such tales as "The Other Gods" and "The Quest of Iranon" (both written in 1921), "What the Moon Brings" (1923), "The Silver Key" and "The Strange

High House in the Mist." Both of these last tales date from 1926. This Dunsanian period culminated in the writing of a bizarre, utterly gorgeous short novel, the famous *Dream-Quest of Unknown Kadath,* which remains Lovecraft's masterpiece in the genre of the imaginary-world fantasy. Still an amateur, Lovecraft made no effort to sell any of these stories but gave them away to his friends in the United Amateur Press Association and elsewhere, where they were published in small private magazines of strictly limited circulation. *The Dream-Quest of Unknown Kadath* itself was published nowhere, dropped out of sight, and was discovered among a trove of Lovecraft manuscripts and papers years after his death. Lovecraft was so dissatisfied with it that he abandoned it and never bothered to revise it; posterity has judged him wrong in his opinion, and today the novella is regarded as a specimen of luxuriant, exotic prose seldom equaled this side of *Vathek.* It has been printed and reprinted at least five times.

Lovecraft used *Dream-Quest* to sum up most of the invented geography and myth he had tossed off in the shorter stories. In it he goes far beyond Dunsany's concept of "little kingdoms at the Edge of the World," and when his hero descends the seven hundred onyx steps and passes through the Gates of Deeper Slumber, he journeys quite frankly into Dreamland.

This short novel (for it is only some 38,000 words long) was written mostly during 1926. Thereafter Lovecraft bade farewell to his dreamworld of twilit forests, perfumed jungles, spire-thronged and opulent cities, passing on to his more commercial period in which he wrote tales of supernatural horror exclusively. The influence of Dunsany, however, left its mark on these later tales as well, for in creating the imaginary pantheon of Cthulhu, Nyarlathotep, Yog-Sothoth & Co. for his Cthulhu Mythos stories, Lovecraft was directly inspired by the pantheon of invented deities in Dunsany's *The Gods of Pegāna.*[5]

THE second of the great *Weird Tales* triumvirate was Clark Ashton Smith, whose first story in The Unique Magazine was a comparatively minor effort called "The Ninth Skeleton," which appeared a year after Lovecraft's first story, in the September 1924 issue.

Smith was born on January 13, 1893, in Long Valley, California, and spent most of his life in a small cabin in the woods near the town of Auburn, only six miles or so from his birthplace. Like Lovecraft, he had an uncomfortable childhood and left school early to educate himself by the "simple" process of reading *every single word* in the Oxford Unabridged Dictionary and the Encyclopedia Britannica. It is certainly an unorthodox method of self-education, but in Smith's case it paid off, for his stories display the most extensive vocabulary of exotic words of any pulp magazine writer I can think of.[6]

Although Smith was no less eccentric a recluse than was Lovecraft, in his younger years he moved freely in the raffish circles of San Francisco's Bohemian half-world of artists and poets, a sort of combination boy-prodigy-*cum*-protégé, under the wing of a distinguished poet of the '20s named George Sterling. Filled with such stellar figures as Jack London, Ambrose Bierce, Bret Harte, and Joaquin Miller, the Bohemian circles of San Francisco rivaled New York's Greenwich Village, and in such sophisticated company the young Smith was exposed to a lot of first-class modern literature which Lovecraft, omnivorous reader though he was, shunned as the plague. Lovecraft's knowledge of modern fiction ended with Ben Hecht's novel *Erik Dorn,* and *The Waste Land* formed the perimeter of his experience with modern poetry, although he had met Hart Crane and moved briefly in the same circles with E. E. Cummings. But Lovecraft's entire life and character was a denial and a refutation of the 20th century, and a deliberate turning-back to the 18th-century world of periwigs and perukes. Smith, however, developed cosmopolitan tastes and learned French in order to translate Baudelaire and other moderns.

It was Lovecraft who urged Smith to send his fantasy verse to *Weird Tales,* and who sent some samples to Edwin Baird, suggesting he try to get Smith for the magazine. Baird was impressed enough to break his own rule against printing poetry; he wrote Smith asking for some, and thereafter Smith contributed heavily to the magazine, both prose and verse, and even an illustration or two. Smith admitted to an intense admiration for Poe, but the influences on his prose seem to have been primarily such bejeweled works as Beckford's febrile and erotic masterpiece of "Baghdad Gothic," the immortal *Vathek,* Flaubert's luxurious Carthaginian extravaganza, *Salammbô,* and stylistic curiosa such as Wilde's *Salome.* Despite the early sale of "The Ninth Skeleton" to *Weird Tales,* Smith did not settle down to work on short stories with any noticeable diligence until the Depression began. Then, in the autumn of 1929, he entered a period of amazing productivity which he managed to sustain until the spring of 1934, by which date he had written about one hundred short stories and novelettes, as well as a number of prose poems. He had also begun and then abandoned two novels.

At that point, for some inexplicable reason, Smith simply stopped writing short stories altogether. In the remaining quarter-century of his life—he died on August 14, 1961—he turned out only a negligible handful of tales. This sudden termination of a remarkable career becomes all the more mystifying if you stop to consider that Smith was only in his early forties when he turned away from the short story; and he was one of the most popular writers in the history of *Weird Tales* as well, having at that point produced twice as many stories as Lovecraft wrote in his entire life.

Whatever his reasons for giving up the short story, we must be grateful for the extraordinary work he did produce, for Smith seems to many, including myself, to be the most brilliant and talented of all the many fine writers who helped make *Weird Tales* legendary. The main body of Smith's work is organized into cycles of stories that are connected by background setting but unconnected, except here and there, by any continuing characters. The earliest of these series he launched in the May 1930 issue with the publication of "The End of the Story." Despite the seeming contradiction in its title, this was the first of a book-length series of tales set in Averoigne, an imaginary province of medieval France. This idea he may have borrowed from Cabell, whose Poictesme is an equally imaginary French province, or from the invented, pseudo-French kingdom of Tryphême, the setting of Pierre Louys' novel, *The Adventures of King Pausole*.

About the same time he also conceived the promising notion of utilizing for his settings mythical prehistoric civilizations. The first of these that came to mind was the obvious choice—Atlantis—but to avoid comparison with the King Kull stories written by his friend, Robert E. Howard, two of which had appeared in *Weird Tales* during the fall of 1929, Smith set his first tale in Poseidonis, "the last isle of foundering Atlantis." Howard's Kull, of course, was a savage from the untamed, primitive Atlantis of the Dawn Age of the Lost Continent; Smith had set his scene in the Twilight Age. A neat compliment, obviously intentional.

The first of these tales of Poseidonis, again ironically titled "The Last Incantation," was published in the June 1930 issue—in the same year, you will notice, as the first of the Averoigne cycle. The following year Smith began a series set in the imaginary polar continent of Hyperborea, a lovely never-never land invented by the Greeks and much touted by occultists such as Madame Blavatsky as the earliest of terrestrial civilizations. The first story in this cycle was called "The Tale of Satampra Zeiros," and it appeared in the November 1931 issue. Having milked prehistory a bit much, Smith set his next series in Zothique, an invented continent here on earth in an inconceivably remote future age in which science has been forgotten and sorcery reborn. He then turned to Xiccarph, a remote planet ruled by a powerful magician, for his next setting; but this was toward the end of that remarkable period of sustained creativity, and only two tales were ever written in this series.

Smith possessed brilliant talents in several of the arts: his poetry stands up to comparison with that of Swinburne, and even approaches Keats and Milton on occasion; as for sculpture, a lifelong interest, he limited himself to small pieces a hand high at most, but even within so minute a scale he created some bizarre and lovely conceptions; his work in color painting has been seen by few and seems largely devoted to fantastical landscapes of bizarre vegetation and fungi, but those of his pen-and-ink drawings that I have seen are interesting enough, although marred by amateurish technique and execution; he also tried his hand at verse drama, without demonstrating any particular talent, but his translations in verse and prose from a number of recent French and Spanish poets are very highly regarded indeed, and I understand that he is considered the finest of the translators of Baudelaire. The broad range of his artistic interests, coupled with the fact that he owned his own home and did not require much of an income to get along, may perhaps explain why he quit writing fiction so abruptly. He may simply have become bored with the story form, and so stopped using it.

THE last of this famous triumvirate was a robust Texan named Robert Ervin Howard, who followed Smith into the pages of *Weird Tales* by one year, just as Smith had followed Lovecraft. Howard's first story in *Weird Tales* —written, by the way, when he was only nineteen—was "Spear and Fang," which appeared in the July 1925 issue.

Howard was born in Peaster, Texas, on January 22, 1906, the son of one of the first doctors in that area of the Southwest. His family settled in Cross Plains after a bit of wandering around, and Howard began writing at the age of fifteen; he sold that first yarn to *Weird Tales* while an undergraduate at Howard Payne College in the nearby town of Brownwood. Those who knew him describe the future creator of that prototype of all Sword

& Sorcery heroes, Conan of Cimmeria, as a rugged six-footer who tipped the scales at two hundred pounds, most of which was solid muscle. He had an explosive temper, and was given to black moods of depression and passionate emotional outbursts.

Howard wrote vivid, colorful stories of terrific verve and gusto—stories filled to the brim with bloody battles, brawny heroes, and barbaric women. He wrote with enormous drive and energy, and in no time he was earning a remarkable income with his typewriter. In fact, at the height of the Depression, Howard was earning more money than any of the fifteen hundred citizens of Cross Plains, including the local banker.[7]

He wrote two-fisted westerns, sport stories, gangster yarns, and an historical series about a dour Puritan adventurer named Solomon Kane who brawled his way through the black jungles of Africa, battering down blood-soaked altars armed with a huge iron-bound Bible. He secretly yearned to write yarns of magic and mystery in Tibet or stories about keen-eyed British espionage agents in India in the vein of Talbot Mundy, or swashbuckling pirate sagas like Rafael Sabatini, or the kind of romantic adventure fiction Edgar Rice Burroughs and Harold Lamb produced. But Howard's rather slapdash, derivative talents could not compete for the major pulps like *Argosy* or *All-Story* against writers like these, to say nothing of Jack London, James Oliver Curwood, and Max Brand, so he settled for *Weird Tales.*

Howard sold all sorts of yarns to *Weird Tales,* but by 1932 he had evolved a formula that seems likely to make his name as immortal as any of the pulp-fiction writers. In the December 1932 issue of *Weird Tales,* a story called "The Phoenix on the Sword" appeared; it was the first of his tales about Conan, a gigantic barbarian warrior of the ancient world. This was not, of course, his first great triumph in *Weird Tales.* By this time, Howard had thrilled the readers of "The Unique Magazine" with an extraordinary succession of vivid, exciting tales, his first success coming, perhaps, with the appearance of "Wolfshead" in April 1926. It was not until the issue of August 1928, however, that he began to find his true *métier:* in that issue appeared "Red Shadows," the earliest of the adventures of that dour Puritan, Solomon Kane. Lovecraft pointed out that it was with the Solomon Kane stories that Howard found his way to "one of his most effective accomplishments —the description of vast megalithic cities of the elder world, around whose dark towers and labyrinthine nether vaults linger an aura of pre-human fear and necromancy."

Having stumbled upon his gift for employing crumbling ruins left over from the elder world as adventure-story settings, Howard swiftly carried the idea to its logical extremity and began plotting stories in the lost, forgotten civilizations of the elder world themselves. In the August and September issues of 1929 appeared two stories, "The Shadow Kingdom" and "The Mirrors of Tus Tuzun Thune," which were set in a mythic age when Atlantis was a raw and savage wilderness and the world was dominated by the immemorial Seven Empires, the supreme realm being that of Valusia. Howard explored the pre-Atlantean world of Valusia and Grondar and Farsun and Thurania in a series of yarns about an exiled Atlantean savage named Kull, who rises to power in the elder world and seizes the throne of Valusia itself. Wright rejected most of these stories, but they eventually reached print in 1967. The character of King Kull served Howard as a sort of rough draft for his later creation, Conan of Cimmeria.

With the birth of Conan in 1932, Howard entered his great phase. Story after story poured from him, painting a vivid panorama of an imaginary "Hyborian Age" civilization that had flourished 15,000 years ago between the death of Atlantis and the birth of Egypt and Chaldea. Using the device of "this sword for hire," Howard sent Conan wandering about primeval Europe, Asia, and Africa, serving here as mercenary warrior, thief, or bandit, and there as guerrilla chief, pirate, or assassin. From yarn to yarn, Conan moves up the ranks, finally becoming a king. The series culminated in the first Conan novel, "The Hour of the Dragon." The readers loved it, because it was something fresh and new, something which combined the heroic action of Burroughs, the black magic and evil demons of Lovecraft, and the fabulous legendary prehistoric kingdoms of Smith. In all, Howard published eighteen stories about Conan.[8]

Burly he-man that he was, Howard had his fatal flaw in a deep emotional attachment to his mother. She fell ill, plunging him into a mood of black despondency. Early in the morning of June 11, 1936, a broiling summer day, told that his mother would never regain consciousness, he sat down at his battered Underwood No. 5 and typed out a couplet—

> All fled—all done, so lift me on the pyre;
> The feast is over and the lamps expire.

They were the last words Robert E. Howard would ever write. He went out, got in his car, and about eight o'clock in the morning put a pistol to his head and blew his brains out.

THE Conan stories were really nothing new: the indomitable warrior battling against monsters and demons in a barbaric world is as old as St. George or Siegfried, Beowulf or Hercules, or Gilgamesh, for that matter. But the color and gusto that Howard brought to his brand of heroic fantasy made for superlative entertainment, and other writers were not hesitant about following in his footsteps. The first to do so was a young girl of twenty-two named Catherine Lucille Moore, who worked for a bank in Indianapolis. Her first sale to *Weird Tales* was a story called "Shambleau," published in the November 1933 issue, in which she introduced a lanky, hard-bitten space adventurer named Northwest Smith, who reappeared in several sequels. These yarns were weird fantasies laid on exotic planets, not unlike some of the stories of Clark Ashton Smith, but they had the rich color and imagery of A. Merritt. The following year, C. L. Moore tried her hand at the kind of thing Howard was doing with his Conan saga, introducing a fiery, red-headed Medieval warrior-girl named Jirel of Joiry in a tale called "Black God's Kiss," which appeared in the October 1934 issue of *Weird Tales*. Readers applauded her idea of a "gal Conan," so Miss Moore wrote five or six sequels.[9]

The kind of story Howard created with his Conan yarns, and which C. L. Moore imitated with her tales of Jirel, we call "Sword & Sorcery" today. The term, however, was not coined until long after the new subbranch of heroic fantasy appeared. It was, in fact, coined by Fritz Leiber (himself probably the finest living writer of Sword & Sorcery) as recently as 1961. The British writer Michael Moorcock had published an open letter in the amateur magazine *Amra,* asking for ideas on a name for the sub-genre, his own suggestion being "epic fantasy." Leiber suggested "Sword & Sorcery," an obvious derivation from such terms as "blood and thunder" and "cloak and dagger." His response first appeared in another "fanzine"—as amateur periodicals are called in the sub-world of fantasy and science fiction enthusiasts—a publication called *Ancalagon,* and was reprinted in the issue of *Amra* dated July 1961. Although some prefer "heroic fantasy," as being more dignified and literary, and a few employ a variant, "swordplay-and-sorcery," the term "Sword & Sorcery" caught on and is now generally accepted. But I am getting ahead of my story here.

Miss Moore was followed in this burgeoning new field by a minor writer named Clifford Ball, who sold only six stories to *Weird Tales,* the last appearing in 1941, whereupon he dropped out of sight. The first of his three unoriginal but lively ventures into Sword & Sorcery was "Duar the Accursed" in the May 1937 issue.

A year later, however, a much more important and talented figure entered the field with a magnificent yarn about a wandering rogue called Elak, an Atlantean prince whose throne had been usurped out from under him. The first of these Elak yarns was a two-part serial called "Thunder in the Dawn," which began in the May 1938 issue of *Weird Tales,* and the author's name was Henry Kuttner.

Kuttner was born in Los Angeles in 1914, and those who knew him describe him as a small, shy, dark, quiet-spoken, and rather diffident man who would never stand out in a crowd. He was, however, a superb craftsman— a born writer—a story-teller par excellence in much the same way that Howard had been; however, Kuttner was capable of a truly remarkable variety, unlike Howard. Kuttner could (and did) write every sort of story, from the Lovecraftian brand of slithering horror, the Howardian fantastic swashbuckler, or the delicately lyric Dunsanian fable, to space opera, coldly cerebral science fiction of the type that John W. Campbell, Jr., preferred for his *Astounding Science Fiction,* or the sort of wacky humor with which Thorne Smith made his mark. He was, simply, a "writer's writer," the envy, despair, and idol of his colleagues—able to turn out such a voluminous number of stories that he employed sixteen pen-names in order to sell them.

Kuttner sold four novelettes about Elak of Atlantis to *Weird Tales*—splendid, rousing yarns filled with color and whirlwind action and spectacular magic. They were, however, written during his apprenticeship as a fictioneer and are not without their flaws. The characterization is hardly developed at all, and Elak remains a cardboard figure, little more than a stereotype. Three of the Elak stories appeared in 1938. In the following year Kuttner launched a similar series for a new competitor of *Weird Tales* called *Strange Stories.* These yarns were set in legendary kingdoms of the prehistoric Gobi Desert region of Central Asia—the occultists call this "Shamballah," although Kuttner does not seem to have been familiar with the name and never used it. He wrote only two of these stories about the adventures of Prince Raynor of Sardopolis, both of which were published in *Strange Stories* during 1939, but the magazine soon folded and no more tales in this sequence appeared.

There would probably have been more stories about Elak but Farnsworth Wright began discouraging ventures into Howardian heroica. He rejected, for instance, the earliest of Fritz Leiber's Fafhrd and the Gray Mouser stories; Leiber gave him the first look at them, one by one, and one by one he bounced them back to Leiber, who then passed them along to John Campbell for his new fantasy magazine, *Unknown,* as we shall see in the next chapter. Wright was an elderly man by this time, and *Weird Tales* was having another of its periodic bouts of money trouble; shortly thereafter the magazine was sold to the firm of Short Stories, Inc. Wright relocated to New York and continued to edit the magazine from its new offices at 9 Rockefeller Plaza, but his health was failing and he soon retired, passing the editorship to a diminutive blond Scotswoman with a wry, Puckish sense of humor named Dorothy McIlwraith, who would be *Weird Tales'* last editor. The final issue to bear the name of Farnsworth Wright on its masthead was dated March 1940.

By 1940 Kuttner and C. L. Moore were married and living in California, making their first home in South Laguna. The final Elak story appeared in *Weird Tales* in the issue dated January 1941. It was the last piece of genuine Sword & Sorcery the magazine ever printed. The Kuttners did not care; Miss Moore never contributed to the magazine again, and Kuttner's last story in *Weird Tales* appeared in 1943. The new husband-and-wife team were busy breaking into Campbell's prestigious magazines, to which they contributed many brilliant, mature, serious works, which quickly placed them in the top rank of science fiction writers. Kuttner died suddenly in 1958 at the age of 44; his wife, since remarried, is still living, but her typewriter has long been silent.

Both facts are to be regretted. But perhaps it is fitting, for the era to which they contributed—the sleazy, gaudy, glorious, golden age of the pulps—has long since ended.

4

The Mathematics of Magic:
Imaginary-World Fantasy in *Unknown*

> "Contrariwise," continued Tweedledee, "if it
> was so, it might be; and if it were so, it
> would be; but as it isn't, it ain't. That's
> logic!"
>
> —Lewis Carroll:
>   "Through the Looking-Glass"

IT has been said of John W. Campbell's great fantasy magazine, *Unknown,* that it was neither a magazine, nor a circle of writers, nor an era of fiction, nor a style of writing, but a state of mind.[1] A state of mind through which some of the most gifted of the fantasy and science fiction writers of the early 1940s passed—a fleeting mood of hilarity and brilliant whimsy and playful fun—before they moved on to the grim realities of writing science fiction in the Atomic Age.

Born in 1910 in Newark, New Jersey, Campbell was the son of an engineer with American Telephone and Telegraph. An early interest in nuclear physics led him to a first-rate scientific education; he studied at M.I.T. and graduated from Duke University with a Bachelor of Science degree in physics. Scarcely out of his teens, he began writing science fiction; his first story appeared in 1930, and he soon became enormously popular with the readers of such pioneering SF magazines as *Amazing Stories*. His super-cosmic space epics were closely compared to those of E. E. Smith, Ph.D., whose immense popularity he soon came to rival.

Although John Campbell was a writer of considerable gifts, his most remarkable talent lay in the editorial field. In 1937 the firm of Street & Smith offered him the editorship of a magazine they had acquired from a foundering publisher. First appearing in the fall of 1929, the little magazine had braved the stormy waters of the Depression but its publisher, W. L. Clayton, had gone under. With John Campbell at its helm, *Astounding Science Fiction* rapidly became the best magazine in its field; the roster of brilliant writers it introduced and the number of superb stories it published have since been equaled by no other science fiction magazine. Those of you familiar with the field will know what I mean; a mere list of the authors who came into print under the direct influence of Campbell reads like a Who's Who of American science fiction—Robert A. Heinlein, Isaac Asimov, L. Sprague de Camp, A. E. van Vogt, Theodore Sturgeon, Lester del Rey, Fritz Leiber, Poul Anderson, James Blish, and others too numerous to name.

Sometime in 1938, Campbell received from the British writer Eric Frank Russell the manuscript of a stunning novel called *Sinister Barrier,* based on the sort of inexplicable freak happenings that Charles Fort spent a lifetime collecting. Campbell was impressed, but the novel did not quite fit in with the kind of material in which *Astounding* specialized. A new, more flexible magazine was needed, a magazine whose parameters were broad enough to include offbeat varieties of imaginative fiction, even out-and-out fantasy. And so Campbell launched *Unknown,* whose first issue appeared in March 1939, with the Russell novel in the top spot. Rather naturally, Campbell encouraged his first-class stable of science fiction talent to contribute to the new magazine, which most if not all of them did.

Now, in revolutionizing science fiction, Campbell had instilled the basic precepts of good writing in his authors. Before him, the field had been largely made up of slam-bang space adventures, colossal intergalactic epics, and serious but dull stories revolving around future technology. Tales in the latter category tended to stop their plots cold at the introduction of a new gadget, in order to explain how it was supposed to work. What

Campbell did was to tell his writers: "We grant you your gadgets—now get on with the story." Following his precepts, writers like Heinlein wrote straightforward, matter-of-fact yarns in which the technological hardware was simply part of the background. In effect, they wrote stories of everyday life that happened to be set in the future, stories that centered on future politics, economics, religion, and so on, not just on gadgetry. Such stories eschewed the wild-eyed wonder and cardboard characterization of early science fiction.

The same sort of thing happened with *Unknown;* when Campbell's writers turned their imaginations to crafting fantasy, they avoided the "gorgeous" prose and verbal poetics that marked most of the *Weird Tales* school. The stories Henry Kuttner and C. L. Moore sold to *Unknown,* for instance, are as unlike the stories they had written for *Weird Tales* as a story can be.

At first, however, the fantasies that *Unknown* printed were fairly stock. L. Ron Hubbard's short novel, "The Ultimate Adventure," which appeared in the second issue, transported a modern Manhattanite to the world of the *Arabian Nights.* Three issues later, Hubbard played a variation on the same notion in *Slaves of Sleep;* in that novel Hubbard's hero dwells in the everyday world during his waking hours but becomes a dashing adventurer in the world of the djinns whenever he falls asleep. Around the same time, Norvell W. Page contributed two short novels, which appeared in the first few issues, that were essentially Sword & Sorcery of the Howardian type, although set in antiquity rather than prehistory. The first of these, *Flame Winds,* introduced a burly, brawling, red-bearded prototype Crusader called Hurricane John, who carves out an empire in the remote East; his adventures were continued in *Sons of the Bear-God,* in which it becomes apparent that the swashbuckling swordsman is the original of Prester John, the legendary Christian monarch of Asia who became part of the folklore of the Middle Ages. Wan Tengri, as Hurricane John is known to his Asiatic friends and foes, differs from Conan in being a more rounded and believable character, possessed of a surprising sense of humor.[2]

But Campbell was not going to settle for printing the same sort of stuff his readers could find in *Weird Tales.* This became obvious when, in the sixth issue of *Unknown,* he published the first of Fritz Leiber's stories about a delightful pair of wandering rogues named Fafhrd and the Gray Mouser. This first tale in the series was a novelette entitled "Two Sought Adventure," which appeared in the August 1939 issue. It began on a singularly promising note—

> It was the Year of the Behemoth, the Month of the Hedgehog, the Day of the Toad. A hot, late summer sun was sinking down toward evening over the somber, fertile land of Lankhmar, the most civilized country in a world which history forgets . . .

The promise implied in that opening, by the way, was faithfully kept. The story was Sword & Sorcery in a deliciously new and original vein that owed more to James Branch Cabell and Lord Dunsany and E. R. Eddison than it did to Howard, Kuttner, or Moore. Leiber, of course, was aware of Howard and had read him, but he was unique among the post-Howardians in that he seemed in no way to have been influenced by the dynamic Texan. He had worked the second major variation on the Conan stereotype, the first having been C. L. Moore's idea of a "gal Conan"; Leiber brought in two heroes, and they were equal partners in swashbuckling deeds, not just the old familiar team of hero-and-sidekick. Fafhrd, the blond, gusty, seven-foot barbarian from the Cold Waste beyond the Eight Cities and the Trollstep Mountains, with his hammered ornaments and huge longsword, and the sly, small, gray-hooded Mouser with his furtive ways and deceptively dainty rapier, were refreshing and different. Readers enjoyed the give-and-take between them and the warm sense of camaraderie they shared.

But those same readers must have been puzzled as to just where—or when—this land of Lankhmar existed, for Leiber left it undefined, floating free in space and time. From that reference to "a world which history forgets," readers may have deduced a prehistoric milieu. But not *too* prehistoric, since the two adventurers ride through "rolling forests of maple and oak" on a dappled gray mare and a chestnut gelding, with jays and catbirds singing in the branches and chipmunks busy in the leaves underfoot. The second story in the series appeared the following year; it was set in "unhistoried Lankhmar" and carried the two adventurers to a grim land beyond the Sea of Monsters, also neglecting to locate this world or age with any precision. In all, Leiber contributed five Fafhrd and the Gray Mouser stories to *Unknown,* the last of them appearing in the issue for February 1943.

BORN in 1910, son of the distinguished stage and screen actor of the same name, Fritz Leiber acted for a couple of seasons in his father's Shakespearian company under the name of Francis Lathrop. He also served brief tours of duty as a college teacher and an editor for *Science Digest.* Although his first sale was to *Weird Tales,* it is with *Astounding Science Fiction* and *Unknown* that his name is most closely associated. For to both of Campbell's magazines he contributed milestone novels, each very different in style and subject, as for example *Gather, Darkness!* in *Astounding* and *Conjure Wife* in *Unknown.*

By 1956 the audience for Sword & Sorcery had grown large enough to support a fanzine devoted entirely to heroic fantasy, and such a magazine materialized in the form of *Amra.* Leiber became one of its staunchest supporters. The full story behind the tales of Fafhrd and the Gray Mouser emerged in articles he wrote for that magazine. The basic concept had been born in 1934 during Leiber's correspondence with his friend Harry Fischer; in the midst of a rambling missive, Fischer had tossed off a prose fragment that introduced the two heroes and Lankhmar itself, which in this first incarnation appeared as a "walled city of the Tuatha

De Danann." Delighted, Leiber responded in kind by sending Fischer a comparable fragment, which, he admits, was "tinged with Lovecraftianisms and Dunsanianisms." Further exchanges of correspondence continued, and the linkages between Lankhmar's world and the world of Celtic myth were soon dropped, as were most of the Lovecraftianisms (although the first stories to be printed contained such Lovecraftian place-names as "the Cold Waste" and occasional references to "the Old Ones" and "the Elder Ones"). The confusion about just where, or when—or even *what*—Lankhmar's world was seems to have been unavoidable. In an article called "Fafhrd and Me," which *Amra* published in 1963, Leiber records that "although 1934 ended with Fafhrd and the Mouser sharply crystalized, their background world or worlds was indeterminate." The next year, under the influence of Robert Graves' *I, Claudius,* Leiber drafted out "a long tale . . . set in early Imperial Rome," but Fafhrd and the Gray Mouser did not seem to fit that milieu and the tale was set aside. Then, "in the fall I began another novella of the twain, this time set in the somewhat mistier period of the Seleucids, and finished it early in 1936. This tale was rejected by several book publishers and by Farnsworth Wright . . . as being too full of stylistic novelties." It went through three or four recastings and rewritings, and was finally published in 1947 as "Adept's Gambit."

After yet more inconclusive fumblings, Leiber finally began isolating in his imagination just the sort of world he felt the stories would feel most comfortable in: it was a composite, "a little like modern Norway in its houses but more like the Roman Empire in its organization; like Thrace because of its city-states and spirit of free inquiry . . . but nomadlike in mind . . . a little like early Japan . . . somewhat resembling Atlantis but with an interest in cats matched only by Egypt." Leiber was on the track of his unique conception, later to be termed "the World of Nehwon,"—which is "Nowhen" spelled backwards—and a map was sketched out. But the writing of stories languished until *Unknown* appeared.

Leiber records that he "took a silver bit in my teeth, devised a somewhat choppier, more action-packed style of narrative that Harry and I had used in our letters, set up for myself the rule that my heroes should not be Conans . . . but earthy characters with earthy weaknesses, winning in the end mostly by luck from villains and supernatural forces more powerful than themselves." For courtesy's sake, since *Weird Tales* had taken a story from Leiber already, he sent "Two Sought Adventure" to Wright, but when it was rejected he took it to Campbell, who accepted it. He also accepted the other stories in the series, which were also bounced by Wright's successor, Dorothy McIlwraith, often with a slightly dubious remark such as "This is more of a *Weird Tales* piece than *Unknown* usually prints. However——"

Fafhrd and the Gray Mouser languished a bit after the disappearance of *Unknown,* but the opportunity afforded by selling his first book of stories to Arkham House in 1947 prompted Leiber to write, or rather polish up, another new one, the above-mentioned "Adept's Gambit." He sold another one to *Suspense* in 1951, and a short-lived fantasy magazine called *Other Worlds* took yet another story of Lankhmar in 1953; in 1959, now a famous author in the field, Leiber sold "Lean Times in Lankhmar" to Cele Goldsmith of *Fantastic,* who accepted several more Mouserian fantasies from that point on. Fritz Leiber is, of course, still crafting tales of Nehwon to this day—in 1971 he won a Nebula award, and subsequently a Hugo, for "Ill Met in Lankhmar," a novelette which had appeared in *The Magazine of Fantasy and Science Fiction.*

Leiber is the only Sword & Sorcery writer in history who has devoted his efforts to one series alone; he has also been at it longer than anyone else. It is now thirty-four years since Fritz Leiber first led us across the portals of his imagination and began conducting us on a guided tour of his world of Nehwon.[8] In story after story he has captained us on a voyage of exploration and discovery through the magical lands where his fascinating pair of delicious rogues dwell. Nehwon remains rather ambiguously situated in time and space; it is contiguous with our own world at certain points, and never very far apart from it—parallel, let us say. If any one thing emerges from a look through these inimitable stories, it is that the true hero, the true central character of the saga, is neither Fafhrd nor the Gray Mouser, but the City of the Black Toga itself—"unhistoried" Lankhmar, that "intrigue-ridden, pleasure-sated, sorcery-working, thief-ruled city, with its fat merchants and cutthroats and rogues," a city whose furtive, crooked alleys and fetid, ill-lit byways have become familiar to us by now, and whose fortunes Leiber has been chronicling for a span of time that is four years longer than the entire lifetime of Robert E. Howard.

Unhistoried Lankhmar, indeed!

NINE months after the first Mouserian fantasy appeared in *Unknown,* John Campbell introduced his readers to the most memorable writing team in the history of fantasy. The story was "The Roaring Trumpet," in the May 1940 issue, and the authors were Fletcher Pratt and L. Sprague de Camp.

Unknown published the work of many writers in its brief but golden time. Some of these were names familiar from the pages of *Astounding*—science fiction writers on a brief vacation from the rigors of cerebral, mature fiction-writing, having pure fun in a magazine whose horizons were so broad as to be out of view. Others were more or less moonlighting from *Weird Tales;* among these were Robert Bloch, Donald Wandrei, Frank Belknap Long, and Manly Wade Wellman. But certain writers were conspicuous in their absence, writers like Seabury Quinn and August Derleth—writers of rather predictable plots and stock ghost-story machinery. *Unknown* wanted originality, ingenuity, a sense of humor, an air of sophistication, and a dimension of literary quality—not "beautiful" writing, but literary quality—unusual in the pages of a pulp magazine. That Campbell had established a quirky, individual magazine devoted to the offbeat, a magazine with a style and character all its own, was by now becoming evident. And to his pages he attracted some impressive names, like Anthony Boucher and Raymond Chandler, whom you would never expect to find in *Weird Tales*.

But of all these writers, the team of Pratt and de Camp most perfectly typified the style of the new magazine. That first collaboration, "The Roaring Trumpet," introduced a most *un*intrepid hero named Harold Shea. It soon became typical of an *Unknown* story that the hero was distinctly unheroic; well, Shea is a flashy dresser, known at times to affect a phoney British accent, and a remarkably unsuccessful ladies' man. He is not even good loking—"a little thinner than average, he would have been handsome if his nose were shorter and his eyes farther apart."

For a hero not without a few psychological hang-ups, Harold Shea has an ideal job working for a research psychologist named Chalmers. Chalmers has the notion that

> The world we live in is composed of impressions received through the senses. But there is an infinity of possible worlds, and if the senses can be attuned to receive a different series of impressions, we should invariably find ourselves living in a different world.

Chalmers' experimental technique consisted of filling one's mind with the fundamental assumptions of the world you desired to visit. The fundamental assumptions of our own modern world are those of scientific law and logic; the assumptions of another world, say, for example, one in which magic worked, would be the laws of magic, which scholars like Frazer have worked out—the Law of Contagion, the Law of Similarity, and so on. By reducing such a world-system to the formulae of symbolic logic, transference from one world to another should be possible. This is exactly what Shea does, aiming for the world of Irish myth. (If you'd like to try it yourself, the formula reads as follows: "If P equals not-Q, Q implies not-P, which is equivalent to saying either P or Q or neither, but not both. *But* if not-P is not implied by not-Q, the counter-implicative form of the proposition . . .")

Well, this being *Unknown,* Shea plays a Wrong-Way Corrigan through an infinity of possible worlds, ending up in the cosmos of the Norse Eddas, complete with Aesir, Jotuns, and Valkyries. Three months later, Pratt and de Camp followed this one with "The Mathematics of Magic," in which Shea, this time accompanied by Chalmers, tries to reach the less hazardous and uncomfortable world of Spenser's *Faerie Queene;* this time the "syllogismobile" does not go astray, and they soon find themselves not only embroiled in a series of quaint adventures but also enamoured of a couple of local damosels. In order to survive the various problems imposed upon them by the plot, they have to master the tricky science of magic. To a logician, this is not as tough a proposition as it may sound, and Chalmers in particular becomes quite—ah—adept at the trade. Having whipped the enchanter Busyrane to a frazzle, Chalmers blandly accepts Harold's words of praise with the remark, "You observe the improvement in my technique? . . . The really important fact about this evening's work is that I've discovered the secret of quantitative control. Frege's definition of number solves the problem with relation to the calculus of classes . . ."

One last villain, who has eluded the general mopping-up, catches Harold and his girl friend, Belphebe, off-guard. Caught in a blast of magic, they are precipitated back into the everyday world, leaving Chalmers and his own fair lady, Florimel, behind in Faerie.

This combination of wacky logic and scientific analysis of magic delighted the readers no end; they ate up both yarns with relish and hungrily howled for more. Pratt and de Camp obliged six issues later with a novel called *The Castle of Iron,* which ran in the April 1941 *Unknown.* The story opened with yet another display of what this incomparable team could do with rational, realistic thinking as against the sloppy romanticism common to pulp writers. In the usual run of pulp adventure yarns, hero and heroine return from their magical adventure and that's that. But Pratt and de Camp opened the novel with a grueling scene in which the cops are interrogating poor Harold under the broiling lights. Not unnaturally, they think he has done away with his boss, disposing of the body somewhere. After all, he and Chalmers were in the lab together . . . and only Harold came out of it, with a girl, probably his accomplice in the murder.

Of course, Harold doesn't have much luck persuading them that Chalmers has accepted a job as chief magician, settled down to married life with a lovely lady made out of snow, and has relocated to Fairyland! In fact, the only thing he can think to do is to try to get back to the universe of *The Faerie Queene*. But everything goes wrong: by accident he takes one of the cops along, and they end up universes away in another literary cosmos, that of the Xanadu of Coleridge's poem, "Kubla Khan." Another hop brings all the characters together in a universe singularly close to that of Spenser's poem, to wit, the universe of Ariosto's *Orlando Furioso*, from which Spenser borrowed rather heavily for his style and many of his ideas.

THE team continued to delight the readership of *Unknown* with some of the most sprightly, entertaining, witty fantasies ever written, fantasies in which romantic adventure took a backseat to rational plotting and interesting characterization. In novels like *The Land of Unreason* and *The Carnelian Cube*, as well as two further Harold Shea stories—in which the syllogismobile journeys into the realm of the *Kalevala* and, at last, to the world of Irish myth—they were far and away the most admired and popular of the writers for *Unknown*.

They were very different in appearance, background, and temperament. Pratt, the senior of the two, was born in Buffalo, New York, in 1897. Damon Knight once described him as "a tiny, goateed wisp of a man who used to be a professional boxer, wore amazing shirts and also kept marmosets." Pratt had translated several interminable pioneering science fiction novels from German for Hugo Gernsback's *Amazing Stories,* for which he also wrote endless potboilers of his own; he had also once worked for the Hearst papers directly under A. Merritt, and had a store of Merritt anecdotes which he would tell over the teacups. He became an expert on Naval warfare and Civil War history. Towards the end of his life (he died in 1956) he wrote two extraordinary imaginary-world fantasies, *The Well of the Unicorn* and *The Blue Star.* The first of these novels showed his indebtedness to Lord Dunsany and William Morris. The second was an astonishingly mature and unheroic work of fantasy, and was set in something quite different from any of the backgrounds used up to then; eschewing the dim scenery of the Middle Ages, all flowery meads and cantering knights, and the opulent Orient, he selected a most unpromising locale: the Austrian Empire of, say, the reign of Maria Theresa. The novel, frankly experimental, was surprisingly successful, and stands today as one of the few uncompromisingly realistic, even downbeat, fantasy novels ever written.

As for L. Sprague de Camp, a lean six-footer who towered over his diminutive collaborator, he has piercing black eyes, a deep voice, and a commanding manner. A native of New York City born in 1907, de Camp holds degrees in aeronautical engineering and economics and a reserve commission as Lieutenant Commander in the navy. An inveterate globe-trotter, on familiar terms with languages like Swahili and Urdu, de Camp bedazzled the readers of *Astounding* and *Unknown* for years, eventually moving on to write superior historical novels which he researched on the spot, as well as many excellent books of formal history, archaeology, and other erudite subjects, including a book on dinosaurs and another one on elephants.

De Camp wrote quite a bit of fantasy on his own for *Unknown.* Employing much the same sort of rational, clear-headed approach to plotting fantasy that he and

Fletcher Pratt had used in their collaborations, he precipitated his hero into Logeia, a world run on strict
Aristotelian terms, in a short novel called *The Un-
desired Princess,* which appeared in the February 1942
issue of *Unknown.* In Logeia, hyperbole and metaphor
are impossible because everything is remorselessly
literal: a red-haired princess is just that, crowned with
locks that are purée-of-tomato *red.* And the world itself
is as formalized as formal could be:

> Thirty feet away began a fantastic jungle. Along a line as
> sharp as if it had been surveyed the red gravel gave way
> to blue moss, and from the moss rose tall, regularly spaced
> trees, every one with an implausibly even tapering cylindri-
> cal trunk . . . the leaves were blue; some were circular,
> some elliptical, some other shapes, but all geometrically
> precise as though cut out of blue paper to go into a store-
> window display.

Notice how de Camp thought everything out carefully, and evolved every implication of his basic premise.
In a strictly Aristotelian world, leaves would not grow
ragged and irregular but would conform to flawlessly
precise geometric shapes. And, of course, only the
primary colors would exist; the various shades and mix-
tures of them—such as green—would be too irregular
to exist!

Another short novel, *Solomon's Stone,* followed in the
June 1942 issue. It involves one Prosper Nash, a staid
CPA who dreams of being a dashing cavalier and gets
a chance to be one when a playful experiment in
ceremonial magic accidentally conjures up a real demon
who sends him to the astral plane. Here, the astral
counterparts of everyone on earth live out their fantasies. Nash finds the life of a cavalier exciting but
hazardous, to the point where he quests for the Shamir,
the talisman of King Solomon, in order to get back to
his dull, predictable existence as an accountant.

Whereas Pratt loathed musclebound heroes such as
Conan and strictly shunned them, de Camp has a sneak-
ing admiration for them, and while the heroes in his

books usually start out with a stammer, incurable gas pains, a mother-fixation, or post-nasal drip, they always, to paraphrase Malvolio, have heroism "thrust upon them" in the course of their adventures.

WHILE the Pratt and de Camp kind of Lewis Carroll logic most perfectly sums up the essence of *Unknown,* other stories were published which indicated new trails in fantasy fiction that might have been followed had the magazine survived longer than it did.

One of these was a short novel by John Campbell himself, written under his favorite pseudonym, "Don A. Stuart." The novella was called "The Elder Gods," and in it Campbell did something quite remarkable: he told an heroic fantasy story of quest and adventure and wars between the gods in plain, simple, everyday English—the sort of flat, unadorned prose Raymond Chandler and Hemingway had made popular.

This may seem like nothing particularly important, but I assure you the story is a stylistic bombshell. How fresh, original, and different the typical heroic fantasy seems when told in ordinary, everyday prose! Suddenly a whole new dimension of story-telling opens up, inexplicably new and different. But this experiment led to nothing; no one followed Campbell's example in this direction, and he himself became too busy editing two magazines to do much additional writing. But the experiment still stands, waiting for someone to try it out with another yarn . . .

Then there was Hannes Bok, an extraordinary fantasy painter and magazine illustrator, who first appeared as a cover artist for Farnsworth Wright in the great days of *Weird Tales.* Unbeknownst to any but his circle of intimate friends of which I was luckily a member, Hannes admired and emulated the great A. Merritt in his rare prose, just as he admired and emulated the equally great Maxfield Parrish in his art. As a young reader, forced to return the magazine in which he had been reading Merritt's *The Ship of Ishtar,* he copied the whole novel out in longhand, uncertain that he would ever find a copy of the story again and very much wanting to have it. Any writer will tell you that, with a writer as distinctively a stylist as Merritt certainly was, such an exercise is bound to leave an indelible mark on your own style; this is what happened to Hannes Bok.

Perhaps it was fated to happen. Visual imagery was Merritt's true forte—gorgeously pictorial descriptions of people and landscapes, cities and monsters, told with crisp precision in singing and evocative words. To this Bok brought the trained eye of a painter, accustomed to think in terms of shape and line and color. Being Bok, it was natural that he should enthusiastically take A. Merritt for his model when he came to write fiction.

And write it he did, but not enough of it, alas! Only one novel appeared in *Unknown,* the gorgeous and utterly magical *Sorcerer's Ship,* in which a young man from our world is thrust by accident into a hazy, mysterious, dreamlike world of islands and oceans and enchantments. Campbell published it in his issue for December 1942; I was only twelve years old when I read it in *Unknown,* but it has lingered with me from that day to this. Bok captured the Merrittesque mood and style and color superbly, but he brought to the story his own glorious romanticism and an unexpected, impish humor as well.

There was to have been a sequel, but Hannes had trouble writing sequels—much as Merritt himself did, always preferring to start a new story rather than return to the well-established and already-explored scenery of an old one. Bok went on to write another strongly Merrittesque novel, *The Blue Flamingo,* for a magazine called *Startling Stories,* which trimmed down the novel to half its original manuscript length. As it was initially printed, it lacks much of the extravagant coloring and elaborate, bejeweled descriptive prose in which Hannes excelled. Luckily, the original manuscript was later discovered in the hands of an agent and found its way into print.

Hannes Bok most perfectly imitated A. Merritt some

years later, when he was given the chance to edit and complete two fragments discovered after Merritt's death among his papers. Merritt had begun two novels but had abandoned them; substantial beginnings had been made, however, and when Bok completed the two posthumous collaborations—entitled *The Fox Woman* and *The Black Wheel*—it was virtually impossible to tell where Merritt ended and Bok began.

In *Unknown* for October 1943 another interesting experiment appeared—a fantasy novel by A. E. van Vogt entitled *The Book of Ptath*. One of *Astounding's* most popular and highly regarded science fiction writers, van Vogt was noted for his intricate puzzle-box plots, his unemotional, realistic prose, and his "hampered superman" characters. The style of van Vogt's fiction could be, perhaps has been, called the science-fictional equivalent of the locked-room mystery—the sort of story where the reader doesn't know what the hell is happening until the final chapter, when all is laid bare.

The Book of Ptath represented an utterly fascinating use of this kind of ultra-complex, convoluted plotting worked out within the milieu of a fantasy world. For his setting, van Vogt selected the imaginary supercontinent of Gondwana in the remote future of our own world; he postulated a ruling class of immortal, invulnerable god-kings, whose power was derived, it turned out, from the fact that when the ordinary folk of Gondwana worshipped them they gave up to them a certain amount of their innate vital energy. A typical van Vogt concept—clever, quite original, not necessarily impossible. What van Vogt was writing, quite simply, was a heroic novel in which all of the magic and the gods could be explained on a scientific basis. What a marvelous idea! The plot gets working when one of these gods, Ptath himself, ousted by a cabal of his peers and exiled millions of years back in time, is reborn again into far future Gondwana, his memory wiped clean.

The novel moves with beautiful logic and is absorbing and entertaining as only a van Vogt novel can be. The Gondwanian milieu was thoroughly new and different, and quite fascinating. The novel was well-received and is, in fact, extremely successful as a piece of writing; I will even go so far as to say that, to my taste—and not overlooking the fact that van Vogt produced, in *The Weapon-Makers,* one of my all-time favorite science fiction novels—*The Book of Ptath* stands out as his single best novel. What do you suppose he might have followed it with, when he wrote his second novel for *Unknown?*

Alas, we shall never know! For *The Book of Ptath* adorned the issue of October 1943, the last issue of *Unknown* ever published. The magazine had survived for a total of thirty-nine issues; it had weathered the opening phase of World War II, but the paper shortage and, I suppose, marginal sales eventually forced Street & Smith to discontinue it. The publishers had tried tinkering with it in an effort to build sales; from an ordinary pulp format they had switched to the "bed-sheet" with the October 1941 issue—the one in which Pratt and de Camp's *Land of Unreason* was published. They had replaced the original pictorial covers with more dignified ones that bore lettering alone; they had gone bimonthly; they had ever changed the title to *Unknown Worlds.* But the doom that comes inexorably to all magazines, it seems, had come to *Unknown,* and it vanished forever from the stands. A bold, promising new age of fantasy had ended before it had more than gotten started.

To give the publishers of *Unknown* due credit, they discontinued the magazine with obvious reluctance. Five years later, with the war over and the paper shortage long since part of history, they issued a large magazine-type anthology called *From Unknown Worlds,* which contained a selection of eighteen stories and poems (including one short novel) from the back files of the magazine. This was obviously done to test the market, in hopes that sales would be healthy enough to warrant their resuming the publication of *Unknown.* After all, John Campbell was still there at the helm of *Astounding,* which had limped through the tight, grim years unimpaired; and the writers who had, in *Unknown,* created something delightful and lively and unique were still around (most of them) and still writing. It was not at all impossible that *Unknown* could be reborn . . .

But this was 1948. Doom hung over all of us; in the threatening shadow of the atom bomb, with the Cold War crackling away on the horizon and solid citizens scurrying to build bomb shelters and mobilize for Civil Defense, this sort of whimsy, though amusing, seemed trivial and somehow out of touch with cruel reality. So the readers would have nothing to do with mischievous elves or enchanted typewriters or the scientific laws of magic.

Unknown died a second time.

And, this time, it stayed dead.

5

From The Night Land *to* Narnia

The Road to *The Lord of the Rings*

No great thing is created suddenly, any more
than a bunch of grapes or a fig. If you tell
me that you desire a fig, I answer that there
must be **time**. Let it blossom, then bear fruit;
for in time the fruit will ripen into that which
you desire.

— Epictetus: "The Encheiridion"[1]

WE have seen how the imaginary-world story, although
founded in England, took root in the foreign soil of
America and flourished there, growing into new forms
and new traditions, such as Sword & Sorcery. But while
these things were happening in the pages of *Weird
Tales* and *Unknown Worlds,* the tradition continued
to develop in its native earth among a rising generation
of new authors—authors ignorant, for the most part,
of the work of their American colleagues. A separate
tradition grew up, uninfluenced by the American writers
we have been discussing.

As early as 1907 the first of these new voices began
to make itself heard. In that year William Hope Hodgson published his first book, a novel called *The Boats
of the 'Glen Carrig.'* Hodgson, the son of an Essex
clergyman, was born in 1877 and spent his childhood
in Ireland. He went to sea as a boy of thirteen and for
nine years he sailed the globe in the maritime service.
He returned to the place of his birth in Lancashire,
where he experimented with a small business, which
failed, and with the writing of horror stories, in which
he achieved an admirable and lasting success. Hodgson

was only thirty when his first novel was published. He
became quite popular in Britain, a country which has
always had a delightful appetite for horror tales and
wherein the greatest of the modern Gothic masters
have flourished.

In 1913 Hodgson got married to his childhood sweet-
heart and moved to the south of France, where he
settled until the outbreak of the First World War,
busying himself with writing a series of strange, darkly
brilliant novels and volumes of verse and short stories.
His family tells that he had a great sense of humor and
loved to play practical jokes on his brothers and sisters
(of which he had eight); his photographs, however,
suggest a sensitive, moody young man, strikingly handsome in a brooding sort of way.

Hodgson at first drew upon the lore and wonder and
mystery of the sea for the theme and setting of his
fiction. *The Boats of the 'Glen Carrig'* is one of the
most peculiar books of its time: an account of a ship-
wrecked party of men whose boats drift into the Sargas-
so Sea, where they encounter a succession of shadowy
terrors. The narrative begins abruptly (almost as if
the first several pages of this first-person journal of
these adventures had been lost, doubtless the effect
Hodgson was striving for), and breaks off just as suddenly.

His next novel, *The House on the Borderland*
(1908), with its dislocation of time, its account of
grim forces which lay uncanny siege to an old house
from Outside, was even stranger and more powerful,
with its cosmic, its Stapledonian, glimpse of enormous
vistas of time and space. The novel elicited high praise
from Lovecraft, who regarded it as Hodgson's masterpiece. His third novel, *The Ghost Pirates* (1908), saw
Hodgson returning to the sea and the unguessed terrors
which haunt its illimitable abysses. By this point in
his career, it became obvious that Hodgson was able
to portray a certain mood of the sea, its immensity and
its brooding mysteries, with a frightening intensity few

writers have ever matched. Not Conrad—not even Melville—could have done what Hodgson did in *The Ghost Pirates*.

Despite his imaginative range, Hodgson would deserve little space in these pages were it not for that appalling masterpiece, *The Night Land*, which appeared on the bookstalls of London in 1912. *The Night Land* must be one of the most stupendous achievements of sheer imaginative power ever set on paper. Again, it wrung words of praise from Lovecraft; Clark Ashton Smith also praised it in glowing terms, in a rare article, and may have done it the honor of imitation in his own tales set on the super-continent of Zothique near the twilight of time.

The Night Land is an immense work of fiction, somewhat more than two hundred thousand words long, set millions of years hence in the last days of mankind. The sun has long since guttered and died like a candle-flame; the cooling earth is a gloom-shrouded wilderness world lost in the immensities of unbroken night, and the surviving remnants of the human race have taken refuge in the Last Redoubt, a mighty pyramid of imperishable metal straddling the Thames. It is the last and greatest of the cities of man: soon it will be his tomb. Over immeasurable ages weird beings have arisen to dominate the dark world. They crouch immobile, held at bay by the impalpable defenses of the metal mountain. For thousands of centuries they have gathered, waiting for those defenses to fail. With subtle, deft strokes of chilling detail, Hodgson sketches in words a nightmarish landscape that would have taxed the pictorial artistry of Hieronymus Bosch to equal:

> And the Watcher of the Northwest. Above its vast head there hung always a blue luminous ring, which shed a strange light downwards, showing a vast, wrinkled brow (upon which an whole library had been writ); but putting to shadow all the lower face, save the ear . . . said by some observers in the past to have been seen to quiver, but no man of our days had seen it.
>
> To the north there stood, very far away, the House of Silence. And in that House were many lights and no

sounds; so it had been through an eternity of years. Always those steady lights and no whisper of sound

The hugest monster of all, a living hill of watchfulness, the Watching Thing of the south. It brooded there, squat and tremendous, hunched over the pale radiance of the Glowing Dome. Much has been writ concerning this Vast Watcher . . . a million years gone came it out of the blackness, and grew steadily nearer through twenty thousand years; but so slow that in no one year could a man perceive that it had moved.

Hodgson was only thirty-seven when he wrote *The Night Land* on the eve of the most enormous and devastating conflict in the annals of human experience. When war broke over Europe, he enlisted in the cavalry, was injured in a fall from his horse, then re-enlisted, ending up in the 84th Battalion of the Battery of the Royal Field Artillery. His battery distinguished itself at Ypres, and again in April, 1918, when the German forces put all they had in a daring thrust; the German advance was blunted when Hodgson, with a few fellow officers and non-commissioned officers, managed to hold firm against an overwhelming number of the enemy.

Not long thereafter, Hodgson and two non-commissioned officers went forward to reconnoitre. While scouting the German lines at Paeschendale, a chance hit by a German shell cut him down. He was literally blown to bits, and his body was never found. He was forty years and five months old, and his entire literary career had occupied only the last decade of his pitifully short life.[2]

Two years after the death of William Hope Hodgson, an Englishman named David Lindsay published a remarkable novel called *A Voyage to Arcturus*. Lindsay remains a fairly mysterious writer, about whom little is known. At the time of his death in 1945, he had published only a handful of novels—*The Sphinx, Devil's Tor, The Haunted Woman*—none of which had been particularly successful, although they display powerful imaginative gifts, the last being (to my taste) quite outstanding supernatural horror. However, only *Arcturus* survives as living literature, leaving the imprint of its vision on other writers. This book is, in essence, a dream-odyssey in the vein of George Macdonald; but it also has elements of science fiction in it, and hovers uneasily in the vague penumbra between that genre and its siblings.

In fact, coming so closely on the heels of the brief career of William Hope Hodgson, it may be worth noting that *A Voyage to Arcturus* has certain parallels to that author's masterpiece, *The Night Land*—just as a novel set in the remote future, a novel which includes an interstellar journey in a crystal spaceship, certainly borders on science fiction. But let me point out once again that books such as these, or *The Worm Ouroboros*, for that matter, which is set upon the planet Mercury, were conceived and written and published before the central body of imaginative fiction became divided into clearly-marked subclassifications.

The Night Land has been hailed as an imaginative achievement of the very first order; it has also been criticized on several points of style. Lovecraft decried its "nauseously romantic sentimentality" and berated Hodgson's "inaccurate and pseudo-romantic attempt" to reproduce 18th-century prose. Somewhat later, C. S. Lewis found the same things objectionable; comparing *The Night Land* to other first-rate masterpieces of fantasy, such as *Phantastes* and *Vathek* and *The Worm Ouroboros*, he remarked that the book is "disfigured by a sentimental and irrelevant erotic interest and by a foolish and flat archaism of style," although he praised it for the "sombre splendour" of its imagery.[3] Both points of criticism are valid, although in considering the first it is only fair to keep in mind that Hodgson was born under the reign of Queen Victoria and that his is no more than the sentimentality common to writers of the Victorian age. As for the second point, it cannot be denied that Hodgson was a euphuist who affected the most florid, elaborate "literary" style, tricked out with verbal ornament, elegant diction, and deliberate archaisms. Modern critics of fantasy and science fiction, like James Blish, tend rather often to complain about such stylistic eccentricities. Blish in particular knocks that school of fantasy writing that produces a sonorous prose fit only to be chanted or intoned. However, not all books need be written in terse, flat prose as if we were all trying to sound like Ernest Hemingway or Raymond Chandler, and fantasy in particular seems to demand a certain lush richness and verbal color to pull off its effects. But it cannot be denied that Hodgson is an extremist and the artificialities of his style *do* get in the way of his story.

No one, however, seems to have found anything in *A Voyage to Arcturus* worth complaining about. I suppose that, like *Lilith* and *Phantastes,* it is an allegory and not a "real story." I suppose Maskull is Everyman and that his wanderings through the weird and wondrous landscapes of the strange planet Tormance in quest of the mysterious Crystalman are as symbolic of man's search for God as anything in the dreary pages of *The Pilgrim's Progress.* As a rule, allegories bore me stiff; I am uninterested in untangling the symbolism of such names as "Surtur" and "Nightspore." James Joyce may be a titan to some, but to my taste he is simply a titanic bore—and a pretentious one, to boot. I suppose I reveal myself here as a crass barbarian instead of a keen intellectual, but I tend to agree with Wilkie Collins that the first business of a novel is *to tell a story,* and that everything else—the sensitive nuances of prose, the delicate peeling-back of layer upon layer of characterization, the exquisite pattern of symbolic overtones, and so forth—comes distinctly second.

Allegory or no, *Arcturus* may simply be read—and enjoyed—for its story alone, and for the richness of imaginative invention with which Lindsay decks his landscapes. For we have no mere Eddisonian "Mercury" here, but a truly strange and alien world. Tormance is different in every way from our own world, and the author has with admirable inventiveness met the obligations imposed upon him by his alien scene. The sun of

Tormance is different from our own, of another hue and a different quality of light, so its spectrum embraces new primary colors—"jale" and "ulfire." Its people are not earth-humans, so he gives them new organs—the "breve," the "poigns." Everything in the book is marked with this freshness of concept, this inventiveness. It is thoroughly brilliant and it has lived, while Lindsay's other novels have faded irretrievably from sight.

The British publisher Victor Gollancz recalls a conversation with Lindsay in which the author remarked that, although he would never be enormously popular, he thought his best work would last and would find its way to a small but appreciative audience. "Somewhere in the world, someone will be reading a book of mine every year," he said.

This is—must be—true of a book as solidly good as *A Voyage to Arcturus*. And few writers could hope for more.

THE next of the modern British masters of fantasy to appear was different in every way from Hodgson and Lindsay. I refer to a strange, irascible, tormented little man of wild comic genius whose name was Terence Hanbury White—"T. H. White" to his readers, and "Tim" to his friends.

White was an only child, born in Bombay on May 29, 1906, with a background in which English, Irish, Scottish, and even a strain of French blood mingled. His childhood was an unhappy one, his father a remote drink-sodden authority-figure, his mother jealous and smothering, and the internecine strife between his parents was vicious to the point of sadism. From this miserable mésalliance emerged a young man emotionally impoverished and lacking the capacity to enjoy normal human relationships, a young man who had to excel in everything in order to compensate for his failure to be anything more than an emotional cripple:

I had to be good at games. I had to be able to win at darts. I had to teach myself not to be clumsy. Com-

pensating for my sense of inferiority . . . I had to learn to
paint, to build and mix concrete and to be a carpenter
and to saw and screw and put in a nail without bending it.
Not only did I have to be physically good at things, I
had to excel with my head as well as with my body and
hands. I had to get first-class honours with distinction
at the University. I had to be a scholar. I had to learn
medieval Latin shorthand so as to translate bestiaries.

These revealing insights are from a lecture called "The
Pleasures of Learning," which White gave in the last
year of his life while on a speaking tour of the United
States. A bitterly unhappy man, he was one of those
rare persons who turn their misery to practical use. "The
best thing for being sad is to learn something," says
Merlyn in *The Sword in the Stone*. That statement may
be seen not only as White's personal credo, but as the
key to his amazing accomplishments. For he was a
man of enormous enthusiasms, and throughout his
richly productive life he defended himself against loneli-
ness and self-denigration by flinging himself into new
areas of interest with passionate and all-consuming
curiosity. These interests might be anything from flying
airplanes to mastering falconry, and each of them left
its mark in one or another of his delightful books.

He was a man with an enormous capacity for loving.
It shows in his prodigious correspondence and in his
affection for dogs and in the bewildered and inarticulate
loves his characters experience in his books; but he had
few close friends, and no genuine relationship with a
woman has been recorded. The only things he dared
to love fully, without reserve, were his red setter,
Brownie, and learning itself.

His first book was *Loved Helen,* a volume of verse
published while he was at Cambridge. This was closely
followed by a couple of detective stories, a clutch of
sporting books, a portrait of Victorian England, a
volume of short stories, and a touching personal memoir
or journal, or whatever you prefer to call it, *England
Have My Bones,* his first best-seller and the book which
brought him to real prominence. And then, in 1939,

when he was only thirty-three, came an indescribably perfect masterpiece that must surely be among the best books of any sort written in this century—*The Sword in the Stone*. This extraordinary novel is the story of King Arthur's boyhood, a peculiar blend of comedy, fantasy, and pathos, packed with the sort of lore only a dedicated scholar could glean from a lifetime of research, and told with such love and warmth and affection, such honesty and authority and understanding, that it transcends its (juvenile) classification to stand as a literary accomplishment of enduring value.

> On Mondays, Wednesdays and Fridays it was Court Hand and Summulae Logicales, while the rest of the week it was the Organon, Repetition and Astrology. The governess was always getting muddled with her astrolabe, and when she got specially muddled she would take it out on the Wart by rapping his knuckles. She did not rap Kay's knuckles because when Kay grew older he would be Sir Kay, and the master of the estate . . .

So opened a completely delightful book, which reads rather as if Kenneth Grahame, instead of Mark Twain, had written *A Connecticut Yankee at King Arthur's Court*. In fact, *A Connecticut Yankee* is about the only book with which *The Sword in the Stone* can be compared. The basic difference between the two is that Twain did not like or sympathize with his characters and thought them absurd and superstitious barbarians, and his ill-will seeps through every page of what is, essentially, a dour and grim and even cruel story. But White understands his Dark Ages thoroughly, knows how the people of the day lived and thought, and deals with them unsentimentally but with honest affection. It makes a very great difference.

The comic scenes in *The Sword in the Stone* are superlatively handled, so much so that they tend to outweigh many lovely minor scenes and less intriguing characters. You come away from the book remembering chiefly things like the wonderful magician's duel between Merlyn and Madame Mim, in which the two transform themselves into a variety of creatures, each transformation an attempt to one-up the other—rather like the old Sicilian hand-game of rock–paper–shears. Madame Mim almost wins the match by turning herself into a sort of super-elephant called an aullay, but Merlyn triumphs by a neat trick:

> The ingenious magician had turned himself successively into the microbes, not yet discovered, of hiccoughs, scarlet fever, mumps, whooping cough, measles and heat spots, and from a complication of all these complaints the infamous Madame Mim had immediately expired.

An even funnier scene comes earlier, the marvelous slow-motion duel between Sir Grummore Grummursum and King Pellinore, in which the two old knights, loaded down with tons of plate-armor, mounted on heavy-footed Percherons, go clumping grandly and ponderously past each other, each charge ending as they thump and crash into trees at opposite sides of the clearing.

A sequel, *The Witch in the Wood,* followed in the same year, 1939. White did not quite manage to pull off the miracle twice in succession, but there are marvelous things in the book. In the last analysis, however, it is rather lumpy and uneven. If Merlyn in the first book is a shrewdly-drawn caricature of White himself, Queen Morgause in the sequel is a portrait of his own mother, and White despised her so much that the whole book is rather soured by his own bad feeling. But again, the comic scenes are superbly handled, as when old King Pellinore, smitten with love for the daughter of the Queen of Flanders, the Princess Piggy, strives manfully to write a poem to her; the Paynim Knight, Sir Palomides, tries to get through the king's dense wits the notion that a true sonnet should rhyme ababcdde efefgg, whereupon Pelly comes up with

> Dear Piggy: I hop you don't mind my calling you Piggy (a)
> It is very nice wether here (b)
> I am very well (a)
> I hop you are very well (b)

I hop the Queen of Flanders is very well (c)
I hop the dogs are very well (d)

and so on, almost driving poor, serious, literal-minded Palomides crackers. White follows this scene of rich comic invention with a gruesome, bloody, deeply touching scene in which the boy princes trap and murder a beautiful unicorn, gorily sawing its head off and dragging the thing home to the castle to give to their mother, who they think wants a unicorn, and who has been neglecting them. The scene is remarkably powerful.

A bleaker and less entertaining third volume, *The Ill-Made Knight,* followed in 1940. In 1958 White trimmed, partially rewrote, and rather arbitrarily cut the three books, tacking on a new novella called "The Candle in the Wind" as the fourth in the sequence, and reissued the tetralogy under the title *The Once and Future King.* The book, most deservedly, was a best-seller in America; it was turned into a spectacular Broadway musical and two very different movies, one a version of *The Sword in the Stone,* a quite disappointing effort by Walt Disney. After a lifetime of poverty and denial, White found himself suddenly a wealthy and famous celebrity. He continued to write marvelously interesting books up to the end of his life. He died quite suddenly of an acute coronary aboard the *S. S. Exeter,* on his way home from an exhausting American speaking tour, on January 17, 1964.

His Arthurian tetralogy does not really belong to the imaginary-world tradition, but I could not bear to leave it out. No book on fantasy would be complete without some notice of one of the most brilliant fantasy novels in literature. In a lifetime devoted to the appreciation of good books I have found hundreds to admire, respect, or enjoy; but I have found only a handful of books I can love with my whole heart, as I love *The Sword in the Stone.*

IN 1946 T. H. White published *Mistress Masham's Repose,* a lovely book which to a large extent does for

Gulliver's Travels what *The Once and Future King* did so superlatively for Sir Thomas Malory. That same year a novel entitled *Titus Groan* appeared on the scene.

The author, Mervyn (Laurence) Peake, had previously been known largely as a poet and an illustrator of books. In both of these arts he had already achieved a certain excellence and even a measure of fame. His several volumes of poetry are highly regarded in England, and his verse has much of the fire and eloquence we find in the poetry of Dylan Thomas—or found twenty years ago, when I was an undergraduate at Columbia University. The similarity lies in both the use of dissociative imagery and the modernity of theme and form, both poets pouring out their speech in a blazing torrent of furious images. Peake's illustrations have adorned several recent editions of some of the standard classics; at least, I have seen his work in printings of *Treasure Island* and the collected *hausmärchen* of the Brothers Grimm, and I own his delightful edition of *The Hunting of the Snark*.

But nothing in his early work had prepared any of us for what lay in the pages of *Titus Groan*.

The novel takes place on barren, mist-shrouded moors, and all the scenes are enacted within the crumbling and labyrinthine walls of a fabulously immense castle named Gormenghast, which is of an equally fabulous antiquity. "Gormenghast" is a superbly Gothic coined name, and for that matter, "Titus Groan" is a name worthy of Dickensian coinage, to say the least. There is something rather Dickensian, as well, in the florid richness of the prose and the cast of human grotesques and fantastic caricatures who people the book.

The outside world beyond the sweep of the moors seems non-existent, is never mentioned, and does not ever intrude into the feverish and complex human drama that unfolds about the birth and infancy of the child, Titus, who will grow up to become the seventy-seventh earl of Gormenghast castle. Rather like that vigorous old novel *Tristram Shandy,* which ends, you may recall, with the birth of the character after whom the novel is named, the hero of *Titus Groan* is not really the child Titus at all, but the immense cast of characters which revolves about him. The child Titus is the center of the book named after him, true; but he remains passive, the story revolving around him like the region of utter calm that exists at the heart of a raging hurricane. In delicious counterpoint to the inactivity of the infant Titus is the ferocious wheeling and dealing of another youth, Steerpike, the Iago of the story, a low-born youth whose complex wiles enmesh most of the other characters in his Machiavellian intrigues.

The writing is rich, vigorous, in vivid strokes of raw color. *Titus Groan* belongs in the imaginary-world tradition in a special sense; for Peake did not create a world in the sense of an immense continuous landscape crowded with kingdoms and cities. Instead, he created an inner world, a universe in miniature, a microcosm. Instead of exploring the traditional terrain of woods and mountains and cities, he delves into the roots of human character via the knotted, tangled, intricately interwoven lives of the many odd, deformed, subtle, monstrous, robust, or decadent creatures who infest the endless warrens of the age-old, world-vast castle. The people in *Titus Groan* are monstrous caricatures, portrayed with the gusto and violent energy of a Dickens; but it is Gormenghast itself that fascinates me: the nightmarish old castle, with its cobwebbed and crumbling maze of corridors and musty suites, its weird collection of human oddities, its fantastic structure of social customs and traditions, enclosing the dark drama of these entangled lives. It is an overwhelming monster of a book, which holds most readers enthralled.

A sequel, called *Gormenghast,* followed in 1950, and the trilogy was rounded off in 1959 with the publication of *Titus Alone*. The third novel is immensely unsatisfactory, so much so that when I read it I seriously regretted that it had ever been written, much less published. My discontent with *Titus Alone* comes main-ly from the fact that it violates certain of the elements that made its predecessors so interesting: in them, Gormenghast exists in utter isolation from the outside world, which is hardly even mentioned and might be presumed not even to exist. But in the third volume of the trilogy Titus *leaves* Gormenghast and ventures into the outer world on his own. Besides this, *Titus Alone* is written in a style somewhat different from its siblings—more harsh, strident, episodic, less rich and robust.

Years later, I discovered what is probably the reason for the appalling imperfections of *Titus Alone*. Mervyn Peake suffered from a rare disease, and had done his best to complete the trilogy during his last years, while his powers waned steadily from day to day. That he should have performed any creative work at all while battling against the disease's inexorable advance seems to me nothing less than an heroic achievement, and I am willing to accept *Titus Alone* for that reason. It has also come to light that the book as it was published was put together by his editors, for by that point he was unable to revise or correct the work himself. On November 17, 1968, Peake succumbed to his long illness, dying at the age of fifty-seven.

IT is here that C. S. Lewis enters this history. His full name was Clive Staples Lewis and he was born in 1898, "the son of a soliciter and of a clergyman's daughter," as he described his parents in his quasi-autobiography, *Surprised by Joy*.[4] Despite the fact that he was born in Belfast, he was not of Irish ancestry; his paternal grandfather was a Welsh farmer, and his mother's family traced their line back to a Norman knight buried in Battle Abbey. Both parents were bookish people, fond of Trollope and Tolstoy, and from them Lewis came quite early to a love of books. His inner imaginative life was quite active from childhood; like the Brontës, with their imaginary countries of Gondal and The Great Glass Town, Lewis and his

brother built worlds of their own, making a continual
game out of the stories they invented concerning these
private kingdoms. Lewis' country was called Animal-
Land and its inhabitants were animals dressed up like
people, just like Toad and Mole and Rat in *The Wind
in the Willows*. From this conception by a busy, imaginative child, perhaps, sprung the original seed that
blossomed into the Chronicles of Narnia.

Lewis went through the usual British public schools—
what we in America, amusingly enough, would consider
private schools—and he so thoroughly detested the experience that when he came to write of those years in
Surprised by Joy he gave his schools fictitious names.
Thus Wynyard School in Hertfordshire and Cherbourg
House in Malvern became "Belsen" and "Chartres" in
the autobiography. But however much he loathed com-
pulsory sports and regulated curricula, he made some
glorious and life-changing discoveries during those grim,
bitter years. The first was a love-affair with what W. H.
Auden calls "the Northern Thing," the mythos of Nordic
Europe, which he first encountered in Longfellow's
poem, "Tegner's Drapa"; his passion was reinforced
later by the chance discovery of Wagner's *Ring*, and
sealed forever by a cataclysmic encounter with William
Morris:

> I had met him first in quotations in books on Norse
> Mythology. That led me to *Sigurd the Volsung*. I did not
> really like this as much as I tried to, and I think I now
> know why: the metre does not satisfy my ear. But then,
> in Arthur's* bookcase, I found *The Well at the World's
> End*. I looked—I read chapter headings—I dipped—and
> next day I was off into town to buy a copy of my own.
> . . . After that I read all the Morris I could get, *Jason,
> The Earthly Paradise,* the prose romances. The growth of
> the new delight is marked by my sudden realization, al-
> most with a sense of disloyalty, that the letters WILLIAM
> MORRIS were coming to have at least as potent a magic
> in them as WAGNER.[5]

---

*Arthur Greeves, a schoolmate with whom Lewis formed a
great friendship when they were at Malvern College ("Wyvern" in
Surprised by Joy) during 1913-1914. The boys shared a common
fascination for Norse mythology/literature.

Not long after this discovery, Lewis made the acquaintance of George MacDonald through a dirty-jacketed shilling Everyman edition of *Phantastes,* picked up by chance in a railway station bookstall. Lewis's head was already filled with Norse and Irish and Greek mythology and the romances of William Morris and H. Rider Haggard, but MacDonald seems to have been the key discovery that established the direction of Lewis' interests for the rest of his life toward fantasy literature.

THE forces that shaped C. S. Lewis are visible and obvious. From a bookish, imaginative child with a penchant for making up stories about talking animals who live in a country all their own, he became a lonely boy trapped in the brutal, hostile public school environment, who turned to myths, legends, and romances for his chief imaginative release. He went on to university and became Professor of Medieval and Renaissance English at Cambridge and a Fellow of Magdalen College, Oxford.

Thirty or so books came from his hands. Of these, at least twelve are popular theological works which hardly concern us here. Of greater interest to fantasy readers is that brilliant and disquieting little book, *The Screwtape Letters* (1943), a sequence of letters written by an elderly devil to his nephew. Quiet in tone, subtle and unsensational, even gently humorous, the book reveals its author as quite well acquainted with Hell. That he was equally familiar with more celestial regions became apparent three years later with the publication of *The Great Divorce* (1946), an extraordinary narrative of a journey through the Heaven of Lewis' own intellectual vision. Also in this period, Lewis wrote the three novels that brought him quite prominently to the attention of fantasy and science fiction readers—the Ransom Trilogy.

The first of these novels, *Out of the Silent Planet,* appeared in 1943. It is the story of a Cambridge philologist named Ransom who is on a walking tour of Britain when two old school acquaintances drug and abduct him to Mars—or "Malacandra," as the new Lewisian cosmology names the planet. This plot element, the unsuspecting traveler duped by two chance-met acquaintances into an interplanetary voyage, resembles—perhaps significantly, perhaps even *pointedly* —the situation we met at the beginning of David Lindsay's *A Voyage to Arcturus.*

Lewis followed this novel with a sequel, *Perelandra,* in 1944, and rounded the sequence off with *That Hideous Strength,* which appeared in 1946. A highly original vision of cosmology emerges through the trilogy: Mars, or Malacandra, is inhabited by beings still in a state of grace, unlike us of earth, or Thulcandra, who were tempted and fell. Venus, too, or Perelandra, is an unspoiled Eden until the Satanic principle enters its paradisiacal gardens. The system as a whole—"the Field of Arbol," Lewis calls it—is run rather according to the notions of occultism, each planet under the dominion of what occultism calls an "Olympian spirit," and Lewis terms an "oyarsa." The trilogy is a curious blend of science fiction, mysticism, theology, and the occult.

Despite the voyage to Mars in *Out of the Silent Planet,* Lewis was not influenced by Edgar Rice Burroughs, whom he seems never to have read. In a letter to the American novelist and professor, Charles A. Brady, Lewis wrote in 1944:

> The real father of my planet books [*i.e.,* the Ransom Trilogy] is David Lindsay's *A Voyage to Arcturus*—it was Lindsay who first gave me the idea that the "scientifiction" appeal could be combined with the "supernatural" appeal.[6]

The genesis of the trilogy, however, dates from much earlier than his first reading of Lindsay. In *Surprised by Joy,* discussing his boyhood reading, Lewis lists some mediocre historicals—*Quo Vadis, Ben-Hur*—and comments:

> They were mostly, as literature, rather bad books. What has worn better, and what I took to at the same time,

is the work of Rider Haggard; and also the "scientific-tion" of H. G. Wells. The idea of other planets exercised upon me then a peculiar, heady attraction, which was quite different from any other of my literary interests . . . something coarser and stranger.[7]

The trilogy was well received . . . I am tempted to say *surprisingly* well received, but such a juxtaposition suggests that the books were unworthy of their critical and popular reception, which is, of course, not at all the case. I *do* mean to imply, however, that such books as these and *Arcturus* and Olaf Stapledon's *The Star Maker,* whatever their excellences, generally appeal to a rather small audience. Science fiction, until quite recently, has been primarily an entertainment medium; a literature of ideas, certainly, but novels such as the above, based upon complex and original systems of theological, cosmological, or philosophical speculation, had previously appealed only to the devout few. Hence, the commercial success of the Ransom trilogy was unprecedented.

The reason for this success was partly that Lewis was a writer of great clarity, narrative skill, and intellectual brilliance. But much of that success can also be traced to his immense popularity; he was, by this time, a distinguished lay theologian, Christian apologist, and a noted essayist and critic—a highly regarded literary figure with an appreciative following on both sides of the Atlantic.

IN 1950, C. S. Lewis revealed yet another of his extraordinary talents. In that year his first children's book, a fantasy novel called *The Lion, the Witch, and the Wardrobe,* was published. It was almost at once recognized as a classic, or, more properly, as the first part of one; for a year later a sequel, *Prince Caspian,* appeared, to be followed in 1952 by *The Voyage of the 'Dawn Treader.'*

With these books Lewis had begun publishing his masterpiece, the Chronicles of Narnia, and successive volumes continued to appear from then on, at yearly intervals, until the seventh and last volume, *The Last Battle,* came out in 1956.

In that first book of the Chronicles, Lewis introduces us to one of the most charming and realistically depicted families of children since the high days of E. Nesbit, for when Peter, Susan, Edmund, and Lucy find their way unexpectedly through the back of an enormous old wardrobe in the house of a friendly but traditionally absent-minded Professor (whose house they have come to share, having been evacuated from their own home due to the War), they become friends of ours—people we know and love and understand. Lewis also, in the same book, introduced us to one of the most wonderful fairylands discovered in recent years, for not since Dorothy and her farmhouse were blown away to Oz in a Kansas cyclone has there been a country quite as much fun as Narnia, or one so chock-full of surprises.

Narnia is under the cruel dominion of the White Witch in that initial book, and locked in the frozen grip of winter; but just as Dorothy and her friends the Scarecrow, the Tin Woodman, and the Cowardly Lion dispose of *their* witch—the Wicked Witch of the West— by tossing a pailful of water on her and thus melting her away, so do Lewis' children and their friends manage to end the reign of Jadis the White. But not so easily as Dorothy, and not until Lewis—a convert to orthodox Christianity in his mature years—puts us through a blatantly symbolic Crucifixion-and-Resurrection scene. The scene—the humiliation and brutal slaying of Aslan, the golden lion-god—is beautifully and simply written, and deeply moving even to a non-believer like myself, but very out of place in these pages.

The friends the children make along their way from the wardrobe to the Stone Table upon which Aslan is murdered are a charming lot. I personally prefer Reepicheep, the gallant and chivalrous Mouse, and Mr. Tumnus the Faun, but other readers speak highly of Rumblebuffin the Giant. There are talking animals here, such as Mr. and Mrs. Beaver; and creatures out of

Greek mythology, such as the fauns and dryads and the great centaur, Glenstorm (who appears in the second book, *Prince Caspian*); and familiar beings from the mythologies of Northern Europe, such as Dwarves and Ogres and Ettins and the Fenris-Wolf, which Peter slays with his enchanted sword, Rhindon. And at the end, with the White Witch slain, her power destroyed, her evil followers scattered, and Narnia freed from its wintry enchantment, the children ascend to the thrones of Cair Paravel, and Peter and Edmund become High Kings of Narnia and their reigns are remembered ever after as a golden age.

The Chronicles of Narnia, being children's fantasies, really do not come within the scope of this history. But they are so much fun, and so very well written, that I cannot ignore them. And if you happen to have passed over them, I strongly suggest that you look them up and read them. Among the many truly fine writers of children's fantasy in this century, C. S. Lewis is far from the least. Narnia belongs with Oz and Andrew Lang's Pantouflia (in *Prince Prigio*) and the delicious countries in Thackeray's *The Rose and the Ring* on a magical continent all their own. Few imaginary worlds in literature can match these for charm and color and excitement.

Before Lewis died in 1963 he added several more books to his *oeuvre,* and among them were some extremely important critical studies of fantastic literature. Lewis is the only critic known to me who wrote at all extensively on the sort of books we have been discussing in these pages. He read his Hodgson and Lindsay and Peake, his Morris and Eddison and Tolkien, and his enthusiasm for their achievements is genuine and well-informed. He knows why such books are good, lasting, well-written, he admires them for all the right reasons, and his literary scholarship is, of course, impeccable. Any reader—and in particular, any *writer*—of fantasy and science fiction would do well to read his appraisal of several aspects of the literature in a marvelous little book called *An Experiment in Criticism* (1961), or the essay "On Stories" in the book *Of Other Worlds* (1966).

Besides his own very excellent stories and his wise and thoughtful critique of other authors' fantasies, Lewis is important to us because of the part he played in the work of his friends. But *that* matter is important enough to deserve a chapter all its own.

6

The Inklings Produce a Classic:
The Achievement of Tolkien and His Influence

> For all these fair people in hall were in their
> first age; none happier under heaven; their
> king, the man of noblest temper. It would be
> a hard task today to find so brave a fellow-
> ship in any castle.
> —Anonymous:
> "Gawain and the Green Knight"

AMONG Lewis' many friends and colleagues at Oxford
were a number of scholars and writers of similar interests and enthusiasms; they made up an informal group,
calling themselves the Inklings, and gathered in Lewis'
rooms at Magdalen College every Thursday evening
after dinner. At such gatherings, the conversation ranged
rather widely—"from beer to *Beowulf,* to torture,
Tertullian, bores, the contractual theory of medieval
kingship, and odd place-names," as W. H. Lewis, the
author's brother, recalled in his preface to an edition
of Lewis' *Letters* published in 1966.

In addition to C. S. Lewis and his brother, the
Inklings included John Wain, Roy Campbell, David
Cecil, and yet others. The novelist Charles Williams,
author of *War in Heaven, The Greater Trumps,* and
other mystico-theological fictions, was an Inkling. And
so was J. R. R. Tolkien, who came to Pembroke College at Oxford in 1925, and remained for the next
twenty years. Tolkien was made a Fellow at Pembroke
a year after his arrival; later he became an Emerson
Fellow at Merton and an Honorary Fellow at Exeter.
(Pembroke, Merton, and Exeter are individual colleges
among the group of twenty-one such that form the

great community of separate colleges we call the University of Oxford.)

Tolkien is of German descent and the name itself is German; opinions on its pronunciation differ, but the Professor himself seems to pronounce it either "tul-KEEN" or "TOL-kin." Both of his parents came from the industrial city of Birmingham in northwestern Warwickshire, but Tolkien was born at Bloemfontein in the Union of South Africa, on January 3, 1892. The initials J. R. R., incidentally, stand for John Ronald Reuel, the last being also a family name. By now we are all rather accustomed to referring to him as "Professor Tolkien," but since he was included in the 1972 New Years Honors List and received a C. B. E. (Commander of the Order of the British Empire), I'm afraid we shall have to get used to calling him "Sir John." With the exception of Haggard, I believe he is the only fantasy writer of modern times to receive a knighthood (Dunsany, of course, was born to the peerage and inherited his titles), although the ranks of science fiction writers boast at least one fully canonized saint.*

Tolkien's father died when he was a child, and his mother brought him and his brother back home to her native city, whose grimy industrial slums and soot-darkened skies doubtless contributed as much to his later descriptions of Mordor as the fresh green countryside contributed to his conception of the Shire.

He was twelve when his mother died, and from then on Tolkien and his brother were raised by a Roman Catholic priest. Tolkien went from King Edward's school in Birmingham to Exeter, but the outbreak of the First World War interrupted his studies, and at the age of 23 he entered the Lancashire Fusiliers. A year later he married Edith Bratt, who was to be the mother of his four children. Tolkien served with his regiment until the end of the war. He returned home in 1918,

---

*St. Thomas More, the author of *Utopia*, canonized in 1935. He was also a knight, by the way, so science fiction is at least one up on fantasy!

took his only degree——M.A. (Oxon)——and worked for two years as an assistant on the famous *Oxford English Dictionary*. In 1920 he became a Reader in the English Language at the University of Leeds; he produced his major scholarly work, *A Middle-English Vocabulary*, in 1922, as well as his critical text of *Gawain and the Green Knight* (with E. V. Gordon), before joining the faculty of Pembroke at Oxford. He remained there for twenty years as Rawlinson and Bosforth Professor of Anglo-Saxon, wrote important works on Chaucer and *Beowulf*, and earned his reputation as a widely respected English philologist.

IT was the pleasant custom of the Inklings to read aloud from their current works-in-progress whenever the conversation lagged. Some of the members, like Charles Williams, would read from their poems——Williams published two excellent volumes of verse on the "Matter of Britain," *Taliesin through Logres* and *The Region of the Summer Stars*——while others would read from stories or essays they had in the works. The members would then comment on the works, and quite a bit of cross-influence probably resulted from this friendly criticism. None of the Inklings' opinions, however, managed to influence Tolkien.

Following the publication of his important monograph *Beowulf: The Monster and the Critics* (1936), Tolkien wrote a children's book called *The Hobbit, or, There and Back Again*, which had evolved out of stories about an imaginary world called "Middle-earth," which he had begun making up perhaps as early as 1935 to amuse his children. Published in 1937, illustrated by the Professor himself, *The Hobbit* was a creditable achievement and has enjoyed a respectable success on both sides of the Atlantic. It was Lewis, who loved nothing more than a good fantasy with dwarves and dragons and magicians in it, who talked his friend into submitting it to a publisher. George Allen and Unwin, Ltd., brought it out in England and Houghton

Mifflin published it in this country, where it promptly won the *Herald Tribune* Prize as the best children's book of the year.

Tolkien was not done with Middle-earth, however, and during those jolly Thursday evenings the Inklings began to listen to early chapters of "Tolkien's new Hobbit," as they called it. Here's a casual note which C. S. Lewis wrote to his brother on November 11, 1939, for instance:

> On Thursday we had a meeting of the Inklings—you and Coghill both absent unfortunately. We dined at the Eastgate. I have never in my life seen Dyson so exuberant —"A roaring cataract of nonsense." The bill of fare, afterwards, consisted of a section of the new Hobbit book from Tolkien, a nativity play from Ch. Williams (unusually intelligible for him, and approved by all), and a chapter out of the book on the Problem of Pain from me.[1]

The Inklings were to enjoy a remarkable honor. Imagine gathering in Lewis' rooms every Thursday evening and listening while Professor Tolkien read aloud to them, page by page, *The Lord of the Rings*!

TOLKIEN set to work on his great masterpiece when he was forty-four. Between 1936, when the first words were set down, and 1949, the work continued at intervals. It is not surprising that it took thirteen years to write *The Lord of the Rings,* for the book is, after all, one of the very longest novels ever written, and works out to something like five hundred thousand words. That is more than eight times longer than the average 60,000-word science fiction paperback.

We don't actually know what the rest of the Inklings thought of the "new Hobbit," although Lewis obviously loved it—as, of course, he would—and wrote a very important review of the trilogy for *Time and Tide* when it finally appeared in print. But whatever criticism the Inklings offered, Tolkien paid no attention. Answering an inquiry about inter-influence among the literary Inklings, Lewis replied in 1959:

Williams certainly influenced me and I perhaps influenced him. But after that I think you would draw a blank. No one ever influenced Tolkien—you might as well try to influence a bandersnatch.³

From all accounts, Tolkien and Lewis seem to have hit it off rather well and one gains the impression that they were quite good friends. Both, of course, were Englishmen born out of the country, both were fascinated by "the Northern thing," both were converts to orthodox Christianity, and fellow scholars and writers deeply interested in myth and legend, fairy tales and fantasy. Unable to influence the writing of *The Lord of the Rings* in any way, due to Tolkien's recalcitrance in the face of criticism or suggestions, Lewis seems to have devoted himself to encouraging Tolkien to finish it and convincing him that it should be submitted to a publisher.

Tolkien seems to have planned the work originally as part of a triptych to be made up of *The Lord of the Rings* itself and two other narratives, the *Silmarillion,* which tells of the First Age of Middle-earth, and the *Akallabêth,* which is laid in the Second Age; *The Lord of the Rings,* set in the Third Age, was to have rounded off the triptych, with *The Hobbit* serving as a sort of preface to it. It is now known that the Professor actually wrote the *Silmarillion* first—an early version of it, anyway—and that Unwin rejected it. Tolkien abandoned it at that point, turning to *The Lord of the Rings* itself, which Unwin did eventually accept, but not without some reservations. They believed the work would not be a commercial success, but that it should nevertheless be published.

Now, *The Hobbit* is a quest story in which the friendly magician Gandalf persuades a hobbit named Bilbo Baggins to leave his cozy home in the Shire and join a party of thirteen dwarves on a wild, adventurous journey. There is a dragon named Smaug, a fabulous hoard of treasure, and all sorts of perilous excitement with trolls and elves and goblins. One incident in the story prepares us for the central theme of the trilogy itself: Bilbo strays from his companions and finds a magic golden ring, the property of a cunning, degenerate, miserable little creature called Gollum. The ring has the property of making its wearer invisible—and certain other properties, not revealed until the trilogy was published.

It all makes for a simply luscious children's book, and it sets the stage for the more important and more serious events which form the theme of the trilogy, which Unwin began publishing in 1954, with good reviews but sluggish sales.

The scenery of Middle-earth seems quite familiar to us; we have visited something quite like this world of untamed forests and adventurous quests and dragon-guarded treasure in the Norse sagas and eddas, the German *Nibelungenlied* epic, Wagner's *Ring* cycle, and —for that matter!—Grimm's fairy tales. It is the familiar heroic or mythological age of Northern European folklore, legend, and epic literature, decked out with newly invented names.

When the Professor came to write the trilogy itself he had some second thoughts about the lore established in *The Hobbit*. The goblins became the orcs, the Necromancer became Sauron, the endpaper maps were tinkered with, and the finish of the riddle game between Bilbo and Gollum was changed. Subsequent printings of *The Hobbit* have been altered to reflect these later developments.

THE first volume of the *Lord of the Rings* trilogy is called *The Fellowship of the Ring*. In it we discover that the magic golden ring Bilbo found in the course of his adventure with Gollum is a very important magical talisman indeed. It is nothing less than the One Ring itself, the great Ring of Power which the lord of evil, Sauron, made in an earlier age and which was cut from his hand when he was destroyed. The Ring was then lost. But Gollum found it, and was perverted by its evil power; and now that Sauron has arisen again, he is searching for it. The Ring has now come into the possession of Bilbo's adopted heir, Frodo. At a great council, the men and dwarves and elves of the West determine that the Ring must be destroyed. The catch to this is that only in the fires wherein it was originally forged can it be destroyed—and those fires are in a volcanic mountain, Orodruin, which is in the dark land of Mordor itself, the dominion of the risen Sauron. Frodo will bear the Ring to the mountain of fire, and a gallant company of men and elves, dwarves and hobbits, will accompany him on this long and very perilous quest. It is this quest which forms the plot of the trilogy.

The story is crowded with incident and has an enormous cast of characters, but—with half a million words at his disposal—Tolkien unfolds the narrative in a richly-detailed manner, at a leisurely pace. I am not going to fill up this chapter with a point-by-point outline of the plot of the trilogy, for I have already done just that in my book *Tolkien: A Look Behind "The Lord of the Rings";* it took me fully thirty-five pages to describe the story in that book, and even so, many dyed-in-the-wool Tolkien buffs criticized me sharply for slighting this or that favorite character, or for skimping on this or that scene which was dear to their hearts.

Tolkien's readers tend towards fanatic adulation of the book and its author, and many of the more dedicated devotees read the trilogy over and over, ten or a dozen times or even more. To me, this seems incredible. I have read *The Lord of the Rings* three times, myself: once when it was first published, and twice in the course of researching my book on Tolkien. I shall probably read it again sometime, but that will be years from now. I happened to discuss this with Fritz Leiber once, wondering why long-time fantasy enthusiasts like us two did not react (or over-react) with the same degree of hyper-adulation as that with which the Tolkien buffs seem to regard the trilogy. It is not that we are less fond of fantasy than they, but that we have read much more of it, and have been reading it longer than they have. Leiber's point of view was refreshing:

There's no arguing that a vast number of people—intelligent, educated, and sensitive people, I mean—young and old (but especially the former)—are tremendously and enduringly enthusiastic about Tolkien's trilogy, yet I do meet quite a few whose reactions are much like my own. We almost always start with, "The ents are great! Oh boy, yes. And that first part of the quest with the black riders in the distance and Strider a mystery—that's great too. Oh and yes, the first appearances of the Nazgûl and the Balrog . . ." At about which point the silence begins and we search our memories and look at each other rather guiltily—exciting things *should* spring to mind, but they don't . . .*

I find what Fritz has to stay on this point interesting because it mirrors my own feelings towards the trilogy rather closely. These days, when I pick up *The Lord of the Rings* again, it is not to re-read the entire work but to re-experience again a few familiar and favorite scenes—the scene in Book II, Chapter 5, "The Bridge of Khazad-Dûm," for example, where the Fellowship flee from the subterranean kingdom of Moria across the bridge and Gandalf confronts and does battle with the terrible Balrog and, locked in mortal combat with the demon, falls into the abyss to his death. A harrowing and magnificently realized scene. Another favorite scene to which I return comes in the second volume of the trilogy, *The Two Towers*. It is the sixth chapter of Book III, "The King of the Golden Hall," in which Gandalf enters the realm of Rohan, puts down Wormtongue and rouses Théoden, King of the Mark, to his old mightiness—a touching and powerfully dramatic confrontation. And I am also deeply moved by the preceding chapter, "The White Rider," in which Gandalf returns from having conquered death itself and tells of the experience in dream-like language that remains stark and grim for all its poetry. Tolkien transcends his own limitations as a writer, I believe, in such passages as these. They are triumphant.

---

*I am able to quote Fritz's remarks so accurately, not because I have total recall, but because he put them in a letter to me, dated June 9, 1969.

But above all, I return most frequently to skim the long scene in the third volume, *The Return of the King,* that recounts the seige of Gondor and the great battle itself; it is one soaring arch of mounting tension and power which rises to a crescendo and fades to a dying fall with a memorable final sentence: "Rohan had come at last."

But in the last analysis *The Lord of the Rings* breaks down into certain favorite scenes and beloved characters, rather than lingering in the memory as a coherent work every part of which is equal to the whole, and the sum of those parts greater than the whole. Such is true, for example, of *The Worm Ouroboros,* in which superb scenes stand out from the continuous tapestry but the tapestry itself remains a thing of irresistible power and beauty. This is, I need hardly say, a purely personal judgment; some of you will perhaps agree and many more of you will disagree, but that's what makes a ballgame.

Part of the trouble with Tolkien's book may lie in what seems to me its essential shallowness. The lack of real philosophical or psychological depth in *The Lord of the Rings* shows up most seriously, I think, in Tolkien's failure to explore the nature of evil. I shall have more to say on this point later, so I will limit myself here to the observation that there is something seriously wrong with Tolkien's villains: they are not really *cosmic* in their villainy, but surprisingly petty. Fritz Leiber noticed this fact, too, and in the same letter quoted above he singles out the villains as a weak spot:

> He's not interested in women and he's not really interested in his villains unless they're just miserable sneaks, bullies, and resentful cowards like Gollum . . . Tolkien (so unlike Eddison) does not explore and even seems uninterested in exploring the mentality and consciousness and inner life of his chief villains.

Leiber further refers to their "flat, two-dimensional" depiction. I think he has laid his finger on what is wrong with Tolkien's use of evil in the book—but more on this point later.

THE general consensus of opinion is that *The Lord of the Rings* is one of the greatest fantasy novels ever written and surely the supreme example of the imaginary-world romance. But when it was first published, its commercial success was still an open question. Cautiously, it was imported into this country by Houghton Mifflin, initially in a small quantity but then in ever-increasing amounts, thus confirming its status in the public domain. However, in fairness, it must be stated that at that time American copyright could not be obtained for any work which had not been manufactured within the United States and *within six months of British publication!* So it is unlikely that the early edition could have obtained protection anyway. Years later, in the 1950s, when Ballantine Books first requested reprint rights, the trilogy was doing so well that Houghton Mifflin preferred to keep it in hardcovers. Later yet, another paperback house, Ace Books, having also tried to buy it, discovering the public domain status of the early *Lord of the Rings,* went ahead without benefit of clergy, as it were. This led to the publication of two competing paperback editions: one, authorized by Tolkien, from Ballantine Books and paying the full royalty; the other, unauthorized, but quite legal nonetheless, from Ace Books, this being the earlier of the two editions.

The loss of copyright protection is generally a disaster, and the unauthorized publication of a book usually a grim event for its author. As it turned out, however, the whole affair proved to be just about the happiest possible sequence of events. For the excitement generated by the appearance of the competing Ballantine edition, with its unequivocal statement by the Professor, and the resultant hullabaloo and controversy, thrust Tolkien's triple-decker novel into the forefront of publishing news, and sales of the trilogy soared to fantastic heights. In the end, Tolkien and all of his several publishers made a good bit of money. Ace Books eventually made a royalty settlement with the Professor and agreed not to publish their now-outdated edition any more (for Tolkien had revised the authorized edition both to eliminate contradictions and to obtain copyright). *The Lord of the Rings* reached an enormous public, which greeted it with vast enthusiasm. I don't know how many millions of copies have been sold in this country by now, but the sales figures are considered quite phenomenal; and the excitement shows absolutely no sign of ebbing.

The Lord of the Rings is surely one of the most remarkable achievements in the history of fantasy. Despite several rather serious flaws, which I will discuss a bit further on, the trilogy succeeds to such a degree, on so many levels, that I am hard put to find the proper superlatives. In the first place, the world Tolkien creates on paper is very much more real, solid, and authentic-sounding than that of any other author, with the possible exception of Austin Tappan Wright. With half a million words to spend, he has the room to pass along to the reader a truly enormous amount of information about his invented world of Middle-earth. Not only do we become quite well acquainted with an immense cast of characters, their history and ancestry, but the quest-plot carries us through a considerable amount of real estate. Along the way we pick up the geography, history, and folklore of Middle-earth, as well as quite a bit of information about, and samples of, the literature of this brave new world.

All of this had been accomplished before, of course, in many another novel. Tolkien gives us, for example, a very detailed map of Middle-earth. Well, we have maps from Fletcher Pratt and E. R. Eddison, and from William Morris himself, for that matter. In the appendices, the Professor gives us an historical summary of key events in Middle-earth for several millennia; but this is in no way different from the chronological lists Eddison tacked onto his Zimiamvian novels. Nor do Tolkien's genealogical tables surprise those of us who are aware that Cabell added an entire volume of genealogical information to his *Biography of Manuel.*[3]

Where Tolkien *does* manage to surprise us is that he is not satisfied to stop at this point, but goes on to reveal a perfectly astonishing wealth of further information about Middle-earth. The trilogy includes so much information about the invented languages of this world, actual vocabularies, actual alphabets, that it is quite possible to learn to write in the Elvish tongues, for example. He goes on to provide us with the calendar of Middle-earth, and with yet more and more information, so that the reader comes away from a perusal of *The Lord of the Rings* in possession of almost as much general information about Middle-earth as he has about the world in which he lives.

That's an amazing comment to make, and may be a trifle overstated, but it really is not far off the mark. Aside from the reams of lore and background information conveyed in the course of the trilogy itself, the Professor has equipped the terminal volume with no fewer than six appendices—a total of *one hundred and three pages of solid, factual data.*

The end result of all this is simply that Middle-earth is ever so much more real than Narnia, Zothique, Tormance, or Barsoom. No author in the history of fantasy has created so convincingly detailed and overwhelmingly realistic an imaginary world, and few have ever created so colorful a story.

THE adulation that young, college-age readers have heaped upon the author of *The Lord of the Rings* must be a delightful recompense for those thirteen years of busy labor. Since 1965, when the trilogy exploded on the literary scene in the form of rival paperback editions, the student sub-culture has adopted *The Lord of the Rings* as a sort of Bible, jostling *The Catcher in the Rye, Lord of the Flies,* and the works of Kurt Vonnegut, Jr., from their hallowed shrines. The Professor himself has become a sort of Superstar to the younger set—a sort of Bob Dylan of the prose narrative—which must be more than a bit embarassing to an elderly Oxford don of sedentary habits and scholarly interests.

Despite the fanatic worship afforded *The Lord of the Rings*—and the passion some of its admirers feel for it is not abated after *thirty* full readings of it—it must be obvious to those thoroughly acquainted with the literature of fantasy outlined here that Middle-earth is not quite so flawless a creation as many believe it to be.

A bit further on I shall discuss fantasy writing to a rather technical degree, and we shall have much to say about prose style, the coining of names, the inventing of imaginary worlds, and the methods of sustaining the illusion of reality. But at the moment I would like to point out that the illusion is unevenly sustained in the pages of Tolkien's masterwork, and that in its creation he made a few serious errors.

In the first place, it must be admitted that Tolkien is not much of an artist when it comes to prose style. He is distinctly mediocre when compared to such brilliant stylists as Dunsany or Cabell or Eddison. Only rarely does his rather pedestrian prose rise to any peak of eloquence or passion or power, although when he does, as in the superbly dramatic scene when Gandalf faces the Balrog on the bridge, he acquits himself excellently. Then again, his characterization is rather stock, and it is all too easy to spot the stereotypes he used—to see behind Aragorn, the exiled, rightful King of Gondor who returns to triumph over his foes and claim his rightful seat, the shadow of Odysseus—or the figure of Christ behind the suffering, humbly noble Frodo, who must bear the burden of the Ring like another Cross—or the image of Sancho Panza behind the lowly, loyal, good-humored, common-sensical Sam. There is not very much in any of Tolkien's characters that comes as a surprise to us. His women characters are particularly weak, almost embarrassingly unconvincing. Tolkien does not seem comfortable when depicting romantic relationships between men and women, and avoids them where possible, making only a perfunctory effort in that direction. For what it's worth, the only character in the entire trilogy that seems to me striking-ly well-conceived or really interesting is the old wizard, Gandalf, a fascinating combination of superhuman dig-nity and majesty and power somehow marvelously blent with cranky, peevish, bad-tempered, and very human common clay. Gandalf is truly a memorable character, and only slightly less so are Treebeard the Ent, and Tom Bombadil. I know of no other character in all literature quite like merry old Tom!

And there is something very wrong with Tolkien's conception of evil. Evil is usually far easier to set down convincingly on paper than good, which is why every reader of Sax Rohmer is much more interested in the villainous Fu Manchu than in the heroic (but rather dull) Sir Dennis Nayland Smith. But in Tolkien the element of evil is singularly shallow and unconvinc-ing. His evil bogies seem somehow flimsy and two-dimensional. They are disposed of all too easily—a flash of light from Galadriel's vial will do it. All through the thirteen hundred pages of the trilogy the grim pres-ence of Sauron the Dark Lord broods in the back-ground, a figure of gigantic menace and power—but at the end he (quite literally) blows away like a puff of smoke! C. S. Lewis knew better: he was grimly aware that evil is tenacious and strong, not easily banished, not without great effort uprooted or slain. The element of evil that is very present throughout his fiction—in *Perelandra,* for instance, but above all in *That Hideous Strength*—is the Real Thing: not lurking shadows or scary faces leering through the window, but something tremendously solid and alive and vigorous. Even in the Narnia books he did not skimp on the reality of evil. Tolkien, however, avoids the issue rather uneasily.

Another flaw, and quite a serious one I think, is the fact that Tolkien's world has no religion in it. When I touched on this point in my book *Tolkien,* several furious Tolkienists sprang to the defense of the Master by pointing out that the shadowy and mysterious Valar are obviously archangels in charge of the world, and that the people of Middle-earth are aware of the One who is supreme over even the Valar—Eru by name, who is God, more or less. To these protests I replied: yes, of course, but that is not what I am talking about. A religion is much more than just the presence of an actual god, or gods; it is also an established canon of inspired writings and an organized priesthood, a system of temples and shrines, and so on.

This element of an hierarchical religion is totally lacking in Tolkien, and its absence seriously injures the credibility of his Middle-earth. During the course of the guided tour Tolkien gives us in the trilogy, we visit a number of societies more or less at the level of those depicted in the Norse and Germanic epic literatures. Organized religions were quite present in those civilizations, as they have been present in every advanced civilization known to us in all of history, from ancient Sumeria down to today. Most fantasy writers know this almost by instinct and include local religions in the apparatus of their imaginary settings. In the Conan stories, Howard's stalwart Cimmerian swears by his primitive god, Crom; Dunsany's early tales are set in those lands wherein the Gods of Pegāna are venerated; Burroughs' Martians have their priests, the Holy Therns, who serve the goddess Issus; a priesthood flourishes in Pratt's *The Blue Star,* and its Pope is called "the Episcopal;" the god Orcher is invoked in Hannes Bok's *Sorcerer's Ship;* Smith's invented lands of Hyperborea and Zothique and Poseidonis have their gods, temples, and priesthoods; in Leiber's Lankhmar, gods as little as Issek of the Jug and as great as Aarth the Invisible are known (and sometimes even worshipped); de Camp's *The Tritonian Ring* opens with a council of the Gods of the West; Cabell's universe has its gods, and they are many and curious; Moorcock's Elric of Melniboné was the last worshipper of the "grotesque and beautiful" gods of Imrryr, but he gave his fealty to Arioch, Duke of Hell; Gardner F. Fox's Kothar the Barbarian swears by the divinity Dwallka; Merritt's

Dwellers in the Mirage centers about the god Khalk'ru, just as *Creep, Shadow* is concerned with the grim worship of the Gatherer in the Cairn; the little Earth Gods dwell in their castle atop the mountain called Kadath in the Cold Waste in Lovecraft's novel *The Dream-Quest of Unknown Kadath;* Cija is the Goddess incarnate, reared by priestesses far from the everyday world, in Jane Gaskell's Atlan Trilogy; the world of John Jakes' Brak the Barbarian is a battleground between the good religion of the prophet Nestoriamus and the dark worship of Yob-Haggoth, lord of evil; in my own Lemurian Books, the warrior-hero Thongor swears by his savage god, Gorm, one of the Nineteen Gods Who Watch the World; a living Goddess appears in the second book of my unfinished epic fantasy, *Khymyrium;* the gods are very real and quite important in my tales of Simrana the Dreamworld.

But there is no religion at all in *The Lord of the Rings*—no temples, shrines, priests, prayers, amulets, scriptures, ikons, idols—*nothing!* None of the many characters, not even the heroic warriors, so much as swears by his gods. Obviously because they *have* no gods. Which is simply incredible in a primitive world of wizards and warriors and walled stone cities.

ALL of which leaves us with an unresolved question: is *The Lord of the Rings* the greatest fantasy novel ever written? If it is not, then what is?

I think Tolkien's achievement is superlative, and that, beyond question, his trilogy stands very high among the few supreme classics of fantasy literature: I will even concede, most willingly, that the novel succeeds brilliantly—on its own terms. The essence of his accomplishment is exactly this: that he has created on paper a "secondary universe" more thoroughly and convincingly detailed than any other writer has done before or after him.[4] I do not imagine that his achievement will be eclipsed in our time by the appearance of a work superior to *The Lord of the Rings* in this respect.

So in this sense, at least, I would say: yes, *The Lord of the Rings* is the greatest fantasy novel ever written.

However (there is always a "however"), in any literary canon the rank of a book or of its author remains a matter of personal taste. The noblest geniuses of literature do not stand secure in their shrines: an Eliot will arrive to dislodge a Milton, a Pound will find the criteria by which to consider even a Shakespeare dispensable. All criticism boils down to a matter of personal taste; there are no fixed or permanent standards. All criticism, in a word, is subjective.

For one thing, are we talking about fantasy in general or merely discussing one of the many traditions that are woven into the tapestry—that of the imaginary world, in this case?

If we are talking about the entire province of fantasy, not just the central tradition, then I would certainly deny *The Lord of the Rings* the premier position. For the single finest fantasy novel written in our time, or for that matter, *ever* written, is, must be, by any conceivable standard, T. H. White's *The Once and Future King.* I can hardly imagine that any mature, literate person who has read the book would disagree with this estimate. White is a great writer.

And if we are limiting ourselves to the imaginary-world tradition, even here my personal taste directs me to another book. For all its undeniable flaws and eccentricities, E. R. Eddison's *The Worm Ouroboros* is still the best, the most durable, the richest, the most exciting, the most splendidly ringing work of heroic fantasy I have ever read. Beyond question, I would agree with the many who find the Eddisonian prose impenetrable: the book *is* difficult. The rewards, however, are very great. It is not a book everyone can read, surely.

For those of us who can, however, it is one of the best books ever written, and certainly the supreme accomplishment in the imaginary world novel.

Chacun à son goût. And *caveat emptor,* I suppose.

TOLKIEN'S achievement, however—these matters of personal taste aside—is unquestionably great. It would be absurd to deny the magnitude of his accomplishment, and, surely, it is enough for any man to have written one of the five or six supreme works in any literary genre.

It has been observed that Lord Dunsany exerted the strongest and widest influence over the fantasy writers of the first half of this century. There seems no doubt that Tolkien will exert a comparable influence on the writers who will arise (and have arisen) to dominate fantasy writing in the second half of our era.

Tolkien's influence became observable quite early. Probably the first newcomer to the field to display this was Carol Kendall, who published her first children's fantasy novel, *The Gammage Cup,* in 1959. Mrs. Kendall hails from Bucyrus, Ohio, earned her B.A. (and a Phi Beta Kappa key, as well) at Ohio University, and is presently married to Paul Murray Kendall, the noted biographer and historian whose excellent life of Richard III will be familiar to many of my readers.

The Gammage Cup shows in particular the influence of *The Hobbit,* as does its sequel, *The Whisper of Glocken,* published in 1965. The story introduces a very Hobbit-like race of small folk who live in quaint houses in a secluded rural valley called The Land Between the Mountains. These mountains are infested by repulsive, goblinish (or Orcish) beings, who are a menace to the peaceful life of the valley. The Five Heroes mount an expedition against them, armed with charmed swords which flash with magic light whenever the goblin-like ogres are near—it's all very much like Tolkien, although it has undeniable charms that are all its own.

To my knowledge, Mrs. Kendall has written nothing since the appearance of *The Whisper of Glocken;* this is to be regretted, for her books have verve and gusto and that indefinable quality that can only be called "good story-telling."

While Mrs. Kendall's books seem largely derived

from (or influenced by) *The Hobbit,* the novels of
Alan Garner are quite a different matter. For one
thing, they are much more serious—at times grim, even
frightening. For another, they are more abundant in
rich imaginative invention. There is also a surer hand
at the controls; and finally, *The Lord of the Rings*
seems to have been a prime factor in their shaping.

Garner hails from Tolkien country: he went to school
in Manchester, the city in which the Professor grew
up, and his college was Magdalen at Oxford. He is
interested in archaeology, history, and the folklore of
his native Cheshire. For the "matter" of his books he
has delved into obscure bypaths: Norse, Celtic, and
Welsh legendry and lore, and even Pictish and Old
British and Highland Scots. Today, with wife and
children, he lives in a "lovely old half-timbered house"
which they discovered lying derelict, mouldering into
decay, and salvaged. The house has now been chris-
tened "Toad Hall," which delights me; but I am much
more pleased by the name of the Cheshire town near
which it stands—"Blackden-cum-Goostrey." Only in
England . . .

Garner's first book was published when he was
twenty-six. It is called *The Weirdstone of Brisingamen*
(1960), and relates the tale of the epic struggle between
Cadellin, the wise old enchanter, and evil Nastrond,
the Great Spirit of Darkness. Into this age-old conflict
stray two children named Colin and Susan from our
own day, and the adventure is as much theirs as it is
the magicians'. Garner has peopled his halfworld with
weird, fabulous new races—the Huldrafolk, the Svart-
mort, the Stromkarl—new monsters, new menaces. The
scene fluctuates eerily between the sunlit lanes of lazy
Cheshire and the strange lost world that is the chess-
board battleground of the opposing forces of light and
darkness. A sequel called *The Moon of Gomrath*
(1963) continues the tale. However, Garner's third
novel, *Elidor* (1965), had nothing to do with the theme
or characters of the first two books and was skimpier
on the fantasy element and lighter in tone. Subsequent

books, like *The Owl Service* (1967), are disappointing.
It is regrettable to see an author of great potential
failing to fulfill that promise.

These are children's books, too, incidentally, as are
the Kendall books. Or perhaps I should say "ostensibly"
children's books; no fantasy-buff should let the label
deter him from seeking out copies of *Brisingamen* and
Gomrath without delay. Publishers are cautious people
and distrust the very notion of "fantasy for grown-
ups"—yes, even in this post-Tolkienian era. Therefore,
most good fantasy published today is packaged as
juvenile.

A case in point is the splendid American writer,
Lloyd Alexander. Alexander and his French wife,
Janine, live in a suburb of Philadelphia called Drexel
Hill. He was writing genuine books "for Children" for
some years before publishing, in 1964, a superb, completely brilliant adventure fantasy entitled *The Book of
Three,* the first in a series of five closely-connected
novels set in the mythic Welsh otherworld of Prydain.
The Prydain books, of course, were "ostensibly" juveniles, but like Garner's books they are the sort of heady
fare that adults will relish with fuller appreciation than
will young readers.

The story begins with a youth named Taran, whose
saga continues for the length of the pentalogy. Lloyd
Alexander and I have met and talked several times,
and I once elicited from him a self-estimate of the
literary influences upon the shaping of the Prydain
books. Tolkien figured into it, of course, but the author
himself believes he was influenced as much by T. H.
White, if not a bit more. At any rate, Alexander is
well-read in the literature, and his long story sparkles
with surprising in-jokes for fantasy-buffs. Young Taran
is a pig-tender when we first encounter him—which
reminds me that when Cabell first brought on stage
Dom Manuel, the future Redeemer of Poictesme, it was
in identical guise. Like his Cabellian counterpart, Taran
also rises in time to heroism and kingship. But not
before he undergoes tutelage at the hands of a kindly

if irascible old magician—just as the boy Wart was tutored by the wizard Merlyn in *The Sword in the Stone*.

The series continued with *The Black Cauldron* (1965), *The Castle of Llyr* (1966), *Taran Wanderer* (1967), and culminated in *The High King* (1968), which won for Alexander the highest award given in this country for excellence in juvenile literature, the Newbery Medal. It was richly deserved. Several elements in the Prydain pentalogy distinguish Alexander as a fine craftsman. The first is sheer good story-telling—crisp, succinct, exciting, with a strong element of tension and suspense. Then again, the characterization is quite outstanding. Taran is the hero of the pentalogy, but in the first couple of books he is just a boy, too young to really hold the center of the stage, and thus with unerring intelligence Alexander places him on the periphery, where he partakes to a degree in the flow of action but also acts as viewpoint-character for the audience. As the youth matures into the man, he moves slowly, book by book, to the center of the stage. As for the last book, *The High King,* well—it is his story all the way.

Another thing that makes the series stand out in my mind is the unexpected element of humor that enlivens every page. This, once again, is the mark of intelligence: the tension is taut throughout, and un-relieved, it would have been harrowing. The humor is present in such amusing characters as the boastful bard, Fflewddur Fflam, whose ensorcelled harp twangs warn-ingly at each exaggeration, and snaps a string when its master forgets himself to skirt the outer limits of veracity.

This humorous element in the Prydain pentalogy may be another thing Alexander learned from the author of *The Once and Future King*. However, as for his heroine, that irresistible tomboy, Princess Eilonwy, even T. H. White could not have envisioned her. She is completely Lloyd Alexander's invention.

For five years the series enriched the publishing trade season, but it ended eventually, as all series do.

Since then, Alexander has chosen, I think wisely, to turn his talents to a kind of story entirely different; and his most recent book, *The Marvelous Misadventures of Sebastian* (1970), bears no resemblance to the tales of Prydain.[5]

7

Post-Howardian Heroica:

The Swordsmen and Sorcerers' Guild of America, Ltd.

Seas crash upon long dragon-guarded shores,
Bursting in crimson moons of burning spray,
And iron castles ope to me their doors,
And serpent-women lure with harp and lay.
  The misty waves shake now to phantom oars—
Seek not for me: I sail to meet the day.
                    —Robert E. Howard:
                    "The Singer in the Mist"[1]

As NOTED earlier in this book, the sub-genre of heroic fantasy that we call Sword & Sorcery was born in the sleazy, gaudy, glorious, golden age of the pulps. To be precise about it—if anyone really cares—the invention might date from August 1929, the publication date of "The Shadow Kingdom," earliest of all Howard's tales in the genre to reach print.

To the surprise of virtually everyone concerned, Sword & Sorcery caught on. It struck a responsive chord in the readers of pulp adventure magazines in general and of *Weird Tales* in particular, so much so that the sub-genre survived the death of its creator, Howard himself—survived even the demise of the great pulp magazine that had been its cradle. The last piece of genuine Sword & Sorcery to appear in *Weird Tales* was Henry Kuttner's "Dragon Moon" in the issue dated January 1941—the last of his aborted "Elak of Atlantis" series.

Kuttner and Moore, as noted in my account of the history of *Weird Tales,* made the jump to Campbell's prestigious *Astounding Science Fiction* and its bright new companion, *Unknown*. *Weird Tales* lasted for another dozen years, but its great days had long since been over; *Unknown* would not itself survive for long, but for a time it housed the raffish, brawling adventures of Fafhrd and the Gray Mouser and of burly, red-bearded Wan Tengri, a creation of Norvell Page. In fact, the age of the pulp magazine was nearly over.

Sword & Sorcery went into the doldrums after *Unknown* fell prey to World War II paper restrictions. The post-war era brought a brief resurgence of its thrillsome, tacky splendors, for fantasy-buffs returning as veterans, pockets bulging with several years' back pay, launched short-lived publishing houses which rescued from pulpish oblivion many a stirring saga of swashbuckling derring-do. Howard's Conan series was one of the gory classics thus resurrected: in 1950 the smallish firm of Gnome Press, operating out of Martin W. Greenberg's home in Hicksville, New York, and from a cubbyhole of a Manhattan office, published a book version of Howard's only Conan novel—the one that was being serialized as "The Hour of the Dragon" in *Weird Tales* at the time of his suicide—under the new title, *Conan the Conqueror*. In due course a reviewer's copy went out to Fletcher Pratt; Pratt read it but did not care for it in the least.

"He despised Howard's Conan stories, whose occasional crudities of concept and lapses of logic exasperated him. He hated heroes who simply batter their way out of traps by means of bulging thews, without bothering to use their brains," remarked Pratt's friend and sometime collaborator, L. Sprague de Camp.[2] At any rate, Pratt passed the book along to de Camp, remarking casually that he thought he might like it. As it happened, de Camp had never encountered the saga of the mighty Cimmerian, and a quick reading of *Conan the Conqueror* burst on de Camp's imagination like a bombshell.

De Camp later described the incident in these terms:

I came into this cultus late. Although I had written some stories of this type in collaboration with Fletcher Pratt [i.e., the Harold Shea yarns], up to 1950 I had never read a Conan story (albeit I had heard vaguely about them) because I had not been a *Weird Tales* reader during Howard's *floruit*, and Miller and Clark had never urged the stories upon me.[3]

When I heard this story, I—rather incredulously— asked Sprague how he could possibly have avoided *Weird Tales* all those years. I suppose I was thinking of those improbably luscious Margaret Brundage covers, with bejeweled kings lolling on ivory thrones, smirking at the undulations of exquisite dancing girls—posed for, I later learned, by Mrs. Brundage's teenage daughters—covers, it seemed to me, completely irresistible to any red-blooded American fantasy buff. Sprague—the redness of whose blood has never been questioned by anyone who has ever met his petite blonde wife and two strapping sons—shrugged humorously and said that somehow or other he had gotten the notion that the magazine was devoted to ghost stories, a genre for which he lacks any enthusiasm whatsoever. At any rate, the upshot of it all was that when *Conan the Conqueror* fell into his hands, "I read it, was hooked, and quickly read all the Howard I could get my hands on."

The "Miller and Clark" to which de Camp alludes above are P. Schuyler Miller, a popular science fiction writer of the era, now for many years a permanent book reviewer for *Analog,* and John D. Clark, Ph.D., an Alaska-born chemist, then on the staff of the Naval Air Rocket Test Station at Dover, New Jersey, whose liquid propellant development program he would soon head, a position he was to hold until 1970 when he retired to write his informal and wildly anecdotal history of liquid rocket propellants, *Ignition!* (New Brunswick, N.J., Rutgers University Press, 1972). Both men were early enthusiasts of the Howardian brand of swash-buckling and ensorcellment and had collaborated on an early "Informal Biography" of Conan published in the rare brochure *The Hyborian Age*.*

At this time Dr. Clark was filling in as a sort of advisory editor for the Gnome Press edition of the Conan saga and had written a brief preface to *Conan the Conqueror.* He knew Pratt and de Camp because they were, the three of them, among the founding members of a small private club known as "The Trap Door Spiders" which met then, and still meets today, more-or-less monthly, at the home or apartment of one of the members, or a restaurant in downtown Manhattan, for a convivial stag evening devoted to cocktails, gourmet dinners, and good conversation.

De Camp wasted no time in hunting down all the Howard anybody knew about. In this he no doubt had the willing help of John Clark, then amiably advising Greenberg on contents for the second volume of the Conan series for Gnome, a volume called *The Sword of Conan,* which consisted of four of Howard's novel-ettes arranged in chronological order and "bridged" by extracts taken from the Miller/Clark "Informal Biography."

The only fantasy magazine of any particular worth then going was an irregular periodical called *The Avon Fantasy Reader,* which appeared three or four times a year under the knowledgeable editorship of Donald A. Wollheim. *The Avon Fantasy Reader,* however, was not exactly a magazine; to be precise, it was a series of paperback anthologies, numbered consecutively, which had for some time been reprinting short fiction by Merritt, Lovecraft, Smith, Dunsany, Chambers, and other writers, including Robert E. Howard. Number 18 included a story by Howard entitled "The Witch from Hell's Kitchen," which de Camp had never seen or heard of. He telephoned Wollheim and learned that the story was indeed a new one, which had originally been titled "The Witch of Arabu." The story had been passed along to Avon by Oscar J. Friend, who had

---

*See Bibliography I: General References.

inherited it from Otis Adelbert Kline. Kline, now dead himself, had been Howard's agent at the time of the writer's suicide, and Wollheim advised de Camp that Friend was rumored to have "a whole pile of unpublished manuscripts" by Howard.

This turned out to be the first of a number of manuscript troves L. Sprague de Camp was to unearth in the course of his new interest in Howard's work. On November 30, 1951, he visited Friend's apartment in Jackson Heights and sorted through the pile. There was an entire carton of unpublished material, including three previously unknown Conan stories, "The Frost-Giant's Daughter," "The God in the Bowl," and "The Black Stranger," which was later retitled "The Treasure of Tranicos." De Camp was eager to get them published, and revised them slightly, finding an eventual welcome for them in the pages of Lester Del Rey's twin magazines, *Fantasy Fiction* and *Space Science Fiction,* where they appeared during 1952–1953.

Meanwhile, Greenberg had published *The Sword of Conan.* He knew of de Camp's interest in the burly Cimmerian and the two got together to plan the sequence of the remainder of the hardcover series. Dr. Clark, whose work on the project had been limited to advising Greenberg on the proper sequence of the then-known Conan canon, which he and Schuyler Miller had worked out, and to writing, for the fun of it, an introduction or two, was happy to step aside and let his fellow Trap Door Spider take the lead in guiding the saga through press.

The Coming of Conan appeared in 1953, followed shortly by *King Conan* that same year. *Conan the Barbarian,* scheduled for 1954, would have been the last of the series had it not been for the new Conan stories de Camp was beginning to find in troves of old manuscripts Howard had left scattered about with various correspondents, friends, and family. A book of these called *Tales of Conan* followed in 1955. Two years later Greenberg's Gnome Press published a brand new Conan novel; it had been written and submitted by

a Swedish Conan fan who had been introduced to the
cult by G. Ken Chapman, the British book-dealer who
for years has specialized in obtaining American fantasy
and science fiction books and magazines for European
readers and collectors, and vice versa. This young author, a lieutenant in Sweden's air force named Björn
Nyberg, had written a booklength Conan novel, which
he submitted to Greenberg quite unexpectedly. De Camp
edited the manuscript, collaborated in rewriting some
portions, and the new Conan novel appeared in magazine form as "Conan the Victorious," and later in book
form as *The Return of Conan*. De Camp recalls the
period with amusement:

> I certainly never imagined, when I first read *Conan the
> Conqueror,* that I should ever become involved to such an
> extent in the affairs of Howard and his super-hero. Nor
> did I ever consciously plan to "take over" this literary
> property. It just happened through coincidence and circum-
> stance. I daresay others could have done better what I have
> done to complete and promote the Conan saga—Howard
> himself, had he lived and matured, would surely have done
> so—but I happened to be the man on the spot.[4]

THE appearance of the Conan books had several kinds
of influence on the future of Sword & Sorcery. When
the terminal volume, *The Return of Conan,* was published in 1957, that might well have been the end of
the story. As it happens, it was not.

For one thing, de Camp had become intrigued with
the potentials of Howardian fantasy. Editing and re-
vising and, in places, rewriting or completing stories by
Howard did not dampen his enthusiasm: he itched to
try his hand at this sort of thing himself. Thus, during
the 1950's he tried writing short stories more or less
in the Howardian mode, creating scenes set in a post-
Atlantean world not really unlike that of the Hyborian
Age. Taking his cue from Clark Ashton Smith, who
borrowed from Blavatsky or Scott-Elliot the name
"Poseidonis" for "the last isle of foundering Atlantis,"
de Camp pretends that the Greek geographers and

mythologists derived "Poseidonis" from "Pusâd," which sounded to them like the name of their own sea-god.

De Camp is very knowledgeable in archaeology, history, and myth, and has written booklength studies of imaginary geography in general and the Atlantis legend in particular; hence, as you might expect, his "Pusâdian Age" world is far more cleverly contrived than Howard's rather slapdash try. Taking "Kernê" from Carthaginian lore and "the Gorgon Isles" from Diodorus Siculus, borrowing "Orgugia" from Homer's "Orgygia" and "Torrutseish" from the historical Tartessus, he constructed a worldscape far more credible than that of the Conan stories, one in which the holes did not show and the sources are far less blatantly obvious. But for the most part he follows Howard's techniques rather closely—as in renaming Africa "Tartaros," after Tartarus, in Greek myth the gloom-shrouded abyss below Hades where Zeus imprisoned the rebellious Titans. This is adroitly Howardian, as the Greek name has long since become an adjective, "Tartarean," indicating subterranean darkness. Five such stories were published during the '50s and early '60s, as well as one important novel, *The Tritonian Ring,* which conducts the reader on a guided tour (or an heroic quest) through a considerable amount of Pusâdian Age geography, and is great fun to read.

Early in the 1960s, de Camp's unquenchable enthusiasm for the Howardian *oeuvres* led him into a new venture. Science fiction had become immensely popular in the burgeoning field of paperback publishing, and Sprague was convinced that Sword & Sorcery could rival its audience. Obtaining permission from Howard's estate, he took the series around to the various paperback firms, eventually interesting Lancer Books in the idea. Gnome Press having gone dormant, if not defunct, in the interval, Sprague had a free hand in reshaping the sequence of stories in the light of further manuscript discoveries. In 1965, for instance, a year after the Lancer editions began appearing on the newsstands, a new cache of previously unknown stories turned up. This one was excavated by Glenn Lord of Pasadena, Texas, who had become literary agent for Howard's estate on de Camp's recommendation. As Sprague recalls the event:

> One story was complete; one was in the form of an outline; one was a three-page fragment; and the rest consisted of the first halves of stories and outlines of the rest. I finished four of the incomplete stories and Lin Carter the remaining one. In addition, Carter and I have collaborated on a few pastiches, based upon hints in Howard's notes and letters, to fill the gaps in the saga.[5]

SINCE this is the point at which I enter the story of Conan, I should perhaps explain here that in 1965 my first novel was published by Ace Books. As anyone might have expected, knowing my tastes, it was an heroic swashbuckler laid in the lost continent of Lemuria half a million years ago, called *The Wizard of Lemuria*. One charitable critic[6] remarked that my book read like "the result of a head-on collision between Burroughs and Howard," a description that rather pleased me, as that is exactly what the story was supposed to be. (Other critics were less charitable.)

De Camp and I were well acquainted at this time, although he had not yet nominated me for membership in the Trap Door Spiders. But we had met and talked many times at science fiction conventions, and I have a hunch that he had developed a certain degree of respect for my familiarity with fantasy literature and my knowledge of its history and traditions. (He once remarked he had never realized the position of William Morris in the imaginary-world tradition until reading one of my fanzine articles on the sources of the Tolkien trilogy.)

At any rate, he had taken a paternal interest in my budding career and had, in fact, read and performed a detailed critique of my *Wizard of Lemuria* in manuscript, volunteering for the task. As I was deeply interested in the fortunes of Conan in paperback, and since he was frequently in Manhattan for meetings with his lawyers and Lancer's editors, we got into the habit of having lunch together. Glenn Lord had earlier discovered a trove containing ten new King Kull stories; these I had touched up, tightened a bit, completed, or revised, and the book, *King Kull,* appeared in 1967. Lord had offered the job to Sprague; too busy with Conan at the time, he had suggested me for the job, and a bit later he asked me to complete the three-page Conan fragment he alludes to above, which I called "The Hand of Nergal."

Our collaboration on the new Conan stories arose from legal troubles with Gnome Press. Considerable time was being wasted while the lawyers of everyone concerned reached an agreement with Martin Greenberg, and Sprague feared that the delay would seriously interrupt the publication of the Conan paperbacks, losing momentum, as it were. During one of these Manhattan luncheons, he rather diffidently asked if I would be interested in working up some new Conan stories with him. I was, of course, delighted at the idea of collaborating with a writer I had long admired and whose stories I had enjoyed since my teens. To date, the new team of de Camp and Carter has published seven short stories or novelettes, including one 30,000-word novella ("Black Tears," in *Conan the Wanderer*), one of the stories being a semi-posthumous three-way collaboration among Howard and the two of us ("The Snout in the Dark," in *Conan of Cimmeria*); there have been, as well, two full-length novels: *Conan of the Isles* (1969) and *Conan the Buccaneer* (1971). At the time of this writing, Sprague and I are completing a sequence of four interconnected novelettes about Conan. The first of these, "The Witch of the Mists," was headlined in the Twentieth-Anniversary issue of Ted White's *Fantastic,* and received the cover spot, with a stunning painting by Jeff Jones; the second in the sequence, "Black Sphinx of Nebthu," will perhaps have appeared in that magazine by the time this book is published. These four

novelettes will eventually comprise the twelfth paperback in the series, under the title *Conan of Aquilonia*.

SEVERAL factors converged at once to touch off a great
renaissance of interest in Sword & Sorcery during the
early 1960s. For one thing, the sudden and dramatic
appearance of the heroic fantasy of Burroughs and
Tolkien rather paved the way for Sword & Sorcery.
The Burroughs boom and the "Hobbit habit" are now
publishing history, and it is perhaps worth noting that
both phenomena were triggered by the release of competing editions of the same works, published by Ballantine Books and by Ace Books. Both explosions into
paperback of the Burroughs and Tolkien works, and
the controversies aroused by the competing paperback
editions, attracted wide public attention and racked
up impressive sales-figures. To those in the know, this
suggested that there was quite a large and enthusiastic
audience for heroic fantasy lurking out there in the
boondocks.

Ace was the first to gamble on this by publishing
comparable works in the genre, hoping they would
catch on and sell as had Burroughs and Tolkien. But
before that, the firm has the credit for publishing the
first recognizable milestone in the revival of Sword &
Sorcery that began sweeping the paperback stands in
the early 1960's. I refer to the publication of *Witch
World* in 1963, a novel by "Andre Norton," the pen-
name used by Alice Mary Norton, a retired children's
librarian from Cleveland, Ohio.

Bitten by the Burroughs bug in her own youth, Miss
Norton decided—quite correctly, as it turned out—that
the young people of today would still be interested in
fast-moving, colorful adventure stories set in fantastic
worlds. Her first novel, *Ralestone's Luck*, was written
while she was in high school, but a later novel, *The
Prince Commands*, was the first of her stories to find
its way into print. It was published in 1934, followed
by *Ralestone's Luck* in 1938. Miss Norton rapidly made
up for this slow start, and with a vengeance, for some

fifty books appeared under her byline in the first twenty years or so following *The Prince Commands.* That schoolgirl enthusiasm for Edgar Rice Burroughs was parlayed into a publishing phenomenon, for she swiftly became one of the most popular of the juvenile trade-book writers, specializing in science fiction adventure stories set against sweeping galactic backgrounds, but involved with the coming-of-age problems of young people.

Witch World surprised us all. For one thing, it wasn't at all a science fiction novel, but straight heroic fantasy set in an earth-like world of sorcerers and enchanters. For another thing, it was in no way a book for juveniles, but a work of excellent adult fiction. (It was also a cracking good bit of storytelling—but that was *no* surprise!) It was followed by a host of sequels, *Web of the Witch World* (1964) and *Three Against the Witch World* (1965) being the first of these. To date, I have seen eight volumes in the series, the most recent being *Spell of the Witch World,* a collection of short pieces, and *The Crystal Gryphon,* a novel.

The Witch World stories are richly told with verve and color, and the element of the supernatural, of fantasy and magic and the gods, is handled with a lively inventiveness, tempered and disciplined by a firm grounding in anthropology. Perhaps Miss Norton writes so convincingly about magical talismans and enchanted swords because she has a scholar's insight into how primitive peoples regarded such artifacts and knows the premises that evolved to account for their presumed powers.

A year after the first book, *Witch World,* hit the stands, Lancer Books unleashed the mighty Conan. The first volume of his adventures was entitled (most appropriately) *Conan the Adventurer;* it had a staggering cover painting by Frank Frazetta which was quickly blown up into a poster three feet high to be sold in paperback bookstores around the country. From a fairly slow, uneven start, the Conan series took off for the high country . . . and today, with three million copies in print and new editions appearing in Japan, France, Italy, and Germany, it has never come down.

The obvious success-potential of Lancer's Conan series may have tipped the scales in favor of comparable books. At any rate, in 1965, my novel *The Wizard of Lemuria* appeared, also from Ace Books. This novel has since been reissued by Berkley Medallion Books under the new title, *Thongor and the Wizard of Lemuria,* and has enjoyed a modest success, with editions published in Japan and in Britain, where the entire series eventually appeared. In addition, a sort of teenage psychedelic folk-rock musical version of one novel, *Thongor in the City of Magicians,* briefly enlivened the London stage a few seasons ago. *Wizard,* anyway, was the first of a series of six novels I would eventually write about the heroic adventures of Thongor the Mighty, barbarian warrior-hero of Lost Lemuria. There have also been a number of novelettes and short stories about Thongor; these will in time, I expect, be gathered into two books, the first and second volumes of the completed saga, which I plan to call *Thongor of Lost Lemuria* and *Thongor in the Land of Peril.* That is for the future to decide, of course. However, recently Thongor has joined his brethren, King Kull and Conan himself, in the comic-books. His story, it would seem, is still far from ended.

In the course of the chapter on the history of *Unknown Worlds,* I mentioned that Fritz Leiber's popular series of tales about Fafhrd and the Gray Mouser did not go down with the ship when *Unknown* foundered, although the roguish duo were marooned for a time in a sort of literary limbo while Leiber went on to garner an armful of Hugo Awards as one of the most brilliant of modern science fiction writers. Spaceships and time warps are weak fare for an author weaned on the heady intoxicants purveyed by the likes of Cabell, Eddison, and Dunsany, however, and during the 1960s Leiber returned in force to claim his Nehwonian empire anew.

Cele Goldsmith, then editrix of *Fantastic,* offered

the swaggering Lankhmarines a hospitable haven in the pages of her magazine, and before long such stories as "Lean Times in Lankhmar," "The Unholy Grail," and "Bazaar of the Bizarre" were brightening successive issues. These new additions to the canon were richer in detail, more succulent and visceral, and told in a more disciplined, mature style superior to that of the earlier, at times less well-woven and even flimsy, adventures. Again, it was Ace Books that took the plunge, and when Fafhrd and the Gray Mouser made their long-awaited debut in paperback it was, as might have been expected, with a loud bang and a whiff of sulphurous dragon's-breath.

In one dramatic splurge Ace brought out *The Swords of Lankhmar, Swords Against Wizardry,* and *Swords in the Mist.* Two years later, *Swords and Deviltry* and *Swords Against Death* followed. That brought the entire saga (so far) into print in matched editions, although, of course, the door is left ajar for any future adventures that may be written. One or two recent additions to the canon have indeed slipped through that door since, and one walked off with the 1971 Hugo and Nebula awards for best novelette.

The story of Fafhrd and the Gray Mouser, too (I pray to Srith of the Scrolls!), is far from ended . . .

Another durable veteran of *Fantastic* found refuge between paperback covers that same year, 1968—John Jakes' popular swordsman-hero, Brak the Barbarian. Jakes is a tall, hefty, affable, Chicago-born ex-advertising-executive with a grizzled crewcut and extensive agency experience in and around Dayton, Ohio, where he and his family make their home. Jakes frankly admits to the Howardian influence clearly visible in his yarns of Brak, the wandering barbarian soldier of fortune. He once discussed the genesis of his character in these terms:

When the first Brak tale saw print, its appearance was followed shortly by a letter to the magazine that had published it. I have lost my copy of the letter since, but I recall its inferences quite clearly—and painful ones they were for an author. That reader's letter expressed the opinion that Brak was but a pale ghost of mighty Conan and, what was worse, had probably been conceived either out of an ignorance of Conan, or with full knowledge and therefore out of sheer cupidity. To the first part of the charge, I plead delightedly guilty. That teller of marvelous tales, Robert Howard, did indeed create a giant in whose shadow other "hero tales" must stand and, sometimes, admittedly, suffer. But be ignorant of all of his work? Or believe that readers would be hoodwinked, and not feel the pulse of common blood which riots through all the warriors who inhabit the world of sword and sorcery? No. My motive for giving birth to Brak and his parallel universe on an old black iron Underwood was much simpler. There just are not enough stories of this kind to go around any more; not enough, anyway, to please me. To help fill this dismal gap well or badly—I hope never indifferently—my barbarian, with the long yellow braid and the light of the south horizons glittering in his eyes, was born.'

That first Brak story, incidentally, was "Devils in the Walls," which appeared in the May 1963 issue of *Fantastic*. Since then, tale upon tale has come out of that miracle-making old black Underwood, and beginning with *Brak the Barbarian* (New York, Avon Books, 1968), they have been making their way, at last, into book form. That first volume was followed with *Brak the Barbarian vs. the Mark of the Demons* and *Brak the Barbarian vs. the Sorceress*, both published in 1969. Since then there has been a hiatus in the appearance of the series, Avon perhaps having pulled in its horns, feeling the crunch of the current economic recession that has pinched most paperback firms in their most vulnerable anatomical portion—the profits. But we who are fond of the blond-braided barbarian can only deplore the absence of subsequent volumes and hope for a resurgence of interest on the parts of the Messrs. Avon.

As a writer myself, and one often denigrated as a mere imitator of Burroughs and Howard, I can certainly sympathize with the sentiments Jakes expresses above, and I wholeheartedly agree with his feelings.

In this well-phrased public credo, I think, John Jakes has put his finger directly on the central ganglion of the whole question of tradition vs. imitation. He also brings up a point my readers may not, perhaps, be aware of: that is, we Sword & Sorcery chaps are generally looked down on as mere imitators of Howard, the implication being that we are wasting our time writing trivial and frivolous derring-do when we should be peeling back layers of character-revelation and grappling with front-page problems like air pollution—which makes the ideal writer sound like an improbable combination of Ralph Nader and Dostoevsky. All kidding aside, gang, I'm afraid we really are generally put down and sneered at by members of the literary establishment—even, Crom help us, by members of the *science fiction* literary establishment. For instance, in that same Twentieth-Anniversary issue of *Fantastic* wherein the Carter and de Camp "Witch of the Mists" appeared, Alexei and Cory Panshin, a Hugo-award-winning newcomer to the literary ranks and his attractive wife, took a meat-axe to the entire genre in their review column, remarking:

> After 1936, when Howard died, Smith retired, and Moore turned to modern sf, sword and sorcery became a frozen form, a ritual dance . . . early Moore and Smith continue to have influence on sf, but the sword and sorcery complex itself is a living fossil with no apparent ability to evolve.

That's the Establishment talking, I suppose, and a reflection of the general party-line taken by those New Wavers who bother to notice us lowly Sword & Sorcery types at all. These guys just don't understand, do they, gang? "Living fossil"? Well, perhaps. But what of it? The stuff is fun to read, and fun to write, and the fossilization of the genre is, I suspect, largely in the eye of the beholder.

To such as the Panshins, modern-day Howardian heroica may seem a sterile school going through the mechanical motions of a ritual dance, but those of us who are fond of it, especially those of us who write the stuff, regard our work as a gnomon—in the sense in which John Barth employs the term towards his own fiction,[8] *i.e.*, something added on to a pre-existing something which enlarges it without distorting or altering its essential proportions, shape, or contour. We think of modern-day Sword & Sorcery as a coherent growth from the sort of thing founded by Howard, Smith, Moore, Ball, and Kuttner in their salad days. That it can be a development beyond the original school is obvious in the work of the superior practitioners of the craft: Jack Vance is more subtle, adroit, and aplombful than even Smith, and Moorcock's doomed villain-hero, Elric, a more dramatically different type of character than even Miss Moore's "gal Conan." (I like to think that my mingling of science fiction and swashbuckling fantasy in the Thongor stories is innovative to a degree: flying airboats and lightning weapons in primal Lemuria are, at least, things neither Howard nor Kuttner thought of.)

The assertion made by the Panshins is, I think, built on a false premise, which is rendered even more shaky by their obvious inability to enjoy the genre. *Must* a school of writing evolve? I wonder why. Evolution implies change into something else. But mere change for the sake of change, experiment for the sake of experiment—the apparent aesthetic of the New Wave school of science fiction writing, to which I suppose Alexei Panshin belongs[9]—seems to a rather backwards-looking conservative like myself a pointless exercise in futility. Must the sonnet sequence evolve into some form other than that of the sonnet sequence, or opera into something that is not opera? Must Sword & Sorcery turn itself into something radically different? Why on Xiccarph should it?

Panshin's assumption is an error, perhaps, because he doesn't understand exactly what Sword & Sorcery is and what it is not. For one thing, it is not and never has been a broad general field of narrative with dozens of stylistic or thematic traditions interweaving to form a complex fabric. That description fits today's science fiction fairly well, but is wide of the mark if applied to Sword & Sorcery. In science fiction, that is, a number of traditions or schools of writing vie for popularity. There is, for instance, the pure gadget story, in which the meat of the tale concerns the impact of a new invention or scientific development on society, as in early Heinlein; the space opera, essentially the swash-buckler retold against a milieu as broad as the galaxy, as in vintage Doc Smith; the intellectual-puzzle yarn, as in certain works by van Vogt; the social-extrapolation story, as in any number of Pohl and Kornbluth collaborations, in which senior citizens or ad agencies or whatever take over in the near future; the (very convoluted) school of variations on the paradoxes inherent in time travel; the superman story, as in various tales by Weinbaum, Stapledon, van Vogt, *et al;* and so on.

But science fiction is several times older, and dozens of times bigger, than Sword & Sorcery, and many, many times more popular. Is Sword & Sorcery a broad general field of narrative, cluttered with dozens of competing styles and schools and traditions? Quite the contrary: Sword & Sorcery is the smallest, tightest literary genre I can think of, and one that is *completely derivative.* We who write it all work within the narrow tradition whose parameters were set down by Howard in the 1930s. And as John Jakes' credo, quoted above, affirms, we write the stuff because we love reading it. And there just ain't enough of it around, the real old-fashioned stuff, and never has been—not enough to satisfy us, at any rate.

There is absolutely no need for Sword & Sorcery to develop new maturities of style and theme and turn itself into sober, responsible "adult fantasy." I say this, of course, because beyond the edges of the Sword & Sorcery field lie the broader acres of adult fantasy itself. The mature stuff is already there; Sword & Sorcery remains a small sub-school within the larger context of the fantasy literature we have been discussing in these pages.

The difference between following a well-loved tradition through fondness and nostalgia for the genre itself and striking boldly out towards new narrative horizons is radical and dramatic. The confusion exists because those who follow a clear-cut tradition, such as Sword & Sorcery, can all too easily be sneered at by Hugo-collecting members of the Establishment as rank imitators of an admittedly great Original. (Of course, Howard himself, who started the whole thing, was engaged in wholehearted and zestful imitation of Talbot Mundy, Harold Lamb, Edgar Rice Burroughs, Rafael Sabatini, and Robert W. Chambers; but Establishment critics find it convenient to ignore the fact as a trivial datum.) The whole question of imitation is a subtle and complex one, and there is no particular point in going into it here. But let's hear what so excellent a writer as C. S. Lewis—much venerated by Establishment critics for his intellectual gifts—has to say on this question:

> "Creation" as applied to human authorship seems to me to be an entirely misleading term. We rearrange elements . . . There is not a vestige of real creativity *de novo* in us. Try to imagine a new primary colour, a third sex, a fourth dimension, or even a monster which does not consist of bits of existing animals stuck together. Nothing happens.[10]

Most of us who write Sword & Sorcery do so out of a nostalgic affection for the genre and have no particular desire to change it, my own feeling being that "change" is not demonstrably synonymous with "improve." It's the sort of thing we loved in our teens (at least I did), and we contribute to the modern-day continuation of the genre out of fondness for what pleased us then. W. H. Auden had something to say about this in one of his essays in *The Dyer's Hand:*

> The work of a young writer—*Werther* is the classic example—is sometimes a therapeutic act. He finds himself obsessed by certain ways of feeling and thinking which his instinct tells him he must be rid of before he can discover his authentic interests and sympathies, and the only way by which he can be rid of them forever is by surrendering to them.

This is certainly true, and can be seen, for example, in the case of Kuttner, whose early work—the "Elak of Atlantis" stories—are lively imitations of the Howardian genre. Kuttner—all too soon, perhaps—went on to other styles. In my own case, while the saga of Thongor continues to be added to, more recent novels and shorter works derive little, if anything, from Howard. I could mention here such novels as *Lost World of Time* (Signet, 1969), *Outworlder* (Lancer, 1971), *The Quest of Kadji* (Belmont, 1971), and such works in progress as *Amalric* and *The Island in the Sky*. These are quite non-Howardian in style and form, and represent new directions in my own work.

IN 1968, deciding that it was about time the handful of active Sword & Sorcery writers organized a mini-guild all their own, L. Sprague de Camp, John Jakes, and myself got together and announced the formation of The Swordsmen and Sorcerers' Guild of America, Ltd., called "S.A.G.A." for short. That original three-man nucleus was swiftly widened to include Fritz Leiber, Andre Norton, Jack Vance, Michael Moorcock, and Poul Anderson.

Unlike most other writers' organizations, S.A.G.A. is strictly forbidden by its constitution, the Sacred Articulorum, to engage in any activity whatsoever of an official nature, including (paradoxically) the drawing-up of constitutions. No meetings, bulletins, conventions, assemblies, publications, banquets, awards, blacklists, campaigns, crusades, ballots, elections, officers, and like that. The SAGAmen pay no dues, fees, expenses, charges, tithes, or weregild. About the only thing the Sacred Articulorum permit the eight members to do is get together in the bar at science fiction conventions and hoist a couple in honor of Absent Friends. We also bestow titles and honorifics on each other at every conceivable occasion, usually for no particular reason at all. De Camp, for instance, is Supreme Sadist of the Reptile Men of Yag, Moorcock is Veiled Thaumaturge of the Mauve Barbarians of Ningg, Jakes is Hereditary Guardian of the Sacred Ruby-Studded Elephant Goad to the Court of Ubbo the Unmerciful, and the present writer enjoys the prerogatives of Exalted Grand Booleywag, to say nothing of the honor of Purple Druid of the Slithering Horde of the Slime Pits of Zugthakya. The recent publication of the two-volume anthology of all-new and original Sword & Sorcery yarns by the SAGAmen, *Flashing Swords!* from Dell Books, is highly *un*official, by the way.

Michael Moorcock was eminently qualified for membership in our exalted guild by reason of his excellent "Elric of Melniboné" tales. Moorcock is a young British writer, born in 1940, whose main hobby outside of writing science fiction and fantasy (and editing the famous British magazine, *New Worlds*) is mountaineering. His earliest Elric stories began appearing in 1961 and thus far there have been four volumes of Elric's adventures, of which the most recent are two novels, *The Dreaming City* and *The Sleeping Sorceress,* both published in 1972 by Lancer Books. The character of Elric is developed with great originality in these stories: Elric is a moody, sardonic princeling, an albino with pink eyes and white skin, who lives in a state of vampiric symbiosis with his enchanted sword, Stormbringer. The popular British science fiction writer, J. G. Ballard, sums up the Elric saga thusly:

> Strange and tormented landscapes, peopled by characters of archetypal dimensions, are the setting for a series of titanic duels between the forces of Chaos and Order. Nightmare armies clash on the shores of spectral seas. Phantom horsemen ride on skeleton steeds across a world as fantastic as those of Bosch and Breughel. Over all these presides the central figure of Elric, the haunted warrior-king whose ambivalent relationship with the magical sword Stormbringer is the author's most original creation. The vast, tragic and sometimes terrifying symbols by which Mr. Moorcock continually illuminates the metaphysical quest of his hero are a measure of the author's remarkable talents.[11]

Moorcock, a very prolific novelist, has also added two other series to the slender canon of Sword & Sorcery:

his "Dorian Hawkmoon" books, and the more recent three-volume history of Prince Corum, which he launched with the publication of *The Knight of the Swords* (Berkley Medallion Books, 1971). At times a hasty, even a sloppy writer, Moorcock's flow of imaginative invention seldom flags, and he is capable of strikingly vivid and colorful images.

Both Jack Vance and Poul Anderson are better known for their skillful and highly professional contributions to modern science fiction; both qualify for membership in S.A.G.A. on the basis of two books in the heroic fantasy genre. Vance is a native Californian, born in San Francisco, raised on a ranch in the center of the state, and for many years now a resident of Oakland. He studied physics, mining engineering, and journalism, but turned about 1940 to the writing of fiction. It was Sam Merwin, I believe, who was the first editor to recognize his talents. Merwin, then editor of a now-defunct science fiction magazine called *Thrilling Wonder Stories,* has recorded that he read and rejected "fascinating but, alas, unpublishable pseudo-Cabellian fantasies" by Vance, starting about 1941. Later he had the honor of purchasing Vance's first commercial sale, a story called "The World Thinker," which he printed in the Summer 1945 issue. Vance quickly became one of the foremost modern sf writers, with such brilliant novels and novellas as *The Languages of Pao, Big Planet, The Dragon Masters,* and *The Last Castle* to his credit.

Those early "pseudo-Cabell" fantasies did not go to waste, however. In 1950 a small and short-lived paperback firm called Hillman Books earned our undying gratitude by publishing them in book form. This slim little book of early Vance, *The Dying Earth,* became almost overnight a minor classic in the genre, and it remains in print from Lancer Books to this day.

Vance is a simply amazing writer. He writes with a great sense of style, with polish, sparkle, and wit. The surface of his polychrome prose glitters with exotic, fascinating names, and with an incredible wealth of ideas and concepts, which he tosses off in careless profusion. He is a "writers' writer," with all the respect and admiration of his colleagues and fellow-craftsmen that the term implies. A sequel called *The Eyes of the Overworld* was published many years later by Ace, and it demonstrated that he could still pull off the miracle of style so ably displayed in the early book.

Vance is nearly alone among modern-day fantasy writers in his intense preoccupation with matters of pure style. "Style," in the present context, does not refer to the characteristic trademarks which most reasonably competent professionals leave on each page, but to an old-fashioned craftsmanship in the use of language. This sort of thing requires a fine ear for tone and coloring in prose, and for the intrinsic cadence of the English sentence. The art of pure langauge regarded as an end in itself is generally considered to have died out with the collapse of the 1920s. In those days, connoisseurs lingered over a well-burnished page of Cabell or Arthur Machen or Edgar Saltus with sensitive appreciation, savoring the bouquet of a book or essay as they might the fragrance of a rare vintage wine. This brief era of *belles lettres* was eclipsed by the stolid rise to prominence of Hemingway and Chandler and gentlemen of similar kidney, exponents of a new fashion for clipped, terse, unadorned monotone that was to replace this leisurely elegance of style. But the belletrists enjoyed their transient heyday, considering style a valid concern for prose artists, equal in importance to plot or content, and perhaps transcending these.

Vance remains one of the last belletrists in captivity, and his popularity may be explained by his wise refusal to subordinate content to surface: in his work neither prose nor plot are dominant—they coexist and are mutually interdependent. I suspect that he learned quite a bit from Cabell, as Merwin sensed: both writers view their characters with wry detachment, at one remove, you might say; both strive for the *mot juste,* writing with suave elegance. Vance has, in fact, considerably more in common with Cabell than with Howard. The grim, humorless urgency typical of Howard is lacking in Vance's sorcerous fables, in which sanguinary coloring is replaced by cool pastel tints. In his dispassionate handling of character, his irony and sardonic understatement, his lapidary surface and delicate precision of phrase, he hearkens back ultimately to a pre-pulp source among the masters of elegant prose. He is a delicious writer, one to be savored, and he belongs to an almost extinct breed. H. L. Mencken affectionately, but accurately, once called Cabell a "lingering survival of the *ancien régime:* a scarlet dragon-fly imbedded in opaque amber." The term is a bit baroque, but it could be applied to Jack Vance.

Like Vance, Poul Anderson is better known for his science fiction, although his heart clearly belongs to his first love, heroic fantasy. In fact, Anderson's first published book was a grim, beautiful Sword & Sorcery novel called *The Broken Sword,* whose roots are more firmly traceable to the traditions of the Scandinavian sagas, strictly speaking, than to the Howardian brand of swashbuckling. Anderson comes by his fondness for the Norse myths and Icelandic sagas quite naturally, being of Danish extraction. He was born in Pennsylvania in 1926 and now lives with his wife and teenaged daughter in Orinda, California. Anderson began selling to John Campbell while still an undergraduate at the University of Minnesota, and he has been writing science fiction ever since, his only other ventures into the realm of swordplay and ensorcellment being a "neo-Carolingian" novel called *Three Hearts and Three Lions* and the not-yet-published *Hrolf Kraki's Saga.* His fondness for the Howardian heroica is well known, however, for he is a frequent contributor to the Sword & Sorcery fanzine *Amra,* and is a member of the Hyborian Legion, as the informal and enormous Conan fan-club is known.[12]

S.A.G.A. has not of late increased its rolls to include any new members, but if it should do so they will doubtless be drawn from among the more recent luminaries of the science fiction firmament who have become converts to the heroic fantasy genre.

Such as Roger Zelazny, for example. Zelazny was born in Cleveland, Ohio, studied at Western Reserve University, and took his Master's degree from my own old alma mater, Columbia. He and his charming wife, Judy, now make their home in Baltimore, where he spends his time fencing, collecting geological specimens, and writing science fiction. This last also involves collecting, for his science fiction (such as *Lord of Light*) has garnered an amazing covey of Hugo and Nebula awards; indeed, Zelazny is considered one of the two or three most brilliant newcomers to the field.

His work, beginning with that modern masterpiece, *Lord of Light,* has been demonstrably verging more and more on the borders of fantasy; with his latest novel, *Jack of Shadows,* he abandoned all pretense and boldly moved right into our preserve. He is no raw recruit to the ranks, however, for some of his earliest stories, back in the 1960s in *Fantastic,* were out-and-out Sword & Sorcery, concerning one Colonel Dilvish, an immortal adventurer in dim, fantasmal realms Zelazny alone has charted. Roger has told me that this early Dilvish cycle was originally intended to make up a book called *Nine Black Doves,* and may yet.

Avram Davidson is another science fiction celebrity whose enthusiasm for fantasy is a poorly-concealed secret. Davidson, who used to edit *The Magazine of Fantasy and Science Fiction,* and who is the only writer known to me who holds both a science fiction Hugo Award and the Edgar Award given by the Mystery Writers of America, has recently begun writing genuine fantasy, and very excellent and subtle work it is. His first novel in the genre was a magnificently original and entertaining book called *The Phoenix and the Mirror* (Doubleday, 1969); it was followed by *The Island Under the Earth* (1969) from Ace Books, and *Peregrine: Primus* (Walker, 1971). By the time the present book reaches your hands, another novel, *Ursus of Ultima Thule,* should also be in print.

Chunks and morsels of Davidson's *magnum opus* have been appearing in Ted White's *Fantastic* for the last couple of years, the earliest being "Arntem of Ultima Thule" in the issue for August 1971, followed by a two-part serial entitled "The Forges of Nainland Are Cold" in the issue dated August 1972. The entirety of *Ursus of Ultima Thule* should be in print from Avon Books shortly before *Imaginary Worlds* is published; since I have not been able to read the full text of the book, it is of course difficult for me to discuss it in any but the most general terms. At any rate, Davidson's use of Ultima Thule as a setting is a splendid notion. The Greeks and the Romans mentioned the imaginary island of "Thule" (pronounced *too*ly) frequently; it was an Arctic paradise, like Hyperborea but still farther north, at the very limits of the world, the farthest north of the known countries inhabited by men—hence the "ultima" they tacked onto its name. In Davidson's hand the realm becomes a sort of Arctic Atlantis, an early Stone Age civilization somewhere among the remotest of the northern islands—"Spitzbergen . . . Nova Zemlya . . . Greenland," hints Davidson, teasingly. It's a charmingly original setting, and it is to Avram's credit that he is the first fantasy writer to employ it.

Avram Davidson is a native New Yorker who recently expatriated himself to California, to join the fantasy colony there. Surprising how that state seems to attract an appalling number of modern fantasy writers; one good earthquake could put fantasy back thirty years. Anyway, when I knew him in Manhattan a dozen years back, he was a rotund, smallish gentleman with a neat, small Vandyke, a gift for spellbinding conversation, and a preference for cats, which I (a dog man to the last drop of heart's-blood) found deplorable. He is a writers' writer, like Vance; I, at least, delight in his sleek, witty, highly individualistic prose as I delight in the work of few of my colleagues. His prime characteristic as a fantasy craftsman—as my above remarks on *Ursus* might suggest—is the brilliant originality he displays in his choice of background or milieux. I find his use of milieux singularly appealing (although it cannot be denied that the action and dialogue going on in the foreground of his novels are fully as fascinating). For *The Phoenix and the Mirror,* for example, he chose a unique and promising milieu unaccountably passed over by all other fantasy writers: that peculiar half-world which medieval romance and legend made out of the misremembered world of the late Roman Empire—in which the majestic epic poet, Virgil, became puzzlingly transmogrified into a sorcerer of towering authority called Vergil Magus. For *The Island Under the Earth,* he pieced together a delicious and entrancing subterranean realm from hints found in such diverse sources as Anaximander, the early Milesian philosopher, and the more obscure byways of Talmudic lore. For *Peregrine: Primus,* a picaresque romance I found irresistible, he turned to the downright screwball world of the *Gesta Romanorum.*[13] Davidson is one of the most unpredictable of all modern fantasy writers, but his one infallible constant is his superb ability to entertain his readers with wit and gusto and spectacular story-telling.

A third potential candidate for S.A.G.A. is the distinguished novelist John Brunner, an Englishman whose most conspicuous recent success was the Hugo-Award-winning *Stand on Zanzibar.* Brunner has published nearly half a hundred science fiction novels and short-story collections, and only those who noticed the Vanceian fantasy-elements in his early novel, *The Hundredth Millennium* (Ace Books, 1959; substantially revised and reissued by the same publisher as *Catch a Falling Star* in 1968), could have foretold what might happen when he turned his attention fully in the direction of straight fantasy.

What happened when he did so can be experienced in a spectacular recent novel called *The Traveler in Black* (Ace Books, 1971), which expertly mingles the

sparkle and invention of early Vance with much of
the sophistication and suave story-telling of vintage
Cabell. For the book's hero, Brunner creates an enig-
matic demiurge who wanders about through that portion of the universe which he (perhaps) created (but
which at least has been allotted to his responsibility),
and whose integrity in the face of the dissolving pull
of Chaos only his untiring vigilance can preserve. The
novel is episodic and ultimately left unresolved, with
many loose plot-strands a-dangle, and the reader is
left with unanswered questions to nag and worry over;
but the brilliant cataract of imaginative invention is
dazzling and the novel succeeds in spite of its inherent
flaws. It's a remarkable job.

This theme of Order (or Law, or Creation) against
Chaos, incidentally, is a favorite one with modern
authors of Sword & Sorcery. Poul Anderson used it in
Three Hearts and Three Lions, Michael Moorcock
uses it in his Elric stories, Brunner employs it in *The
Traveler in Black,* and I have used it myself in my
Lemurian books, where it forms the overplot which
binds together the first four novels, culminating with
the destruction of the Black City of Zaar in the final
pages of *Thongor in the City of Magicians.* Although
Howard did not employ it, the theme has become by
now part of the tradition of the whole Sword & Sorcery
school.

This is the sort of thing I am talking about when I
say that no matter how diverse the various S.A.G.A.
members may be in terms of individual style or milieu,
we are still to be considered all one school of writing
and one close-knit tradition, forming a gaudy but fairly
important strand in the fabric of fantasy today. It is a
tradition that aspires to do little more than entertain
and stretch the imagination a little, that remains sub-
limely immune to tackling the problems on the front
pages of your daily newspaper, unlike modern science
fiction, which rather self-righteously feels that it is
somehow frivoling away its readers' time if it is not
grappling solemnly with overpopulation, environmental

pollution, race relations, and other bugaboos of the hour. These days, science fiction takes itself awfully seriously and strives to pretend it is a Serious Literary Genre, hoping nobody will remember that its roots lie in a bunch of gaudy, horrendously vulgar thirty-year-old pulps.

We Sword & Sorcery chaps, however, have few such pretensions. Nor do we worry much that we still re-use for the umpty-'leventh time plot devices and story-stratagems which Burroughs and Howard and Merritt first stole from Haggard and Scott and Stevenson when we were lapping up porridge and listening to Little Orphan Annie on the cabinet Philco. A good idea is still a good idea thirty years later. And in this context I am reminded of a morsel of advice to young writers that Archibald MacLeish proffered in his book *A Continuing Journey* (Boston, Houghton Mifflin, 1968):

> A real writer learns from earlier writers the way a boy learns from an apple orchard—by stealing what he has a taste for, and can carry off.

The Young Magicians:

Some Modern Masters of Fantasy

The army of weird and beautiful works could
well do with recruits.

—C. S. Lewis[1]

WHERE will the fantasy writers of the first rank come
from in the years and decades ahead? That's a foolish
question to ask, I suppose, but at least it is an easy
one to answer: they will come from among the fantasy
readers of today.

Some of them may well be onstage already, however
many may still be waiting in the wings. Of the writers
of modern Sword & Sorcery discussed in the last
chapter, one at least has it in him to produce a genuine
masterpiece. I hope I do no disservice to the other
writers discussed in that chapter if I single out Avram
Davidson as the possessor of a talent whose fullest
potentials have not yet been released.

But beyond—or above?—the ranks of the Swordsmen and Sorcerers' Guild of America, Ltd., is a handful
of writers who have worked, or are working, in regions
of fantasy literature somewhat broader than the pulp
adventure genre. Let us look briefly at some of these
men and women and their work before passing on to
discuss the writing of fantasy itself.

As for my own personal taste, I have read three
absolutely first-class fantasy novels published since *The
Lord of the Rings* first appeared in print in this country
during the mid-1950s. And *only* three—for however
many decent, good, or even excellent new novels have

been printed in the last twenty years or so, there are three that seem to me to tower above all the rest.

The first of these is *The Last Unicorn* by Peter S. Beagle. I cannot in the least explain my reaction to this book, which seems like an ingenious and entertaining but fairly ordinary fantasy novel when you examine its components in the light of cool reason. When these components are assembled between a single set of covers, however, cool reason goes out the window and I am helplessly lost in a story that sweeps me along with breathless urgency and stunning beauty. Doubtless other readers have found a comparable enchantment in *The Last Unicorn,* and perhaps they too find it impossible to analyze and pin down the unique magic of that book. For me, it is in a class all by itself—one of the inexplicable curiosities of modern fantasy, as is *The Circus of Dr. Lao* and *The Dying Earth* and *The Tale of the Land of Green Ginger.* It is, in a word, a book totally unlike any other I can call to mind.

I first encountered Beagle's name on an excellent short review of the Tolkien trilogy in (I believe) *Esquire.* When a writer as appreciative of Tolkien's skills as he came to turn his own hand to fantasy writing, we might logically have expected a "Tolkienian" fantasy, of sorts—just as *The Gammage Cup* or *The Weirdstone of Brisingamen* or *Taran Wanderer* are "Tolkienian" fantasies, of sorts. Not so, however, with *The Last Unicorn:* from first to last, Peter S. Beagle has written a book completely his own; in fact, from the evidence of that narrative, one cannot even discern whether Mr. Beagle had ever so much as dipped into the pages of *The Lord of the Rings,* much less set forth to compose his own novel with the trilogy as model and inspiration.

Beagle was born thirty-four years ago in New York City; he graduated from the University of Pittsburgh at twenty, and published his first novel, *A Fine and Private Place,* the following year. That book, which garnered admiring reviews, was followed in 1965 by a second called *I See By My Outfit,* which described a cross-country trip via motor-scooter. His third book was quite another thing.

The Last Unicorn was published by The Viking Press in 1968. The story is, as you might suppose, about a unicorn, and it centers around her pathetic and wistful search for her lost fellows. This search, or quest, is led (or stage-managed) by one Schmendrick, a Magician by trade. Even in its brevity this sketchy outline suggests that the novel is a peculiar, even unique, blend of exquisite lyric beauty and low comedy—rather like Thurber's *The Thirteen Clocks* or *The White Deer* or *Many Moons,* you might say. Well, yes and no; it is and it isn't. *The Thirteen Clocks* is a lovely book but essentially a sort of joke in that the prose scans remarkably close to iambic pentameter and even, occasionally, breaks into rhyme. It's as if someone bet Thurber he couldn't write a story in prose than scans.[2]

The Last Unicorn is a lot more than an offbeat media-mix of poetic fantasy and slapstick comedy, though. It has beauty and terror and pathos and tenderness and paradox and philosophy, and, thank Gorm, it never really takes itself seriously or pauses to admire what it is doing. The seductive danger for a writer of this sort of thing is to admire one's own cuteness; Beagle never does, however, and the story as a whole is told in a straightforward manner filled with vivid poetic imagery and playful high-jinks. This blend of down-to-earth and Beyond-the-Fields-we-Know can be suggested with a single quotation from the opening page. Describing the spiral-fluted horn of his unicorn, Beagle remarks briefly:

> The long horn above her eyes shone and shivered with its own seashell light even in the deepest midnight. She had killed dragons with it, and healed a king whose poisoned wound would not close, *and knocked down ripe chestnuts for bear cubs.*

The italics are my own. The book is Beagle's own. Entirely his own, as far as I can see, owing nothing to any particular author or school or tradition. I have not seen another book from him in the five years since *The Last Unicorn* appeared; I sincerely hope that it is not the last novel in the genre we shall see from his hand.

THE second of the three first-rate fantasies I have seen since *The Lord of the Rings* is a remarkable first novel by an Englishwoman named Joy Chant. The book is called *Red Moon and Black Mountain*—a perfectly splendid title, by the way—and it was published in this country by Doubleday in 1970, through arrangement with Ballantine, who got an advance look at the manuscript from George Allen & Unwin, the British publishers who discovered Tolkien.

Miss Chant lives in Essex in a town called Leigh-on-Sea. The book began growing in her youth, when she and a girl friend named Ann Walland vied with each other in inventing the magic world of Khendiol, much in the same way that C. S. Lewis and his brother played with Animal-land and "India" during their boyhood, or the Brontë sisters played with Gondal and Verdopolis during their own childhood. *Red Moon and Black Mountain* is about the end of the House of Kendreth—that was Miss Chant's original title, by the way—and the story is a complex one, written on many levels, the most obvious one being a sort of children's book essentially like the Narnia books of Lewis, which, I strongly suspect, played an important role in shaping the original conception. It starts off like a children's book, at least, with three children named Oliver, Nicholas, and Penelope who bicycle down an English lane straight into the perilous and magical world of Khendiol, where they become caught up in the epic struggle of the Lords of the Star Magic against the renegade magician, Fendarl, the exiled master of Black Mountain.

The two younger children are taken under the wing of a party of Tolkienian elves, led by the Princess In'serinna, and stand by during the so-called "Battle of the Eagles" in Chapter Three, a gripping, superbly realized scene that gives the book not only its cover scene but its most powerful single episode. The older boy, meanwhile, who entered the world of Khendiol at a different point, is sort of adopted by a nomadic people called the Hurnei, in whose ranks he rises to manhood and grim responsibility. It is one of the major pleasures the novel affords to watch him grow and develop into a man; these scenes among the Hurnei are splendidly realized, with a wealth of apparently authentic anthropological detail. Curiously, time moves at a different rate for the young nomad warrior than it does for the littler children; despite this, the novel is straight story-telling, with strong narrative sweep and drive, devoid of gimmickry. The only disappointment, a minor one, is that the antagonist, Fendarl, is little more than the familiar (by now) Tolkienian Sauron-stereotype—a forgivable flaw in what is otherwise a work of masterly imaginative force.

Miss Chant is one of a number of women writers who have come to the fore in modern fantasy in recent years. Just before we signed *Red Moon and Black Mountain,* I read another first novel by a woman writer, which impressed me greatly. The writer's name was Katherine Kurtz and the book, *Deryni Rising.* Miss Kurtz is a native Floridian who graduated from the University of Miami with a major in chemistry, a minor in biology, and honors in the humanities. A vivacious blonde—in her twenties, I should think—she now lives in California and works in law enforcement. *Deryni Rising* and its sequel, *Deryni Checkmate,* are laid in a world very near in space/time to our own—right next door, so to speak, both worlds sharing a common history up to some point in the Middle Ages. Her kingdoms have a flavor more of the Welsh than anything else, although this element is not overly stressed. It is a very believable world, and the story she develops is most interesting. The Deryni, a secret race of people with "wild talents," once ruled these realms but lost their hold and were crushed through savage persecutions, although they linger on, dwelling among their superstitious fellows, "passing for human," you might say.

The story is filled with powerful and richly-developed characters, and Miss Kurtz has an impressive gift for depicting dramatic person-to-person confrontations. The overplot that binds these two novels together, and will connect the further volumes she plans to add to the series, revolves about the religious hierarchy of Gwynedd (which is closely similar to the Roman Church of the Middle Ages) and a mysterious being, long-dead but still active, canonized as St. Camber and probably himself a Deryni.

Another woman writer of enormous promise, which is already being fulfilled by a brilliantly imaginative trilogy, is Ursula K. LeGuin. Like Leiber, Vance, and Anderson, Miss LeGuin has a dual talent, able to turn off first-rate science fiction, such as her Hugo-Award-winning *The Left Hand of Darkness,* and superb fantasy, such as *A Wizard of Earthsea,* with equal facility. *Wizard,* published in 1968 by Parnassus Press, was the first book of a (thus far) trilogy that gets stronger and deeper and better as it goes along. The books are set in quite original worldscapes—Earthsea is one immense ocean filled with many islands but apparently devoid of continents. *A Wizard of Earthsea* describes the coming-of-age of a youth named Ged and his student years at the famous college for magicians on the isle of Roke. Early in the tale his richly promising career goes darkly awry when Ged, or Sparrowhawk, as he is called, is tempted by arrogant pride to summon a dangerous demonic force whose control is beyond him. From that point on, it seemed on first reading, a potentially fascinating story went wrong; what I wanted to do was eavesdrop, as it were, on a sorcerer-in-training, and it annoyed me that the novel did not complete the enormously entertaining course indicated in its opening chapters.

In light of the sequels, however, I now realize that it was not a case of the author turning aside to explore a sidepath, and that Miss LeGuin had matters firmly in hand from the start. The second novel of the set, *The Tombs of Atuan* (Atheneum, 1971), turns from Roke to an island in the Kargads, on the periphery of the invented geography of Earthsea, an island merely mentioned in *Wizard*. It develops the stark, grim story of Tenar, or Arha, a girl under training to become eventual high priestess of the ancient and nameless Powers of the Earth. Sold by her parents to the cult as a child, the girl grows up to a sterile, gloomy life of severity and denial, bound in service to forces she dimly comes to understand as enemies of life and wholesomeness. Ged enters the story as a young man seeking in the catacombs of Atuan for a long-lost talisman of tremendous power.

The third tale, in many ways the most dramatic and imaginative yet, is called *The Farthest Shore* (Atheneum, 1972). In it we again encounter Ged, now grown to maturity, even to old age, and supreme Archmage of his old school on Roke. In this novel, which reaches extraordinary heights of narrative power, Miss LeGuin does something quite remarkable, for Ged must descend into hell itself, the netherworld of the dead, in order to do combat with a dark magician who has opened a certain door and is slowly drying up the wells of magic in Earthsea. The entire sequence of events as Ged and his young squire traverse the underworld to its uttermost depths is a harrowing masterpiece of emotional intensity, held under tight control and told in terms of quiet understatement. The terror of the realm of death is conveyed with stark, numbing power. It's quite a passage! And it makes the reader look forward eagerly to the books that will follow, for I suspect that Miss LeGuin is not yet done with Earthsea.

THE third and last of my choices of the best fantasy novels to appear since *The Lord of the Rings* is a book that has received virtually no recognition as yet, overlooked alike by reviewers and fantasy buffs. The novel is called *The Face in the Frost,* by a writer of amazing brilliance and charm named John Bellairs. Although it was packaged as a children's book, don't let that stop you from hunting it up—so were all three of the Ursula K. LeGuin books discussed above.

The Face in the Frost opens in a mood of wacky hilarity. There is this cranky old magician named Prospero, see—"and not the one you are thinking of, either"—who lives in a wacky country called "the South Kingdom," which is split up into scores of vest-pocket kingdomettes with grandiose names like "The Grand Union of the Five Counties," "The Duchy of Irontree-Dragonrock," and so forth (not unlike the comic-opera hodge-podge of miniature duchies and princedoms in Lloyd Alexander's *Marvelous Misadventures of Sebastian,* or the crazy-quilt landscape of Oz, for that matter).

Prospero lives in "a huge, ridiculous, doodad-covered, trash-filled two-story horror of a house," with gutter-spouts carved into "whistling sphinxes and screaming bearded faces" and a front porch decorated with "carved bears, monkeys, toads, and fat women in togas holding sheaves of grain," a house cluttered with Victorian bric-a-brac and thaumaturgical paraphernalia—jars of mandrake roots, alembics, a brass St. Bernard dog with a clock in his tummy, Hands of Glory, grimoires, mahogany chests covered with fat cherubs and tiger mouths "that bit you if you put your finger in the wrong place," a library of books with titles such as *Nameless Horrors and What to Do About Them,* and, "of course," the dreaded *Krankenhammer* of Stefan Schimph the Mad Cobbler of Mainz, as well as a magic mirror gone zany from boredom which shows the eighth inning of the 1943 game between the Chicago Cubs and the New York Giants, and sings madly to itself,

> "O-ver-head the moon is SCREEEEEAMING,
> Whi-i-te as turnips on the Rhine . . . ."

until poor old Prospero feels like blowing out its brains, if it *had* any brains, which, of course, being only a mirror, it hasn't. Along comes an old crony of his called Roger Bacon—"one of Prospero's best friends and a pretty good sorcerer in his own right"—with a tale about a mysterious and long-lost grimoire and a supposedly equally long-dead magician named Melichus Magister. And the plot begins to thicken on the spot . . .

The tale is rich, hilarious, inventive, filled with infectious good-humor, grisly horrors, slithering Evil, bumbling monarchs, and enough Various & Sundry Menaces of the supernatural variety to keep the now-defunct Gothic soap opera *Dark Shadows* running for another decade. Bellairs is a marvelous writer who has obviously read all the right books with enthusiasm, and his own venture into the genre is one of the most exciting debuts in a long time.

A graduate of Notre Dame and the University of Chicago, he is a teacher-turned-novelist who now lives in rural Massachusetts, where he is busily concocting further adventures of Prospero and Roger Bacon. I wrote to him after reading *The Face in the Frost*, and we have been exchanging letters off and on for some time now. An affable chap, he has let me look at his sketchy maps of the South Kingdom and some unpublished scraps, notes, and outlines for these further adventures; and, in fact, he has produced for my yet-unpublished anthology of juvenile fantasy, entitled *Magic Kingdoms*, a new short-story which tells how his diabolic duo first became friends. I confess myself hopelessly smitten with the South Kingdom, with Prospero, with his house (which sounds like the sort of place I'd like to live in myself), and very much infatuated with his jolly, mad mirror—even if it does show nothing else but the eighth inning of the 1943 Cubs-Giants game.

SIDE by side with the contemporary creators of imaginary worlds that we have been discussing are some writers of great skill who confine their work largely to a parallel genre, the novel of heroic myth. The novel of myth is, at best, a neighboring province in the

Empire of Imagination, but it corresponds in many ways with the sort of fiction we have been exploring. Two contemporary novelists in that field seem outstanding enough to demand brief mention here.

The first of these is Thomas Burnett Swann, who has taken the world of Classical mythology for his personal domain. Born in Florida in 1928, Swann is a former college professor, with an A.B. from Duke University, an M.A. from the University of Tennessee, and a Ph.D. from the University of Florida. His first novel was *Day of the Minotaur* (Ace Books, 1966), followed by *The Weirwoods* from the same publisher in 1967, and several other books at approximately yearly intervals: *Moondust, The Forest of Forever,* and so on.

In such books, Mr. Swann has detailed a most interesting and original milieu: where most writers before him were content merely to retell in novel form the famous myths and legends of Greece, Swann turned to prehistoric Crete, the ancient Etruscans, and the very earliest days of Rome when the children of Aeneas ruled a little hilltop town and shared the primeval woods with nymphs, fauns, and satyrs. Swann is unique among such writers also in that his stories are rarely told from the viewpoint of his human characters; very often the story takes place largely within the forests themselves and concerns itself with the peculiar prehuman civilization of the various mythological hybrid creatures who live there. Both his first novel, *Day of the Minotaur,* and his recent book, *The Forest of Forever,* (Ace Books, 1971) tell the story of Eunostos the last minotaur, for instance. Swann has delved deeply into the few fragments we have of Cretan myth and Etruscan lore and has painstakingly constructed a fascinating milieu peopled with remarkable semi- or non-human creatures such as the Thriae or bee-folk, the friendly Bears of Artemis, the faunlike Panisci, the tree-dwelling dryads, and so on. He writes of the various races of beast-people with insight and sympathy, and through their eyes he depicts the early Bronze Age humans as rapacious and barbaric interlopers in an ancient world of mighty forests whose weird and simple way of life has existed for untold ages, is now near its twilight.

His most remarkable feat, I think, is his success in portraying his human characters as all-but-incomprehensible aliens, and he accomplishes this, for the most part, without any overt attempt to slant the story against his humans, consistently resisting the obvious temptation to draw them in brutal caricature. The main defect, at least in those of his novels I have seen to date, is an element of cuddly cuteness that creeps into his depiction of the mythological hybrids and beast-people, as if they were something left over from a bad Walt Disney film. There is also a sort of parochial narrowness of scope in his mythological novels: the gods seldom enter into them, and there is seldom any note of cosmic grandeur or epic conflict. They are, however, unfailingly pleasant to read and consistently entertaining, demonstrating a considerable talent for imaginative invention, especially in picturing the personality and life-style of alien creatures who inhabit a prehuman civilization far closer to nature than that of man. Despite the cloying sweetness that obtrudes at times into these stories, and the lack of scope and grandeur in his plots, I have long been convinced that Swann has it in him to produce a truly first-rate work of fantasy, that he has yet to tap his full potential.

Another, very different writer who has exploited mythological settings is Evangeline Walton. Miss Walton, who lives in Arizona, belongs to the early school of mythological fiction characterized by John Cowper Powys and James Stephens. Her first venture into fantasy was a superb novel called *The Virgin and the Swine,* published in 1936 by Willett, Clark & Company of Chicago in a handsome hardcover edition. She was about thirty years ahead of her time, however, and despite some glowing reviews from knowledgeable critics, the book was a commercial failure.

Like Thomas Burnett Swann, Miss Walton selected a mythological milieu largely left untouched by other

writers. She turned to the mythological literature of
ancient Wales, and her first novel retold the Fourth
Branch of the *Mabinogion,* the great collection of
Welsh mythic tales. Her original intention was to retell
all Four Branches of the *Mabinogion,* but the failure of
her first book caused her to turn aside to other fields,
such as the historical novel and the novel of Gothic horror. The trouble with *The Virgin and the Swine* is that
the title is singularly ill-chosen: the title of a novel ideally
should reflect its essential nature, but to me *The Virgin
and the Swine* suggests a steamy Erskine Caldwell
sizzler about illicit love on a backwoods Georgia pig-
farm, not a powerful and brilliant novel of the godlike
heroes of Welsh mythology. Accordingly, when the book
was reprinted in paperback after thirty-four years of
oblivion, it was retitled *The Island of the Mighty.*

The revival of that book inspired Miss Walton to
turn again to the yellowing manuscripts of its sequels,
which she had begun and then abandoned decades
earlier. She has thus far published two brilliant sequels,
The Children of Llyr (1971) and *The Song of Rhiannon* (1972), drawn from the Second and Third of the
Four Branches of the *Mabinogion,* as the divisions of
that book are known. The First Branch is now being
retold, and the book she is making from it may be
in print by now.

Miss Walton is clearly one of the three or four
finest artists working in fantasy today. Considered purely as a writer, she is without peer, a novelist of incredible perfection and power; her controlled and
disciplined narrative line is pure, serene, and sinewy,
with not so much as a single dispensable page or
superfluous paragraph. Her control is breathtaking;
among her fellow living fantasy-artists, only Ursula K.
LeGuin is comparable, although the differences between
the two writers in theme and form are perhaps more
striking than their accidental similarity of style.

For example, let's look briefly again at *The Island
of the Mighty,* in which she retells the old tale of
Gwydion. As told in the Fourth Branch of the *Mabino-*

gion, the tale is crude and rough-hewn; it is unfinished, in the sense of lacking literary polish. Welsh mythology was abandoned early in its history, owing, I suppose, to the incursions of Christianity. Unlike the great mythologies of Greece and Rome, it did not remain viable long enough to reach the hands of those sophisticated poets and story-tellers from whom a body of national myth usually receives its final form. But in Miss Walton's hands the crude, loosely-spun narrative achieves heroic stature as it attains beautifully controlled form. The sheer momentum of the novel, the inevitability of its sequence of cause and effect, reminds me of the most polished examples of Greek tragedy. The interactions of the characters are linked as smoothly and cleverly as in a good modern psychological detective story, and the flaws of character in Miss Walton's people make each twist and turn of the ancient plot logical and inescapable.

If anything, *The Children of Llyr* represents an even higher degree of artistry and control. The prose is still lean and sinewy, but here the story—the dark tale of the wedding of Branwen to Matholuch, King of Ireland, his mistreatment of her, and the godlike wrath of her magnificent brother, Bran—is grim and stark, an utter tragedy as merciless as any I have ever read in a novel. If the second book in the sequence lacks something of the magical freshness and wonder of the first, it redeems itself in the presentation of a cast of superbly realized characters. The most remarkable of these is Evnissyen, whom I find unforgettable. Evnissyen represents total evil, completely without any redeeming feature; this sort of character is perhaps the most difficult of all for a writer to make real and credible, for evil is negative and total evil almost unbelievable, since all human beings are a mixture of good and evil, strength and weakness, courage and cowardice. A complete villain is almost as difficult to depict as a complete hero, both extremes being beyond the experience of most of us. It is a testimonial to Miss Walton's brilliant talent—I really want to use the word "genius" here, but it is a word I hesitate to employ—that she succeeds gloriously in making Evnissyen a thoroughly real and believable character. Under her remarkable control he emerges from the page a living, breathing man of flesh and blood, not just a leering caricature; she illuminates the one terrible flaw in his character, permitting us to understand him, and understanding the twisted motive that drives him inexorably on from one enormity to another, you can almost—not quite, but *almost*—forgive him. This is an amazing achievement, and one that in my opinion is beyond the power of any living fantasy writer I can think of.

In her third novel of the sequence, *The Song of Rhiannon,* Miss Walton performs another miracle of brilliant art, one almost comparable to the creation of Evnissyen. *Song* follows closely upon the heels of *Children,* an overwhelming tragedy ending with the destruction of the godlike family of heroes, the fall of the Island of the Mighty, and the end of its heroic age. After this, to write a sequel that is itself a complete and interesting novel is close to an impossibility. Well, Miss Walton achieves the impossible, and in many ways *The Song of Rhiannon* recaptures something of the springtime charm and color and freshness of the first book, but without distorting or ignoring the cataclysm that engulfed the heroes in the second book. This trick, too, must have been tremendously difficult to bring off, and she achieves it splendidly. I am left with a feeling of complete awe for her abilities as a writer and am eager to discover what she will do with the First Branch, which is one of the most delicious stories ever told.

What the future holds for fantasy in general or for Miss Walton's work in particular, I am unable to predict. I know that Evangeline Walton originally intended to follow her Welsh tetralogy with an exploration of the Greek myths about the hero Theseus, lover of Ariadne, battler against the Minotaur, conqueror of Minos of Knossus. In mid-1971, Miss Walton traveled to Greece and the island of Crete to explore the territories her proposed trilogy would use as its settings. Twenty years before this she had planned to begin work on the first book about Theseus, but before she had gotten very far beyond the note-taking and early research stage, by one of those unforeseeable coincidences that make a writer's life a thing of such uncertainty, Mary Renault published her memorable retellings of precisely the same cycle of legends, *The King Must Die* and *The Bull From the Sea,* so Miss Walton abandoned her proposed trilogy even as she had abandoned her Welsh tetralogy still earlier. As things worked out, however, after a hiatus of thirty-four years, work on the tetralogy was resumed after all. I hope the same thing will happen with the Theseus trilogy, and there is every reason to expect it within the next year or two. Miss Walton is no longer young, but she is at the height of her creative powers, and I wish her every kind of good fortune in the fruitful years ahead.

WRITERS continue to appear out of nowhere, and the history of fantasy extends beyond our point of time into the unborn tomorrows ahead. Only the other day I received a manuscript from a writer unknown to me, a first novel called *Excalibur* from a woman named Sanders Anne Laubenthal, whose rehandling of the materials of Arthurian legend are fresh and exciting and filled with promise. There are many new fledgling writers like her whose work will come to our attention in the years ahead.

To this history of fantasy, as to the history of any genre of literature, there can be no real ending. All we can expect to do is what I have done here: to bring the story up to today, and leave the rest of it unwritten.

9

Of World-Making:

Some Problems of the Invented Milieu

> **Pooh-Bah:** Merely corroborative detail, intended to give artistic verisimilitude to an otherwise bald and unconvincing narrative.
> —Sir William S. Gilbert: "The Mikado"

Now that we have traced the evolution of the imaginary-world fantasy through the major writers in the genre, it might not be amiss to devote some thought to fantasy itself—how it is written, and in particular, how it is written *well*.

If you stop and think about it, you will realize that fantasy writers face a variety of technical problems that authors working in most other genres seldom have to worry about. The problem of creating an imaginary world on paper is the largest and most serious of these, and it is a complex problem involving many different factors.

In the first place, this problem is virtually unique to fantasy, although science fiction can, and often does, involve similar difficulties. But a writer busy at the concocting of, let's say, a modern espionage or adventure novel, while he has his own technical problems to worry about, at least has it easier than we fantasy writers in this respect.

That is, if Ian Fleming wishes to get his character from here to there, he can have him pick up a phone, call a cab, ride to the airport, and hop aboard a jet for Lisbon. In fact, if he really wants to he can accomplish this transition in about as many words as it has just taken me to describe it. He can do this for the simple reason that he and his reader share the same world: he does not need to define any of the above terms, because his reader is already familiar with them. Unless his book should happen to fall into the hands of an Australian Bushman or an isolated Eskimo, the espionage writer can safely assume that his reader has used a telephone and ridden in a taxicab; and while he may not have flown in a jet himself, he should be familiar with them from television commercials; and although he may not have visited the city of Lisbon, it can be assumed that any literate person has a fair idea of where and what it is.

Now suppose that, instead of Ian Fleming, the writer we are talking about is Lord Dunsany, and instead of an espionage thriller he is writing a work of adult fantasy, such as "The Fortress Unvanquishable, Save For Sacnoth." In that story, the young hero Leothric slays the dragon Tharagavverug in order to obtain the enchanted sword Sacnoth, so that he can destroy the evil magician Gaznak. From this it should be quite obvious that the fantasy writer must solve problems the author of thrillers doesn't have to fret over: far from sharing the same world with his reader, the fantasy writer is involved in *creating a new one*. And he has to do it the hard way, without being able to count on his reader's easy familiarity with what he is talking about. For unless his reader is extremely far-traveled indeed,[1] he is not likely ever to have seen a dragon, even in the most exotic of zoos, or to have faced an evil magician. Nor are enchanted swords like Sacnoth on public view even in the most celebrated of this world's museums.

Each of these exotic elements—dragon, sword, magician—must somehow be made to seem real to the reader, if only for the moment. This is far more complicated and difficult than it may at first sound: in the first place, the writer is asking his reader to take seriously a number of things that he knows to be absurdities—to believe in dragons. In the second place, he is asking the reader to become involved with his hero, to actually worry about whether or not Leothric can and will slay the monster instead of being slain himself.

Now the second of these is a problem that *all* fiction writers, of whatever genre, must solve as best they can. It is not really to the point to say that the reader knows Leothric to be a completely imaginary young man who does not in any sense exist except as words printed on paper; he knows the same to be true of Soames Forsyte, or Ivanhoe, or James Bond himself, as far as that goes. All fiction writers have to involve the reader in the fortunes of their characters. No, it is with the first part of the problem that we are chiefly concerned here—to somehow persuade the reader *to believe in dragons,* if only for the duration of the tale. What every fantasy writer must ask of his reader is *the willing suspension of disbelief,* in Coleridge's famous phrase.[2] The phrase is quite apt here: although Coleridge was talking about poetry when he coined it, he was talking in particular about *the supernatural element* in certain of his poems, and the manner in which it might be made temporarily credible.

There is also a larger phase of the problem, namely, the world in which the tale takes place—the problem of the invented milieu itself, with which we shall concern ourselves in this chapter. To define the problem briefly, the writer not only has to persuade his reader into a temporary willingness to believe in dragons, enchanted swords, and evil magicians; he must also paint a convincing portrait of a world or land or age in which these things naturally fit. Why "world"? Because the *setting* is, or should be, larger than just the *scene.* Leothric might slay the dragon in a gloomy, wooded region—like the forests of Bavaria, say. But to set the scene in modern Bavaria would be very difficult, since modern Bavaria, gloomy wooded hills and all, is only an item in the larger context of this planet in this century. Not very far away (as the jet flies) are twelve-lane highways, television sets, air conditioners. Dragons and twelve-lane highways are mutually contradictory:

it is hard to believe they could coexist. But *ancient* Bavaria . . . well, that's a different matter. The Rhineland forests of the mythic age, the age of Siegfried and Balmung and Fafnir, are a context much more convincing. But best of all would be the world that our author in question, Dunsany, actually did use for the story.

He used, of course, an imaginary world of his own invention.

BUT why an invented world, if the milieu of the Norse sagas and the Germanic *Nibelungenlied* is available and quite suitable? The reason is, simply, that this milieu is most suitable to a retelling of the Siegfried epic, less well suited to the inventing of a new and original story. Those writers who have used the world of this or that epic or legendary story have usually used it for a modern redaction of the original tale. For example, David Chaney recreated the Mycenaean world of Theseus and the Minotaur for his novel *Son of Minos* (1930); Evangeline Walton revived the world of Welsh mythology for her retelling of those myths in her novel *The Virgin and the Swine* (1936); Robert Graves recreated the world of Hercules from Greek mythology for his novel *Hercules, My Shipmate* (1945); Ruth Collier Sharpe recreated the land of Lyonesse from the Arthurian legends for her novel *Tristram of Lyonesse* (1949); Marvin Borowsky recreated the Camelot of Lancelot and Guinevere for his retelling of their story in his novel *The Queen's Knight* (1955); Ernst Schnabel recreated the world of Daedalus and Icarus from the Greek myths for his version of that story in his novel *Story for Icarus* (1958); Rosemary Sutcliff recreated the world of Cuchulainn from the Irish myths for her retelling of that story in her novel *The Hound of Ulster* (1963); Frank G. Slaughter recreated the world of Queen Dido from the *Aeneid* for his retelling of her story in his novel *The Purple Quest* (1965); Mary Stewart recreated the world and age of Merlin the magician, Aurelius Ambrosius, and

Uther Pendragon from the pages of Geoffrey of Monmouth for her novel *The Crystal Cave* (1970); Poul Anderson recreated the heroic age of Danish national legend for his retelling of the *Hrolf Kraki's Saga* (1973); and so on, *ad infinitum.*

Borrowing an already established world of myth or heroic legend for the setting of a new and original story, involves the author in historical and literary research which can sharply curtail and influence his own imaginative concept, since his new story should not violate any strictures of the original world-picture the writer is using. Such being the case, writers from William Morris to Joy Chant have generally preferred to invent their own *weltansicht,* designing its configuration to fit their own special needs and purposes. It is a lot easier to do this, actually, and you avoid making errors in historical or geographical lore; you also avoid embarrassing anachronisms, the primary bugaboo of the historical novelist.

Writers of imaginary-world fantasies enjoy immense freedom in scenery and locale, incomparably more than that enjoyed by the purveyors of any other kind of narrative. In general, these settings tend to sort out into four broad classifications. The first is to set the tale on our own world but in the remote past before history began. Examples of this kind of setting may be seen in Avram Davidson's use of Ultima Thule, Jane Gaskell's Atlantis trilogy, Robert E. Howard's post-Atlantean world of the "Hyborian Age," Tolkien's Middle-earth, or my own six novels of the adventures of Thongor the Mighty, which are set in the lost continent of Lemuria.[3]

Then there are those stories that are laid on our own planet but in the inconceivably remote future— such as Clark Ashton Smith's stories of the future continent Zothique, or William Hope Hodgson's novel *The Night Land,* or A. E. van Vogt's *The Book of Ptath,* or Jack Vance's marvelous tales of the "Dying Earth," or my own novel *The Giant of World's End,* which is set on the future super-continent of Gondwane.

Other writers have chosen to set their scenes in a world that is essentially akin to our own world, and very close to it in space/time, but separated from it along some alternate dimension. Into this group fall Andre Norton's Witch World novels, John Jakes' tales of Brak the Barbarian, Fritz Leiber's Fafhrd and the Gray Mouser saga, which is set in a world he calls "Nehwon," and L. Sprague de Camp's *The Goblin Tower* and its recent sequel, and my own tales of Simrana the Dreamworld.

The final classification includes those fantasies definitely situated on another planet. Here Edgar Rice Burroughs' Barsoom, Clark Ashton Smith's Xiccarph, Eddison's Mercury, and Lindsay's Tormance deserve mention; and I might also list my imaginary planet Zarkandu, setting of my heroic fantasy novel *Lost World of Time*.

These four groups, however, do not represent all the varieties of locale available to the fantasy writer. Not by a long shot. There exist interesting anomalies, stories which do not precisely fit any of these classifications. Austin Tappan Wright's novel *Islandia,* for instance, is set in our own world and time, but on an imaginary continent; John Myers Myers' novel *Silverlock* is set somewhere on earth in our own time, but in a region of allegorical symbol; Dunsany's stories are set "at the edge of the world" (whatever that means!); and some of Clark Ashton Smith's stories, such as "The Abominations of Yondo" or "The Epiphany of Death," are vague and nebulous in their setting. And, of course, the "lost race" genre, touched upon earlier in my survey of Haggard and Merritt, falls into none of these four categories with any precision. To say nothing of Cabell's fiction, which often strays into Heaven, Hell, Asgard, and elsewhere.

You see what I mean by "freedom of scenery and locale"?

Now let us examine another question: Precisely what does an invented world consist of?

In the first place, of course, it has a system of invented geography. And herein lies the first major hazard the beginning fantasy author must deal with. Even when you are inventing a world all your own, you are not really free to let your imagination have its own untrammeled way. Despite my earlier observations regarding the author's freedom in scene and setting, this freedom must be kept under intelligent discipline, for you are not free to set it down just any old way, exactly the way it comes to you. Geography does not just *happen*—natural features are where they are due to certain causes. It behooves the would-be author of imaginary-world fantasy to think a little before sketching out his map.

You cannot really have a lush rain-forest smack up against a parched desert of burning sands, you know; it pays to do a bit of reading into climatology so as to understand the interplay of forces that create deserts and rain-forests, jungles and grasslands, and so on. Nor can you stick mountains about your map in a helter-skelter fashion; mountains have good reasons for being where they are, and a fantasy writer should know something about them. Pooh-Bah's immortal words about artistic verisimilitude, quoted at the head of this chapter, bear on this, as does Coleridge's line concerning the willing suspension of disbelief. The fantasy author should do *everything possible* to convince his reader that his invented world is real and genuine. A cursory understanding of the climatological causes behind deserts and the geological causes that raise up mountains makes an invented world more convincing, less difficult to swallow, easier to accept as real. Anything the fantasy writer can do to persuade the reader to accept his story and his world, to take them seriously, is well worth the time and effort involved.

Most fantasy writers would agree that in plotting out a story it is wise to construct a map of your invented world, even if such is not to be published in conjunction with the tale. To do this is simply good sense, a good professional work-habit; otherwise, in chapter nine you may have your heroes traveling *south* to the city of Qzytxio, when in chapter two you clearly remarked that the direction was *north*. Authors are as forgetful and absent-minded as the lesser breeds of humankind, and a simple precaution like taking a moment to sketch out a map helps prevent such errors and inconsistencies (upon which eagle-eyed readers are bound to swoop with gleeful cries, thereafter sitting down to write nasty letters to the poor author). In addition, a short-cut past all that research into geography which I advised a moment ago would be to buy a good atlas and simply take a corner of Europe or wherever as your guide. This way you will have forests thinning out into grasslands, or deepening into soggy swamps, or rising into foothills and mountains, or drying up into desert regions in a manner consistent with reality. And it saves a lot of research, too.

There are several things the fantasy writer generally keeps in mind while inventing his geography. One of these is that, just as there are *reasons* for mountains being where they are, cities also do not just spring up without cause. Most of the world's great cities are where they are for reasons of trade, and most of the important cities of antiquity were founded in locations having easy access to the sea, ocean trade being a major factor in their prosperity or decline. Some cities, of course, are on the seacoast itself, but those that are not were often built on rivers leading to the sea—Rome on the Tiber, London on the Thames, Paris on the Seine, Thebes on the Nile, and so on. Many other cities, although also built on rivers, are further inland; but cities built at or near the mouths of major river systems could control and tax the trade of these less fortunate cities, which is often one of the reasons why the great cities became great in the first place. In planning the location of the cities in a fantasy novel, it is a good idea to keep this firmly in mind. It is not accidental that the greatest of the world's most ancient cities became great because of where they were. Ur of the Chaldees, for instance, was built at the very head of the Persian Gulf, at the mouth of the Tigris-Euphrates river-system. There were many other cities built on the Tigris and Euphrates also, but further inland; Ur, however, became rich and powerful, while few of the inland cities are more than names to us. The famous seaport of Basra is another example of this; it is mentioned in the *Arabian Nights* almost as frequently as Baghdad itself. And those cities far inland which were *not* built on rivers—such as Samarkand, for instance—probably became strong and prosperous because they were built at the juncture of major overland trade routes.

The fantasy writer, then, should beware of scattering his cities all over the map on pure whim. A modicum of reason should prevail, even in creating a magic world.

BESIDES cobbling together a world composed of oceans, islands, rivers, valleys, mountains, forests, deserts, lakes, cities, and so on, the fantasy writer goes beyond mere geographical invention to the sphere of politics—for most fantasy worlds are divided into nations. It helps to know a little about the historical forces that shaped the growth of individual nations—to know, for example, how the decay and collapse of the world empire of ancient Rome influenced the rise of the various nations of Europe, since many of the older political divisions of Europe were originally provinces of the Roman Empire. The situation in Europe between the collapse of ancient Rome and the rise of France, Britain, Germany, and Spain was one in which semi-civilized tribes or clans having a brief heritage of Roman overlordship suddenly became their own masters as the legions were withdrawn home to Italy one by one. The actual number of Romans in any one province of Gaul before the collapse of the Empire was in general surprisingly small; a few administrators ran things by overseeing a large number of native clerks and minor officials. After the legions withdrew, it probably seemed only natural for these administrative systems to continue in opera-tion; since the Roman system of provincial government worked better than rank savagery or barbarism, the early Frankish-Gothic states tried to keep it going as best they could. Because the Frankish-Gothic clerks and bureaucrats had had to learn Latin, the emerging nations that we now call France, Germany, Spain, Britain, and so on, used that language to a considerable degree. Today, French and Spanish and Italian are called "Romance languages," being all interrelated, each having grown out of the decay of Latin.

In creating a fantasy world, the author should know a lot more about it than he sets down in his story. Specifically, he should know something about the ancient history of his various kingdoms or empires. Nations rise to a sense of identity and national purpose for *reasons;* some nations grew out of tribal or clan organizations, others were the result of successful invasions from without (as England today is the result of a Norman aristocracy imposed upon an Anglo-Saxon peasantry, due to just such an invasion). I don't say that a detailed summary of past historical events has to be written into the novel; but it pays for the author to have some idea, however vague, of how his invented kingdoms and empires arose in the first place. It makes a world hang together better; it makes it more consistent and believable.

It is also a good idea for the fantasy writer to know something about how actual historical countries were organized and run. Not all of them were as simple as you might think, with a king on top, a bunch of powerful dukes and barons in the middle, and farmers, tradesmen, and peasants at the bottom. Such a view is simplistic. Think of the Joan of Arc story: Joan's Dauphin was the one true and rightfully born King of France, but he was poor and completely powerless compared to some of his dukes, such as Burgundy. In England, a strong central monarchy had been established quite early, but for the better part of France's history the monarch had been little more than a figurehead. Oh, there was usually a King of France around, at least nominally, but the nation was fragmented, divided up between the great landowners, the dukes, some of whom were far more rich and powerful than any king since Charlemagne; and it took quite a bit of history before the monarchial power was firmly centralized.

It helps to know just a little about the actual organization of such kingdoms—exactly how they were governed. It also helps to know the difference between a kingdom and an empire, for instance, for an empire is really something quite different from a kingdom. Technically, an empire is a coalition of independent states or tribes brought under a unified central government one way or another. Great Britain did not become the British Empire until it acquired sovereignty over the many states and princedoms of India. Germany did not become the German Empire until the many small Graustarks and Grand Fenwicks and Ruritanias which made up Germany were brought together under one sovereign; this was accomplished, by the way, by an extraordinary statesman, Otto von Bismarck, who persuaded or coerced members of the loose federation of German principalities to accept William II, then King of Prussia, as their Emperor. If an empire is the setting of your fantasy novel, it is a safe bet that it had a Bismarck in its past somewhere.

But the Fields We Know, to use Dunsany's charming phrase, have been ruled by all sorts of different governmental forms, ranging from theocracies, such as Tibet, pre-Columbian Peru, Mexico, or ancient Egypt, in which the monarch was recognized as a divinity of one kind or another, to republics, such as our own modern United States. Of particular interest to the fantasy writer might be some of the more unique forms of government: the Hanseatic League, the Venice of the Doges, the peculiar "empire" of the Mayans. In this respect, I recommend a careful reading of a novel by L. Sprague de Camp called *The Goblin Tower* (New York, Pyramid Books, 1968). In this book and a recent

sequel, *The Clocks of Iraz,* de Camp escorts his reader
through a veritable guidebook of governmental systems,
such as the Twelve Cities, wherein each state has its
own, often very peculiar, form of government. There
is the stiff, proper, rather blue-nosed Republic of
Vindium, for example, ruled by a Senate; and Zolon,
which is an island and hence a maritime power, aptly
ruled by a High Admiral. In Othomae, the rule is
divided: the eldest legitimate son of the late Grand Duke
becomes Grand Duke in his father's place and has
charge of the civil administration, while the eldest
illegitimate son becomes the "Grand Bastard," who is
hereditary commander-in-chief of the military. Other
forms of government are explored, or at least touched
upon, in this charming, whimsical novel; we are introduced to the Tyrant of Boaktis, the Syndics of Ir, the
Hereditary Usurper of Govannian, and the Theocrat of
Tarxia, among others.

The book was obviously designed to run the gamut
of governmental systems, and is certainly a genuine
tour-de-force in this area. Some of the systems are
quite amusing, such as Metouro, which is run by a
secret society under the control of a masked council
known as The Faceless Five. De Camp informs me
that this notion is based on the secret council which
ruled Venice during the High Renaissance, the Doge
being but the elective president of this council.

There are several kingdoms, so-called, in the world
of *The Goblin Tower,* and each has solved the old
problem of lawful succession in its own way. In the
kingdom of Xylar, for example, the succession is non-
hereditary: the Xylarians ritually behead each monarch
at the end of his five-year term of office and toss the
former monarch's noggin out into the crowd like a
wedding bouquet. Whoever is lucky (or unlucky)
enough to catch this grisly prize becomes the next
King of Xylar and is free to enjoy the several pleasures
and prerogatives of the royal office until his turn beneath
the headsman's axe.

YET another element in the makeup of imaginary civilizations deserves attention, namely, that such worlds or realms will have a literature all their own. It should be present in the story, touched upon, however briefly, and made part of the background information. A master at handling this component of the craft is L. Sprague de Camp. In his several novels and short-stories about Krishna, an imaginary planet revolving about Tau Ceti, he works literary information into his invented lore in a remarkably clever and unobtrusive manner. Sometimes he has his characters refer to scenes or situations in the Krishnan epic literature during casual conversation—the sort of thing literate people often do—as in *The Hand of Zei,* when the heroine asks Barnvelt, "What ails my captain? You look as sour as Qarar when he's been deceived by the King of 'Ishk," and a bit further on remarks, " 'Tis one thing to talk big, like the heroine in Harian's *The Conspirators,* of casting aside the comforts and prerogatives of rank for love." At other times, he works similar data into the actual scene itself, as in *The Tower of Zanid,* when Mjipa declines an invitation to go out, saying,

"As for me, these brawls merely make my head ache. I'd rather stay home reading *Abbeq and Dangi.*"

"In the original Gozashtandou? All two hundred and sixty-four cantos?"

"Certainly," said Mjipa.

"Gad, what a frightful fate to be an intellectual."

A bit further on in the same book, Fallon remarks, "There's a revival of Harian's *The Conspirators* opening at the Sahi tonight. I'll pay for the seats," thus precipitating the background lore directly into the flow of action. Notice, too, how cunningly de Camp maintains his system of background lore by careful cross-references: this is the same play referred to in the other novel, *The Hand of Zei,* quoted above.

This sort of thing Tolkien handles quite effectively, too. In *The Lord of the Rings,* however, the local literature is often right there in the actual dialogue, as

in the first volume of *The Fellowship of the Ring,*
the scene in Chapter 3 in which Frodo and his companions meet a party of Elves while traveling through
the woods. They are singing an old Elvish song, and
it is their singing voices Frodo hears first—

> *O Elbereth! Gilthoniel!*
>   *We still remember, we who dwell*
> *In this far land beneath the trees,*
>   *Thy starlight on the Western Seas.*

There are many such songs, and even ballads, in *The
Lord of the Rings,* as well as references to old books,
epics, tales, and legends—all worked into the texture of
the trilogy itself. This casual use of references to the
literature of an imaginary world adds an entire new
dimension of reality to the story, and most of the major
writers in the genre have realized this (although Burroughs and Merritt are somewhat deficient in this aspect
of world-making).

Howard, for example, often uses quotations from
an invented Hyborian Age literature for his epigraphs
(chapter-headings), as in "The Phoenix on the Sword,"
in which the chapter-headings consist of snippets from
invented history ("The Nemedian Chronicles"), ballad
literature ("The Road of Kings"), and so on. He also
understood the de Campian notion of strengthening
the illusion of a genuine historical context by the use
of cross-references between stories: the same ballad,
"The Road of Kings," is used epigraphically in another
Conan story, "The Scarlet Citadel," as are some
Aquilonian proverbs and a marching-song sung by the
Bossonian Archers.

I learned this trick from Howard, and my Lemurian
Books use for their chapter-headings quotations from
various historical documents such as "The Lemurian
Chronicles" and "The Tsargol Records," magical or
occult works such as "The Scarlet Edda" and the
grimoire of Sharajsha, epics like "Thongor's Saga,"
pieces of Lemurian literature such as "Diombar's Song
of The Last Battle," and any number of folksongs, sea

chanteys, sayings and proverbs, and war or marching songs such as "Drum-Song of the Kodanga Tribesmen," "Battle-Song of the Black Dragons," and "Caravan-Song of the Jegga Nomads."

I wasn't very far into my work on the Lemurian Books before I realized that I had better write out some of this literature in advance, to avoid errors. The entire text of "The Lemurian Chronicles," for example, stands complete in my notebooks, and in one of the novels, *Thongor in the City of Magicians* (New York, Paperback Library, 1968), I thought it would be fun to use one full canto of "Thongor's Saga" for my chapter-headings; thus, in that book an entire canto is quoted piecemeal—thirty-one stanzas, adding up to one hundred and twenty-four lines of epic verse. However, neither "The Scarlet Edda" nor "Testaments of Yaa" or any of the songs exist in my notebooks as complete works, although "Diombar's Song" stands as a finished ballad, has been published in *Amra,* and will be reprinted in my forthcoming book of poems from Arkham House, *Dreams from R'lyeh.*

SOME imaginary-world fictions confine themselves to a limited sphere of action within the borders of one state, but most of the better ones broaden the scope of their plots to cover a continent or even a hemisphere. Howard's Conan stories, for example, carry their reader from the proto-Scandinavia of Cimmeria, Asgard, Hyperborea, etc., to a proto-Cathay in the far east called Khitai, south to the primal realms of what we would call Africa, and so on, including a visit or two to Vendhya, Howard's name for India.

In constructing an imaginary milieu for purposes of fantasy, it is generally a good idea to suggest the presence, at least the off-stage presence, of an entire diverse world. Although the romances of Morris include continent-spanning quests to the World's End and such, none of the realms through which his heroes travel are particularly strange or alien to them. He was working, of course, in the tradition of the Grail romances,

Malory, the *Parzival* of Wolfram von Eschenbach, and to a certain degree, the world-view of Ariosto, Spenser, and *Amadis*. In such medieval fictions, the world was envisioned as a continuum of the culture familiar to the reader, and there is no attempt to make foreign lands seem actually foreign. The inhabitants of the world of *Amadis of Gaul* or the *Parzival* all speak the same language; in Boiardo and Ariosto, the Princess of far Cathay is named "Angelica." Morris worked in this tradition: his world, or worlds, are one continuous tapestry of Medieval Europe.

Modern world-makers, however, adopt a more realistic view. In Pratt's *Well of the Unicorn,* the action centers in Dalarna, a country very like Medieval Scandinavia which is under the tyranny of the Vulkings, a closely-knit military caste like the Medieval Templars or the Knights of Malta. However, even though the story centers in Dalarna, Pratt makes the reader understand that Dalarna is only one small part of an entire world. Southwest, he tells us, lies a realm simply called "the Empire," which closely resembles the Holy Roman one of mundane history; to the south lies Dodekapolis, a confederacy of free cities classically Greek in substance; and to the west dwell the "blond heathen of Dzik." Likewise, de Camp's *The Goblin Tower* centers around states adjacent to Novaria which are, like Novaria, Medieval European in culture. But to the north dwell the nomads of Shven (blond Nordics with a nomadic Mongol-type culture), while to the south are the nations of Feridun (Arabs, more or less) and an immense but static empire called Mulvan (India, more or less). Although the action of these novels is necessarily limited, we are dealing with entire worlds here.

There are several ways of suggesting a worldscape in this kind of fiction. One is to employ the guided-tour plot: that is, to have the central matter of your novel concerned with a quest. Tolkien did this, and so did Eddison. Of course, they were working in novel lengths; but it is possible to use the quest plot even in the short story. For an example of how this can be done, see Dunsany's story "Idle Days on the Yann." In that tale a remarkable amount of real estate is explored, although the story is a brief one.

But even if your story is concerned with the internal problems of a single state, the presence of cities or kingdoms off-stage, so to speak, can still be suggested.

Let me illustrate this by referring to some of my own fiction. The second volume of my Atlantis trilogy (whose first volume, *The Black Star*, has not yet been published as I write this) will be called *The White Throne*. The scene is laid, of course, in Atlantis, and the story opens in the great bazaar of Adalon the White City. In the course of the first three manuscript pages the young hero, Crysarion of Ith, strolls through the bazaar and asks directions to the house of the magician, Herpes Zoster. The man he queries is a jewel-merchant named Borochan, who tries to interest him in "emeralds from the mountains beyond Daqualoth," "rubies from old Pythontus," and a black opal "brought at great difficulty and expense from the furthest north, beyond fabulous Ith where the Hills of Mir march down to the black shores of Khom Mur Paz, the Hyperborean Sea." Such gems, he shrewdly notes, eyeing the youth's rather slender pocket pouch, are, although rare, less expensive than one might think, even in these troublous times "when Malidorn the bandit-king of Kerné has closed the mountain passes to all caravans." Crysarion buys nothing, elicits directions, and strides off, leaving the old merchant suspicious. Borochan summons a lounger "in faded Stryphax kilt" idling nearby in an unobtrusive manner, and bids him:

> "Go, tell the Master that a warrior in the mercenary's scarlet of the Free Swords seeks out Herpes Zoster, the old wizard from Ulphar. He wears the badge of service of the House of Istysis on his trappings. Although a mercenary, his features and carriage denote high—even noble—breeding. From the hue of his skin, he's a Turanian; yet he wears his hair in the fashion of the North Kingdoms, and speaks with the accents of Illurdis. This may be of importance, so don't loiter!"

I cite this passage, not as a model of deathless prose, but to show how easily and unobtrusively quite a bit of background geography can be worked into even a scene of conversation. Note that from just these few pages the reader learns of the cities or kingdoms of Adalon, Ith, Daqualoth, Pythontus, the Hills of Mir, Khom Mur Paz the Hyperborean Sea, Kerné, Ulphar, Turan, the North Kingdoms, Stryphax, and Illurdis. I have suggested a busy, crowded mapful of countries, a whole world out there beyond the borders of the page.

Note also the variety of the names introduced, which vary from the monosyllabic "Mir" to the polysyllabic "Crysarion." Note also how the invented names are distributed fairly evenly across the alphabet:

Adalon, Atlantis
Borochan   Malidorn, Mir
Crysarion
Daqualoth   Pythontus

Herpes Zoster, Hyperborea   Stryphax
Illurdis, Istysis, Ith   Turan
                                  Ulphar
Kerné, Khom Mur Paz

But this brings us to the second phase of our discussion of the invented milieu, the coining of names, and for that we will need a new chapter.

A Local Habitation and a Name:

Some Observations on Neocognomina

> And out of the ground the Lord God formed
> every beast of the field, and every fowl of
> the air; and brought them unto Adam to see
> what he would call them: and whatsoever
> Adam called every living creature, that was
> the name thereof.
>
> —Genesis 2:19.

In one of the essays in *The Dyer's Hand,* published in New York in 1962, W. H. Auden touches upon the problem that confronts us in this chapter:

> It was Edward Lear, I believe, who said that the true test of imagination is the ability to name a cat, and we are told in *Genesis* that the Lord brought to unfallen Adam all the creatures that he might name them and whatsoever Adam called every living creature, that was its name, which is to say, its Proper Name. Here Adam plays the role of the Proto-poet, not the Proto-prosewriter. A Proper Name must not only refer, it must refer *aptly,* and this aptness must be publicly recognizable.

Mr. Auden is wrong about the source of that remark about the naming of cats—it is from Samuel Butler, not Lear[1]—but the rest of his statements ring true, save only that the distinction he would make between the poet and the prosewriter makes no sense to me. In the province of fantasy, at least, the inventing of names—the finding of "the Proper Name"—is of the very first importance.

In creating an imaginary world with words, the

author is thrust into the role of Adam. Everything must be named—kings, gods, and men, as well as kingdoms, cities, rivers, oceans, mountains, forests, deserts, islands, and all of the birds and beasts who inhabit this world. Adam had it easy—all he had to name were the beasts!

And the *kind* of names they are, their weight and color and taste and music, are of enormous importance, too. I admit to being a fanatic on this topic; I have always been hypersensitive to the ring and shape and savor of made-up names. Some people have a superlative ear for it—Dunsany is the Old Master in this department, and Jack Vance a modern genius of the art. Others are less competent, some lacking the skill altogether; these unfortunate writers either have no ear at all for the sound of neocognomina, or they fail to prepare themselves in advance by carefully working out a list of fifty or sixty invented names to have on hand when the need arises—a system I would recommend to all new workers in the art of fantasy. The hastier of such writers—and I might place Gardner F. Fox among them—when faced with the need to insert a coined name into a passage, do either one of two things. Either they snatch a noun carelessly out of history, geography, or legend and transmogrify it by knocking out a syllable or altering a vowel; or they simply coin a name on the spot, generally a gawdawful one, full of X's, Z's, and Q's.

Neither of these practices is to be recommended to the beginner. As for plucking a name out of the history book, Robert E. Howard himself was addicted to this unhappy practice, and the quality of his work suffered because of it. Let me expand on this a bit. Howard was able to coin perfectly good original names, but all too often he was liable to borrow a name rather than invent one. In part, this was a good idea because of the partly historical nature of the invented world in his Conan stories: that is, although the Hyborian Age presumably existed before our own ancient history and was demolished in a cataclysm, its memory lingered into historical times in the form of vague and distorted legends.

There is nothing wrong with this idea at all, used properly. Howard picked over Classical mythology for grim, stark names redolent of dark evil, employing these as the names of ancient kingdoms given over to the practice of primordial black magic. I guess he meant to convey the notion that the names of these empires of black magicians became virtual synonyms for evil and horror in later years, lingering down the ages and passing into "early" myth as half-forgotten symbols. Thus, in "The God in the Bowl" he mentions the kingdom of Acheron, and elsewhere he refers to Stygia and Dagonia, both named in "The Devil in Iron." (Acheron is the "River of Sorrows," one of the five rivers of Hades; Stygia derives from the Styx, another river in the infernal regions, the word becoming a synonym for darkness; Dagonia is from the Philistine sea god Dagon, whose temple Samson pulled down in Judges 16:23-30.)

Now, as I said, this was a very good idea—one of Howard's best ideas, in fact. But when he got away from using this naming technique *for a specific purpose* (e.g., to suggest a kingdom of evil so terrible that its very name lived on in myth for ages as a synonym for darkness or the Inferno) and just used it because it was *an easy way to coin names,* it became a flaw in his style, and a glaring one at that.

The position of Greece on his imaginary map of the world during the Hyborian Age, for example, is occupied by the kingdom of "Corinthia." The name was picked, obviously, because it sounds like the name of the Greek city Corinth, and was therefore supposed to "suggest" the idea of ancient Greece to the reader. It is an absolutely awful idea; Corinth was a minor city of no particular importance, situated on a small and infertile strip of the isthmus between the Saronic and the Corinthian gulfs. Until the tyrannies of Cypselus and Periander, 657–581 B.C., it enjoyed neither power, prosperity, nor any particular world role. Even in Homer's time it was a small town under the thumb of Mycenae. To suggest that primal Greece was known as "Corinthia" is to commit a logical absurdity. Howard would have done better to call his proto-Greece "Hellenica"—even "Achaia" (Homer's name for the oldest Greeks) would have been a better idea—but he was just slamming this stuff through the typewriter and snapped up the first Greekish name that popped into his head. He didn't take the time to think about it; he just didn't care.

He did this over and over again in the clumsiest manner imaginable in his Conan stories. In "Black Colossus" he introduces the city of "Akbatana." This is nothing more than Ecbatana, the historical capitol of ancient Media. In "Queen of the Black Coast" he mentions a city called "Asgalun," which is nothing more than the old Biblical city of Ascalon. Even worse is his use, in a story called "The Scarlet Citadel," of "Khorshemish," which is the name of the old Syrian city Carchemish, mangled just a bit for effect.

Howard simply used what was immediately *on hand;* he couldn't be bothered to go to the extra effort of coining his own names. This is also true of most of the names of his characters, and it was singled out by readers of the time as one of his major flaws. H. P. Lovecraft, in a letter to Donald A. Wollheim, discussing Howard's famous essay "The Hyborian Age," observed:

> The only flaw in this stuff is R. E. H.'s incurable tendency to devise names too closely resembling actual names of ancient history—names which, for us, have a very different set of associations. In many cases he does this designedly—on the theory that familiar names descend from the fabulous realms he describes—but such a design is invalidated by the fact that we clearly know the etymology of many of the historic terms, hence cannot accept the pedigree he suggests.

L. Sprague de Camp also discussed this annoying trait of Howard's, in the preface to his essay "An Exegesis of Howard's Hyborian Tales," first published in the famous Sword & Sorcery fanzine, *Amra*. De Camp sums it up thusly:

> Many of the personal names used by Howard in his Conan stories are ordinary Latin personal names (Publius, Constantius, Valeria) or Greek names (Dion, Pelias, Tiberias) or modern Italian versions of these (Publio, Tito, Demetrio). Others are modern Asiatic or Arabic names, sometimes modified (Aram Baksh, Yar Afzal, Jungir Khan, etc.) while still others are . . . Aztec or pseudo-Aztec [and] pseudo-Iroquois.

Even the name "Conan" itself—that of Howard's mightiest hero—was borrowed, not invented. It is a common Celtic name, there having been any number of Duke Conans in Medieval Brittany and a King Conann of the Fomorians in Irish myth. And it appears in modern times, of course, as the middle name of the creator of Sherlock Holmes.

This is really not the way to do it; it does not pay to make it too easy for the reader to guess the source from which your names are derived. A case in point here are the delightful Brak the Barbarian tales that John Jakes has been writing since 1963. These stories are enormously entertaining examples of good Sword and Sorcery, penned with verve and gusto and rich color, but they do not exemplify good name-inventing techniques. For example, Jakes' wandering barbarian warrior is searching for "the golden kingdom of Khurdisan," which lies somewhere to the south. Now, "Khurdisan" is a nice enough name, but it does not take very much geographical knowledge to recognize that Jakes casually (and carelessly) lifted the name from Kurdistan, a plateau region in southeastern Turkey, northwestern Iran, and northern Iraq. Once you spot the source of the name—*poof!*—all the romance and mystery the author strove to weave about it go out the window.

Similarly, Jakes postulates two opposing religions in his parallel world (which I privately think of as "Para-

Terra"): dark cults which worship the devil-god "Yob-Haggoth," and pseudo-Christian followers of "the ecstatic goatherd Nestoriamus." Again, the idea is a good one, essentially, but Jakes' failure to think through the problems of neocognomina impedes his readers' willing suspension of disbelief. For he lifted "Yog-Haggoth" from Lovecraft's Cthulhu Mythos divinity "Yog-Sothoth," and as for "Nestoriamus," Jakes got him from the 5th-century Syrian ecclesiastic Nestorius, founder of the Nestorian church (or heresy, as you will). In the introduction to one of his books about Brak, Jakes frankly admits taking Howard as his model. There's nothing wrong with that, but influence is carried to the point of idolatry when one imitates even the bad habits of one's model.[2]

Unfortunately, many another writer has followed Howard in this very bad habit. So excellent a writer as Leigh Brackett was not immune to the contagion; able to toss off fine names of her own coinage—like "Valkis, Jekkara, Sinharat, and the trade city of Kahora" in her marvelous Mars stories—she all too often threw in a couple of easy ones, like "Barrakesh" (from Marrakesh, a city in Morocco) and "Boghaz Hoi" (from Bogazköy, a major archaeological site for the excavation of the Hittite civilization in Turkey). And in *The Sword of Rhiannon* she has "Caer Dhu," while in *Shadow Over Mars* she presents us with "Caer Hebra." These are certainly poor choices for the names of ancient cities on the planet Mars, "caer" being a Welsh prefix commonly found in such place-names as Caerleon, Caernarvon, and so forth. Come to think of it, "Rhiannon" comes from the Welsh too, as in Evangeline Walton's recent novel, *The Song of Rhiannon.*

Gardner F. Fox, in his Kothar the Barbarian novels, is guilty of the same fault. A writer with real zip and dash, a master of colorful, exciting action, he dates back to the old *Planet Stories,* and I remember with fond nostalgia reading his entertaining swashbucklers when I was about fourteen. He is, however, one of those writers who turns the stuff out at dazzling speed, making it up as he goes along, which is not the way to do it. His coining of names is a dead giveaway of sloppy writing habits, and although he has mastered a swift-moving and colorful style of pulp adventure writing which I essentially approve of, he reveals himself as a writer of indifferent talents and slender skills through his habit of bad name-coining.

This fault has shown up most recently in a spate of Sword & Sorcery novels of his, a series that began with a novel called *Kothar—Barbarian Swordsman* (New York, Belmont Books, 1969) and was continued to the tune of at least five volumes, of which the most recent known to me is *Kothar and the Wizard Slayer* (Belmont, 1970). The tales take place on a planet called "Yarth," which seems to be a fairly earthlike planet in the remote future, but I am a bit hazy about whether or not Fox intends us to understand it as our own world aeons hence (he is a bit reticent on the point, for some reason). Yarth, anyway, is a barbaric world of warriors and wizards, and the saga of that mighty adventurer, Kothar, as he swaggers from one epic peril straight into another, armed with his charmed sword Frostfire and eternally endangered by his old enemy, the she-devil and temptress Red Lori, is jolly fun, if a bit routine.

Fox has no particular trouble with exciting incident or swashbuckling derring-do, but he is weak on the fantasy techniques, and terrible with cognominal invention. He just grabs the first name that comes along, changes a vowel or a consonant, and pops it down on the page, never caring how obvious the derivation may be, seemingly convinced that the reader will never notice. This is very careless. In a recent example, *Kothar of the Magic Sword* (Belmont Books, 1969), his wandering hero, armed with an enchanted blade given him by the wizard "Afgorkon" (from Clark Ashton Smith's "Aforgomon," most likely), attempts to steal a magic treasure from the emperor of "Avalonia" (from the island "Avalon" in the King

Arthur stories) but is caught by the emperor's "Prokorian" guards (from the Roman "Praetorian Guard"). Swearing by his god "Dwalka" (borrowed from King Kull's god "Valka"), he fights his way free and escapes to the parallel world "Nirvalla" (from the Buddhist term, "Nirvana"), where the "giant Cumberian" (from Howard's "giant Cimmerian") runs the gamut of supernatural perils before getting home again. Sloppy, clumsy hackwork.

This is not the way to do it.

WHEN it comes to making up names, as I remarked a bit earlier, some writers seem to have a tin ear. Howard, who did occasionally make up a good name (such as "Kull" and "Valusia"), may have been wiser than we assume when he borrowed names from history rather than coining them himself. For generally, when he *does* make up a name it is a pretty uninspired one. Here are a few typical gems culled from his sanguinary pages: Thak, Thaug, Thog, Yog, Yara, Yogah, Zang, Zogar, Sag. To which I respond, with Churchy la Femme—*oog.*

Michael Moorcock is another writer of undeniable talent who has what it takes to coin a delicious and melodic original name—when he wants to. The trouble is that he doesn't always want to, and turns out clinkers as often as not. In a new story called "The Jade Man's Eyes," which I have read in manuscript but which has not at the time of this writing been published, he produces a neat synthesis of the best and the worst of his abilities in a single passage. Duke Avan is questioning Elric about his travels:

"One of those legends speaks of a city older than dreaming Imrryr. A city that still exists in the deep jungles of the west," says Avan.

"You mean R'lin K'ren A'a?" Eric pretended a lack of interest he no longer felt.

"Aye. A strange name. You pronounce it more fluently than could I."

Now, as for Imrryr, "the Dreaming City of Melniboné," it is a name so beautiful as to be worthy of Dunsany himself.

But R'lin K'ren A'a . . .

R'lin K'ren A'a!

If names were meant to be eaten, that one would give you indigestion.

Now what, exactly, are the criteria we use in judging invented names? "Aptness," suggests Auden, correctly enough. This quality of aptness is an elusive one, hard to define. But we recognize it when we hear it—the Proper Name—and no other name will do. For an example of this, we turn to the first page of Burroughs' novel *Thuvia, Maid of Mars,* and we read:

> Upon a massive bench of polished ersite, beneath the gorgeous blooms of a giant pimalia, a woman sat. Her shapely, sandaled foot tapped impatiently upon the jewel-strewn walk that wound beneath the stately sorapus trees across the scarlet sward of the royal gardens of Thuvan Dihn, Jeddak of Ptarth, as a dark-haired, red-skinned warrior bent low toward her, whispering heated words close to her ear.

Acknowledging the self-evident fact that this is a simply brilliant way of opening a story—scene, setting, mood, and characters all sketched out in one swift stroke of the verbal brush—notice those invented names. "Pimalia" and "ersite." The blooms of the flowering pimalia tree. Massive bench of polished ersite stone. We recognize it when we hear it—the Proper Name—"and no other name will do."

"Pimalia" *sounds* like the name of a flowering tree; "ersite" *sounds* like a kind of carven stone. This is precisely what Auden meant by aptness.

Now let's try it this way:

> Upon a massive bench of polished pimalia, beneath the gorgeous blooms of a giant ersite, a woman . . .

NO. That simply will not do at all. The invented words
—purely nonsense words, without derivation or mean-
ing—just cannot be used interchangeably.

Let me employ a further example of aptness in name-
invention, turning this time to the Fields We Know.
Amid the brooding starkness of the great Salisbury
Plain of England rises that tremendous stone monument
dating from neolithic times that we know as Stonehenge.

Stonehenge . . . taste the word on your tongue; roll
it around in your mouth; listen to it . . . *Stonehenge*.
The word has a slow, stately grandeur to it. The syllables are ponderous, weighty as the great stones themselves.

Now imagine it called "Piccadilly"!

It simply doesn't fit, does it? The true name has a
ponderous and mysterious grandeur to it—it is right
there, in the slow, heavy roll of the evenly accented
syllables. But "Piccadilly" is a brisk, almost humorous
word; it sounds trivial, jingly. You simply cannot sub-
stitute it for the real name.

For the real name, Stonehenge, is the Proper Name,
and somehow we recognize it as such when we hear it.

Now, beyond aptness, what other criterion comes to
mind by which to judge invented names?

In a letter dated September 2, 1957, to the youthful
fantasy novelist Jane Gaskell, our old friend C. S. Lewis
touched on many interesting topics concerned with the
craftsmanship of fantasy writing. Prominent among
these was the topic of invented names: Lewis concluded
that they "ought to be beautiful and suggestive *as well
as strange;* not merely odd." (The italics are my own.)

Moorcock's "R'lin K'ren A'a" is certainly strange,
certainly odd; with equal certainty, I can say it is
neither beautiful nor suggestive.

Leigh Brackett, when she avoids the Celtic glossaries,
can coin beautifully. In *The Secret of Sinharat,* such
names as Berild, Narrabhar, and Delgaun are fluid and
lovely. Clark Ashton Smith is a master at this, coining

names at once odd and beautiful: Malygris the Magician, Satampra Zeiros, Phaniol, Tirouv Ompallios, Maal Dweb, Ralibar Vooz in "The Seven Geases," Tsathoggua, Mmatmuor, and Sodosma.

And Dunsany, of course, the master of them all. Remember the heroes of the City of Victories?—"Welleran, Soorenard, Mommolek, Rollory, Akanax and young Iraine." Or Thangobrind the Jeweller, or Lorendiac in "The Fortress Unvanquishable," or Lirazel and Alveric and Ziroonderel, the witch who dwelt among the thunders in *The King of Elfland's Daughter*. Or the warriors in that fine tale "Carcassone," who dwelt in days "when Camorak reigned at Arn, and the world was fairer . . . Gadriol the Leal, and Norn, and Athoric of the Sleety Sword, Heriel the Wild, Yarold, and Thanga of Esk."

And Vance, the current reigning master, can turn off some beautifully polished names when he has a mind to. There is "Dorwe Coreme" in *The Eyes of the Overworld*, and "Claude Glystra" in *Big Planet*, and "Pharesm the Sorcerer."

In my own stories, I try to match the savor to the sound and the sense: "Thongor," has grim weight to it, solidity, and the ring of clashing steel. The character is obviously a fighting-man; you can sense that from the sound of the name alone. "Sharajsha" suggests, at least to my ear, a mysterious and vaguely Oriental magician —which is exactly what the character is. The name has weight and importance: it is *impressive*. Elsewhere, in my newly-launched series of stories laid in the legendary isles of Antillia, needing a name for a wealthy and fabulous metropolis, I coined "Palmyrium." The name was derived from an extinct nation of the Near East called Palmyra, whose queen, Zenobia, was crushed by the Roman Emperor Aurelian—but that is irrelevant. The name of the capital of an empire should sound like what it is, and to my ear something in the very sound of "Palmyrium" echoed the music of the imperial.[8]

How do professional fantasy writers invent names? They use a number of different systems. Some of them, more linguistically talented or experienced than the rest of us, build their neocognomina by scientific techniques. Professor Tolkien, a linguist by avocation and a philologist by profession, invented the languages used in *The Hobbit* and *The Lord of the Rings* before he ever turned his mind to inventing the world in which these languages would be spoken, much less writing stories about his world of Middle-earth. (Such, at least, is the persistent rumor, which has yet to be denied officially.)

Few of us have ever gone to the length of inventing an entire language for our imaginary worlds, Tolkien being the rare exception. However, if a series continues long enough, the author generally tends to work up a sizable vocabulary of coined words. Burroughs did this in his Mars books, for example. Such words usually are made up for specific needs—"jed" for king, "jeddak" for emperor, "haad" for mile, "od" for foot, "safad" for inch. Burroughs, you see, was clever enough to realize that to employ modern English terms in his narrative would "break the mood," so to speak. He had a difficult enough time convincing the reader to accept his Martian locale, without tossing in jarringly anachronistic terminology. Coleridge would have understood his reasoning, surely!

"Anachronism" is not quite the word for this sort of thing, but no one has coined a better one. "Anamundism," perhaps.

So Burroughs, as I said, avoided breaking the mood, the "sense" of his extraterrestrial scene, with such anamundisms. Although I doubt that he ever drew up his invented Barsoomian languages systematically, in the course of writing his eleven books about Mars he had to coin quite a few words. Wherever he felt that a modern, familiar term would jar the reader, he introduced a neologism—"kaor" for "hello" is an example. And he was smart enough to devise these words with *a suggestion of linguistic relationship:* if "jed"

means king and "jeddak" means emperor, we can
deduce that the syllable "dak" indicates superior degree.
He worked the same trick in inventing his Martian
equivalents of terrene military ranks: "padwar" for
lieutenant, "dwar" for captain, "odwar" for general.
"Pad," according to his system, must mean "lesser
than" or "subsidiary" or simply "sub." Thus, "padwar"
means "sub-dwar," or "sub-captain." There is considerable fascination in unraveling this sort of internal
data—it is a part of the lasting fascination of such
series as the Mars books, the Oz books, the Sherlock
Holmes stories, etc.[4]

When I began working out the milieu of my Lemurian
books, I followed Burroughs closely in this, for I could
see that his use of neologisms was not governed by
arbitrary whim but clearly dictated by need. Thus, in
my Lemurian terminology "sark" means king, "sarkaja"
means queen ("aja" being the feminine ending), and
"Sarkon" means king of kings, or emperor. I followed
his lead in denoting military ranks, too; thus, in my
system "otar" means the leader of a hundred warriors
("captain"), while "daotar" means the leader of ten
such companies, i.e., a thousand men ("colonel"), and
"daotarkon" means "colonel-of-colonels," or "general."
You will notice that I am consistent in employing the
suffix "kon" to denote superiority. (I also, and just for
the hell of it, made up the Lemurian version of "kaor,"
the Martian greeting: in my system it became "belarba"
—*be-lar-ba:* literally, "I greet you," from which it can
be deduced that "be" means "I" and "ba" means
"you.")

I have now evolved a working vocabulary of about
fifty or sixty words in the Lemurian language, not including the invented names of beasts, flowers, trees,
and so on. I suggest this system to anyone who seriously
intends writing a fantasy novel set in imaginary sur-
roundings—and *work out your terms in advance*.

NOT all fantasy writers are conscious of the problems
of the anachronism and the anamundism, unfortunately.

The British writer Jane Gaskell is, I'm afraid, a case in point. Her "Cija of Atlan" trilogy is excellent stuff and quite absorbing to read, but her casual and unthinking use of familiar, everyday terminology in heroic novels which purport to be set in lost Atlantis are, to say the least, terribly jarring. I am not talking about terms like "king" or "general" here, although it might be pointed out that the word "general" is a modern European term for which a noncommittal variant like "commander" could easily and unobtrusively have been substituted. No—she commits far worse bloopers than these.

In discussing Zerd's army—again, I would have preferred a term with less modern connotations: "host," perhaps, or "legion"—we are treated to a positively staggering collection of anachronisms. "Uniform" and "poncho," "regiment" and "battalion," "the big brass" (used, of course, as a euphemism for "superior officers") and "civilians" are bad enough; but before long the reader is asked to swallow anachronisms such as an army "goose-stepping to a blare of pompous bands" (*The City*, p. 47), soldiers wearing "shakos and epaulettes" (*ibid,* p. 50), and soldiers that "weren't in formation" and "looked off-duty in spite of their proud uniforms."

Still further along we find terms like "H. Q.," "frontline duty," and "ration-allowances," and by this point we are too numb to wince at the appearance of "noncoms," "barracks," or "sergeant." There can hardly be any excuse for this sort of sloppiness. Surely Miss Gaskell knows that in antiquity there was no such thing as soldiers in uniform, marching to, God help us, brass bands. As her story leaves the army camp behind and moves into what I am sure she would not have hesitated to call "civilian life," the barrage of mindless anachronisms continues. "Dandruff," "vacuum," "honeymoon," "breakfast," "pneumonia," "Gosh!"—it's almost as if she were doing everything she could think of to break the mood of her own story. "O.K., sonny, you're hired," says a shopkeeper in *The Serpent*. Another character has "a prominent adam's apple." She does this sort of thing interminably—whether from sheer ignorance, pure insensitivity, or downright carelessness, I hardly dare guess.

As might be imagined, C. S. Lewis took her to task for this in severe terms: "In a fantasy, every precaution must be taken never to break the spell, to do nothing which will wake the reader and bring him back with a bump to the common earth," he says pointedly in the letter to her mentioned earlier, concluding, "All magic dies at the touch of the commonplace."

Miss Gaskell errs blatantly in this manner, but the grand championship in the anachronism department goes to an otherwise virtually unknown writer named Karl Edward Wagner for the use of a single word. In 1970 a paperback firm called "Powell Sci-Fi" issued his Sword & Sorcery novel *Darkness Weaves;* at once inept and amateurish, the book was not without a certain narrative drive and a sense of pace and color. However, I wish someone had informed Wagner that in an imaginary Medieval-type world of sorcerers and swordsmen, no one is about to offer an assassin "two hundred *dollars*" to perform a dirty deed.

IN the preceding chapter I pointed out, in reference to my novel *The White Throne,* how invented names could be worked into the flow of a scene. I also suggested that they be scattered throughout the alphabet with deliberate evenness.

This is a point of some importance, I think. Beginners tend to invent names as exotic as all get-out, names beginning with Z's or Q's or X's. A little of this goes a long way. Exotic-sounding names should be used carefully and with a precise purpose, as when naming alien gods, for example. Lovecraft and his colleagues did this quite well in their Cthulhu Mythos stories, "Cthulhu" itself being a good example. The name is difficult to pronounce, as the name of a thoroughly alien entity ought to be. Recall as well Lovecraft's name for a subterranean city of the Deep Ones: "Y'ha-nthlei." The name sounds and looks as if it was never meant to be pronounced by the human throat, which was more or less the idea Lovecraft was trying to get across.

A worldscape filled with similar names, however, would impede the reader's ease in following the story, and there is no good reason for doing that. It is far better—assuming that your world is one inhabited by human beings, or reasonably human beings, anyway—to develop the habit of coining names with a purpose. For example, in the opening section of *The Lord of the Rings,* Professor Tolkien tries to create in his reader a sense of *being at home.* He makes the Shire sound very like the familiar English countryside, not only by including in the minutiae of the Hobbit culture such everyday items as umbrellas, doorknobs, visiting cards and fireworks (for which he *could* be criticized, since these are glaring anachronisms), but also by making the names sound "Englishy." "Shire" itself is an Old English term, while other nearby places bear names like "Bree" and "Rivendell" and yet others have suffixes familiar to the English countryside: "Trollshaws," "Hoarwell," "Ettenmoors." Another clever device he uses to good purpose is to *translate* some of his names into their English equivalent meanings: the river "Baranduin" or "Brandywine," the "Cuathlo" or "Greyflood," the "Brunen" or "Loudwater," Lake "Nenuial" or "Evendim."

Other writers have employed similar devices. Some have focussed on "the English look" of names: that is, so many British names are bisyllabic, each syllable consisting of a consonant followed by a vowel followed by a second consonant—Milton, London, Carter, Parker, Harlow, Warren, and so on. One writer who did this rather well was Isaac Asimov: in his famous Foundation Trilogy—an example of world-making which shows that the rules hold as true for science fiction as for fantasy —he creates a familiar sense of "at-home-ness" through coined place-names like Kalgan, Trantor, Dorwin, Hardin, and so on. Invented names of many of the characters have a very "familiar" sound to them: Hari Seldon, Hober Mallow, Lathan Devers. If anything,

Asimov may have used this style of names a bit to excess, for his future galactic civilization lacks "alienness."

At any rate, a worldscape should include not only a few exotica, like "Unmoiqh," but also familiar-sounding names like "Mallow" or "Rivendell." But Englishy names have a deadly sameness of look and sound, and occasional words with un-English elements should be introduced, if only for variety. A glance at the nearest Rand McNally atlas suggests the enormous range and variety of names our own world offers as example to those who would create new worlds: not only is there London and Rome and Paris, but also Teotihuacan, Budapest, Cairo, Algeria, Paramaribo, and Walla-Walla. Note that some of these end in vowels and others do not, that they vary from being monosyllabic to having five syllables, and that while some have familiar English sequences of consonant/vowel/consonant, others include exotic double-vowels, called diphthongs—the "ai" in Cairo and the "eo" and "ua" in Teotihuacan.

Since a novel-length story in the genre could or perhaps should include up to one hundred invented names, sameness of look or sound or syllabic length must be avoided. Another gem from "Powell Sci-Fi" demonstrates how *not* to do it: in the course of a dismal heroic fantasy called *Swordmen of Vistar,* author Charles Nuetzel commits virtually every error imaginable in the delicate art of name-invention. Not only does he give male characters names with feminine endings, like "Xalla" and "Thoris," but almost without exception the names in his book are bisyllabic: Thoris, Illa, Xalla, Opil, Muda, Rota, Vistar, Tagor, Rusis, Vayis, Fada, etc.

Another example of "how not to do it" turns up in Ted White's novel *The Sorceress of Qar* (New York, Lancer, 1966). White takes us on a guided tour of his invented world, but there is a rather depressing sameness to the sound of his names: Qar, Qanar, Zominor, Zanor, Azanor, Tanakor, Shanathor, Vagar—do so many of them *have* to end with an "R"? In all fairness to White, though, it should be pointed out that no less an author than Tolkien himself commits the identical error. A glance over the map of his Middle-earth shows country after country with annoyingly similar-sounding names: Mordor, Gondor, Harondor, Arnor, Eriador, Erebor—again, do they *all* have to end with "or"? As far as I can figure it out, Tolkien was operating on the principle that everybody in his imaginary world speaks the same language, or spoke it when the countries were named, anyway, because "or" means "land," according to his system. This rings false to me and I am tempted to consider it a mistaken operating principle on his part. Anyway, it was a mistake in style.

One more example and we shall move on to other matters. Newcomers to the craft should be alerted to the fact that when coining names there is an almost irresistible tendency to make up names which begin with "T." Frankly, I haven't the slightest idea why, but I am aware of the tendency and have to watch out for it in my own novels. Beginners, however, not having noticed this, often go overboard with T-names. As an example, Dave Van Arnam's novel *The Players of Hell* (New York, Belmont, 1968) demonstrates what can happen when this tendency gets out of hand: in the first *twenty* pages of his book, Van Arnam throws no fewer than *eleven* names beginning with "T" at his reader— Taher, Thranor, Tron, Tza, Tir'u, Touraj, Tormitan, Tarmisorn, Tassoran, Tchambar, and Tholk. There is simply no excuse for this; Van Arnam's novel is a short one of about thirty or thirty-five thousand words, and eleven names beginning with the same letter would be too many for even a novel twice that length. Authors who commit this sort of error are simply going to confuse their readers, who can hardly be expected to keep these names straight in their minds, especially names that look and sound as much alike as "Tormitan" and "Tarmisorn" and "Tassoran."

Another letter to watch out for is "S." Again, there

seems to be an almost irresistible tendency for fantasy writers to coin names beginning with that letter. In the same twenty pages, for instance, Van Arnam tosses out Sezain, Shaiphar, Samand, Shagon, and Shassa. Van Arnam fairly rubs his reader's nose in this: in a single sentence in *Players of Hell* (page 83), for instance, he clutters a single phrase with four such names ("deep in the mysteries of Tron and Lord Tir'u and Touraj of the God Lands of Tormitan"), while in the opening sentence of another novel, *Star Gladiator* (Belmont, 1967), he risks seriously confusing readers at the very start of his story by presenting them with two very similar names, this time beginning with "K" ("It was midnight in the capital city of Kallor when the Star Guards . . . struck the planet Kalvar.").

This sort of error is understandable, even forgivable, in the first work of a beginner. In fairness to Van Arnam, I should remark that he has a remarkable talent for name-invention, despite his overuse of names beginning with "S" and "T." *The Players of Hell* offers its readers excellent and memorable names, such as "Azelteram," a fine name for a magician, and "Zantain," which sounds like what it is—the name of a godlike immortal being of unguessable power.

But never underestimate the importance of coined names. "What's in a name?" asks Shakespeare; to which I could answer, "Plenty!" Sometimes a superb name can all but rescue an otherwise inept story. A case in point here is a very forgettable novel by Robert Moore Williams called *King of the Fourth Planet* (New York, Ace Books, 1962), which is almost redeemed—but not quite—by a single brilliantly invented name: "the mighty mountain Suzusilmar."

I have been concentrating on what happens when name-coining is done poorly. When it is done well it is an enduring delight. Much of the magic and beauty of well-coined names lies in the element of mystery, for it seems beyond the power of imagination to *explain* the secret of the charm and lure of such names.

Take, for example, "Barsoom" and "Oz," which are

to me two of the most magically evocative of all names
—but why I feel this I do not really understand. Or the
bizarre rhythm and music of "Uzuldaroum" and "Com-
moriom," the capitals of Hyperborea, or the unearthly
weirdness of "Zothique" and "Xiccarph" and the
"Eiglophian Mountains" and "Mount Voormithadreth,"
and many another name coined by the incomparable
Clark Ashton Smith. The very sources of such magnificent names are beyond conjecture, happily unlike the
over-obviousness of Howard's names, which de Camp
in his exegesis traced to their origins with almost
embarrassing ease.

Burroughs also stands splendidly in the company of
the masters of the naming craft. His "Warhoon" and
"Zodanga" have a wild, barbaric ring of "strangeness"
to them, and he was capable of extraordinary precision
in such names as "the Great Toonoolian Marshes," a
name worthy of Klarkash-Ton in his prime.

And also Lovecraft, who communicated a flavor of
the weirdly alien in such thick, Hebraic-sounding
names: Yuggoth, Yog-Sothoth, R'lyeh, Shub-Niggurath,
and so on. (I have elsewhere discussed at length what
I see as the Hebraic element in such names.)[5] But in
another mood, Lovecraft was also capable of lyrical,
singing, beautifully exotic names, as in those coined
during his early Dunsanian period: the Peaks of Throk,
Pnoth, Mnar, Ooth-Nargai, Thalarion, Ilarnek, Kada-
theron, Aphorat, Oriab, Baharna, and Hlanith on the
Cerenerian Sea.

These are rich and lovely and musical names, and
purely Dunsanian in tone and quality. Which brings us
to Lord Dunsany himself, in this, as in most other
techniques, the supreme artist of the genre. The endless
profusion of gorgeous and exotic names that poured
from his swan's-quill pen are so satisfying, so melodious,
so savory, they beggar comparison:

Goolunza and Poltarness and Babbulkund the City
of Marvel; Allathurion and Sacnoth and Pondar Obed;
holy Zaccarath and Bethmoora and Sardathrion; Peol
Jagganoth and Pungar Vees and that mysterious great

jewel called Ong Zwarba; fair Belzoond and the
Athraminaurian mountains, and Zretazoola the city of
Sombelënë the Centauress . . .

Such names are beyond imitation and their magic is
beyond our ability to explain.

11

The Tricks of the Trade:
Some Advanced Techniques of World-Making

> Every writer making a secondary world . . . wishes to be a real maker, hopes that he is drawing on Reality, or that the peculiar quality of his secondary world (if not all the details) are derived from Reality, or are flowing into it. If he indeed achieves a quality that can fairly be described by the dictionary definition: "inner consistency of reality," it is difficult to conceive how this can be, if the work does not in some way partake of Reality.
>
> —J. R. R. Tolkien: "On Fairy-Stories"

1. The Problem of Magic

WHEN a writer first begins evolving in his imagination, and his notebooks, the raw materials that he intends to shape into an imaginary world, he should think the problem through to its logical ramifications. An imaginary world, one clearly not intended to represent our own either in the remote past or the equally-distant future, is likely to be very different. For one thing, the inclusion of the element of the fantastic, of magic and supernatural forces, presupposes a world governed by a variant system of natural law. That is, despite the convictions of occultists and the *religiosi* of the several faiths, in the actual world magic simply does not work, ghosts simply do not exist, curses are ineffectual, and science has yet to prove the existence of any gods, demons, or genii. An invented world, therefore, that includes the supernatural element must be—has to be

213

—very different from our own. Any writer working in the genre should realize this and should think through all its implications.

For example: *how does magic work?* A detailed literature can be found in our larger libraries on the theory, philosophy, and practice of ceremonial and talismanic magic as believed in and employed throughout the Middle Ages. But that is not quite sufficient for the purposes of fiction: a magician should not be omnipotent in a story, for the possession of absolute power makes him an unbeatable adversary or, if the magician is the protagonist, a hero who cannot possibly get into any tough spot that he cannot easily escape from with a snap of the fingers and a quick "Abracadabra" (or "Shazam"). This, obviously, would rob any story of the important quality of suspense, and can be fatal to sustaining reader interest: who cares what happens to a hero who can't be beaten?

Fantasy writers have usually dealt with this problem by inventing a new system of magic all their own, one with built-in flaws or limitations. The problem is identical with that faced by the writers of the comic strip "Superman": a hero who is invulnerable and super-strong needs some kind of Achilles' heel, hence the invention of *kryptonite,* an imaginary mineral that robs the cloaked crime-fighter of his powers.

Jack Vance, in his brilliant and highly-inventive "Dying Earth" stories, devised an original science of magic consisting of vocalized spells of terrific power. In his story "Turjan of Miir," Vance explains the system thusly, indicating the built-in limitation: "These were volumes compiled by many wizards of the past, untidy folios collected by the Sage, leather-bound librams setting forth the syllables of a hundred powerful spells, *so cogent that Turjan's brain could know but four at a time.*" The italics are my own, but you get the idea. A hundred such spells are known, Vance explains, but the average human brain, upon which they must be impressed by a terrific act of will, *can only hold a few at a time.*

A bit later in the same story, Turjan prepares to set forth on a journey. Any magician who ventures forth from the safe precincts of his tower or palace exposes himself to the myriad perils of this strange future world; Turjan attempts to select only those spells he anticipates he may need:

> He robed himself with a short blue cape, tucked a blade into his belt, fitted the amulet holding Laccodel's Rune to his wrist. Then he sat down and from a journal chose the spells he would take with him. What dangers he might meet he could not know, so he selected three spells of general application: The Excellent Prismatic Spray, Phandaal's Mantle of Stealth, and the Spell of the Slow Hour.

The limitations of this magical system are obvious. Either the magician will encounter perils for which he is unprepared, or he will exhaust his magical armament (since each spell can be used only once), which will make him helpless in the face of further hazards. You will observe that Vance has admirably thought through the implications of the invulnerable magician problem.

Somewhat the same sort of thing may be found in my novel *The Giant of World's End* (New York, Belmont, 1969). My magician, Zelobion of Karchoy, is a master of the School of Phomenic Thaumaturgy—a fancy way of saying he uses spoken spells or cantrips. Although his powers are remarkable, and I have imposed no limitations on the number of thaumaturgies he can wield, it can easily be seen that he would be rendered magically impotent if his enemies simply gagged him— which they do in the ninth chapter, tying him up to be eaten alive by the insatiable Myriapod, from which he is rescued by the superhuman warrior, Ganelon Silvermane. Also (although I did not use the notion in this novel) a simple attack of laryngitis would render him helpless as well.

Similarly, in *The Lord of the Rings,* Professor Tolkien faced the problem of Sauron, a black magician of such immense power that he long ago transcended mortality to become virtually indestructible: he is described almost as a god of evil. Now, any hero, no matter how gallant, is obviously going to be helpless against an antagonist of such strength. Tolkien anticipated the objection by having the greater part of Sauron's power center about his possession of an enormously potent talisman, the "One Ring"; his entire plot revolves around the dual problem of keeping Sauron from obtaining the Ring and, if possible, destroying it before he does gain possession of it.

Another method of handling this technical problem has yet to be demonstrated in my unfinished epic fantasy, *Khymyrium*. Although it is essentially akin to Jack Vance's solution, it has some unique properties. In the world of *Khymyrium*—which is known as "Istradorpha," by the way—a new variety of talismanic magic is employed by which a wizard embues an artifact with Power by a method called Enstarrment. Magical potency derives from the wizard's own life-force, drawn from his flesh by a feat of will. The vital energy resembles a pure, star-like flame through which the talisman is passed; the "charge" can be exhausted through repeated use of the talisman; it can also be drained by use of a conflicting talisman. And, of course, nature itself imposes a limit to the number of talismanic artifacts any wizard of Istradorpha can "Enstarr with Power," since each Enstarrment vitiates a portion of his life-force.

But let us pass on to a brief consideration of some other technical problems of world-making.

2. *The Problem of Realism*

THE fantasy writer, as I have said, must work out the implications of world-invention. For one thing, there must indeed be that "inner consistency of reality" of which Tolkien speaks in his fascinating essay quoted as epigraph to this chapter. A world that has magic in it, *magic that really works,* ought not to have gunpowder. If you have a system of what might be called "practical magic"—magic that does things in the physical world—the physical sciences, such as chemistry, are not only superfluous but somehow out of place.

To coax readers into that mood Coleridge labeled "the willing suspension of disbelief" requires a high order of literary craftsmanship. The fantasy elements in a story that does this are somehow made to seem real, solid, credible. One factor in accomplishing the trick is what I call, for lack of a more appropriate term, "fantastic realism." C. S. Lewis discusses this factor in his insightful little book, *An Experiment in Criticism* (1961):

> This is what I call Realism of Presentation—the art of bringing something close to us, making it palpable and vivid, by sharply observed or sharply imagined detail . . . We should all describe as realistic the exact specifications of size which are given by direct measurements in *Gulliver* or by comparison with well-known objects in the *Divine Comedy*.[1]

The careful use of precise, vividly realized, on-the-spot descriptive detail can work miracles in bringing to life on the page imaginary beings, fantastic scenes, supernatural events. Lewis goes on to list a few examples of what seem to him to be outstandingly realistic imagined details—

1. The dragon "sniffing along the stone" in *Beowulf*.

2. The Arthur, in Layamon's *Brut*, who, on hearing that he had become king, sat very quiet and "one time he was red and one time he was pale."

3. The castle pinnacles in *Sir Gawain and the Green Knight* that looked as if they were "pared out of paper."

4. The fairy bakers in *Huon of Bordeaux* "rubbing the paste off their fingers."

The obvious anomaly about these sample bits of descriptive detail is that none of them are drawn from the kind of fiction we would call "realistic," in the sense that Hardy, say, or Hemingway wrote realistic fiction. Lewis himself was aware of this: "It will be noticed that most of my examples of presentational realism, though I did not select them for that purpose, occur in stories which are not themselves at all 'realistic' in the sense of being probable or even possible."

Lewis goes on to delineate the differences between *realism of content* and *realism of presentation,* two quite different things. He further demonstrates the adumbrations of these: realism of presentation *without* that of content, as in medieval romance; realism of content without that of presentation, as in the dramas of Racine or Sophocles (what we would call "psychological realism," I suppose); the use of both forms of realism together in the same story, as in *War and Peace;* and, finally, the *absence* of either, as in Johnson's *Rasselas* or Voltaire's *Candide.*

To Lewis' list of examples, I would like to add a few of my own:

5. The dragon in Dunsany's story "Carcassone" that had caught a bear and "was playing with it, letting it run a little way and overtaking it with a paw."

6. The new colors, "ulfire" and "jale," visible in the daylight of Tormance, in *A Voyage to Arcturus.*

7. Leigh Brackett's Martian women, who are graceful as cats, bare to the waist, and wear no ornaments but "tiny golden bells woven in their hair" that fill the air with "delicate, wanton chiming" when they move.

8. The stuffed and mounted unicorn's head above the door of the Atlantean magician, in Clark Ashton Smith's story "The Death of Malygris."

The telling bit of realistic detail can be seen again and again in the work of the masters of the genre. Dunsany, for instance, seems to have intuitively grasped the essence of Lewis' argument. Leaf through his pages at complete random and you encounter the vivid touch of realistic observation frequently: the desert city in

"Bethmoora," where "window after window pours into the dusk its *lion-frightening light.*" Or his description of the Inner Lands, in "Poltarnees, Beholder of Ocean," beyond which to the east lies a desert "forever untroubled by man: all yellow it is, and spotted with shadows of stones, and Death is in it, like a leopard lying in the sun," to which he adds the clincher, the small unnecessary detail that says so much—"to the south they are *bounded by magic.*" Or the travelers in "Idle Days on the Yann," who reach Astahahn, a city of ancientness so remote in origin that its carven walls picture "beasts that have long since passed away from Earth—the dragon, the griffin and the hippogriffin, and *the eleven species of gargoyle.*" Or the cottage of the witch Ziroonderel in *The King of Elfland's Daughter,* high in the uplands "near the thunder, which used to roll in Summer along the hills," and how the witch forges for Prince Alveric an enchanted sword made from seventeen thunderbolts "gathered from *under her cabbages.*" Or the ivory gate of Perdóndaris, also in "Idle Days on the Yann," which was carved out of *"one solid piece"* of ivory. How much he conveys in that single phrase! Imagine the Behemoth so incredibly huge that an entire city gate could be carved from *one tusk.* Or the archers of Tor, in "The Probable Adventures of the Three Literary Men," who loose ivory arrows "at all strangers, lest any foreigner should alter their laws"— which are bad laws, but *"not to be altered by mere aliens."*

It is for touches such as these that we consider Lord Dunsany, quite simply, the greatest fantasy writer of them all.

AT first thought, the intrusion of realistic, even homely detail into splendid scenes of high heroic fantasy would seem almost a contradiction in terms. "All magic dies at the touch of the commonplace," Lewis remarked to Jane Gaskell in the letter quoted from earlier. But the more you think of it, the more obvious it becomes that we enjoy reading a fantastic scene all the more when it is intensely realized on the page, brought into sharp visual focus, rendered with sensuous immediacy through imaginative effort. There is a certain innate pleasure in reading of dragons and castles and magicians *per se,* but that pleasure is intensified when the scene is made vivid through carefully-chosen, crisp detail.

"All magic dies at the touch of the commonplace." *Au contraire:* far from withering before the homely bit of detail, Faërie can actually be enhanced by it. In fantasy *of a certain type,* anyway. The factor that enlivens Pratt and de Camp's charming "Harold Shea" stories, and the so-called *Unknown*-type fantasy in general, is the application of *reason and logic* to the element of pure fantasy.

In other words, it is not always enough just to put a traditional fire-breathing dragon into a yarn; in certain kinds of fantasy it is often most effective to rationalize your dragons, to envision exactly how they work, to visualize them within the story-context as if they were actual zoölogical specimens encountered amidst a genuine landscape. (I am not saying that this can or even should be done in *all* fantasies, only in some.) Robert A. Heinlein accomplished this trick quite cleverly in his sole venture into heroic fantasy, a richly entertaining novel called *Glory Road* (New York, Putnam's, 1963). His hero, Oscar, reacts incredulously to the assertion that he is shortly to encounter a real live fire-breathing dragon out of the storybooks. The heroine, Star, explains the nature of the beast thusly:

> They don't exactly *breathe* fire. That would kill them. They hold their breaths while flaming. It's swamp gas —methane—from the digestive tract. It's a controlled belch, with a hypergolic effect from an enzyme secreted between the first and second rows of teeth. The gas bursts into flame on the way out.

The tale, by the way, is a slangy modern variant of heroic fantasy rich with colloquial detail and most of the components of fantastic realism we have looked at so far. If the draconian digestive process seems at all unlikely, Heinlein forestalls your critique by remarking: "No evolutionary quirk can be considered odd if you use the way octopi make love as a comparison"—an aside that sent me scurrying to a text on marine biology, I might add.

Heinlein, of course, cut his teeth (professionally speaking) on realistic modern science fiction—not at all a bad training-ground for fantasy writing. Poul Anderson is another graduate of the John W. Campbell School of Realistic World-Making, and oddly enough, he took a similarly factualizing look at "how dragons work" in the course of his fantasy novel, *Three Hearts and Three Lions,* published two years before *Glory Road.* In that book, Holger Carlsen is attacked by a fire-breathing member of the species while crossing a stream; he snatches off his helmet, scoops it full of water, and gives it to the brute right in the kisser. A muffled explosion ensues, and the dragon limps painfully away—

> Look, if the creature breathed fire, then it had to be even hotter inside. So I tossed half a gallon of water down its gullet. Caused a small boiler explosion.

3. The Problem of "Business"

INTIMATELY associated with the above techniques of infusing a story with "fantastic realism" is another trick for which I have found no better name than "business."

"Business" is what theatre people call the little extra touches actors put into their stage activities. That is, while one actor is speaking to another, the second attempts to "react realistically" to the situation. He strives to infuse his stage presence with the illusion of normalcy: he may fidget with a clutter of tabletop ornaments, light a cigarette, scratch his knee. I recall Ingrid Bergman listening through a long scene in a recent Broadway performance of Bernard Shaw's *Captain Brassbound's Conversion.* Another character had a speech of considerable length; Miss Bergman had nothing to do, script-wise, but had to be on stage throughout the scene. Where a lesser actress might have just sat there woodenly, waiting for her next cue, Miss Bergman made a casual production out of removing her hat, adjusting her coiffure, brushing the dust of travel from her skirts, and neatening the folds and ruffles of her gown, all the while listening and reacting to the other actor's words with the mercurial play of expression across her features.

That was "business."

Now, by "business" in fantasy I mean the added touch of vivid detail that some writers omit but wiser artists daub into a "dull but necessary" stretch of prose. For example: suppose, for sheer plot-reasons, you must get your characters from "here" to "there." Some writers will simply "cut" to the next scene, as in a movie dissolve. Others, obviously more sensitive to style and mood, will suggest the passing-through-scenery with a telling flash of detail that illuminates the magical mood and atmosphere so vital to a fantasy.

Frequently, the better artists in the genre will use "business" to make memorable, to "characterize," a geographical place. Lovecraft is among the masters of this technique: in "Celephaïs," Kuranes strolls down a street—not just any street, but "the Street of Pillars"; in "The Silver Key," a passing reference to Narath is enriched by reference to "its hundred carven gates and domes of chalcedony"; in *The Dream-Quest of Unknown Kadath,* mentioning Ulthar, Lovecraft remarks that in that city, "according to an ancient and significant law, no man may kill a cat"; in the same novel, mentioning a city called Sarkomand, he singles out its "huge winged lions of diorite."

As you can see, the margins between "fantastic realism" and what I call "business" are blurred and dubious. However, the pertinent thing here is the vivid descriptive detail that makes an image or scene memorable, as opposed to just real. In this respect, at least, the same novel, *The Dream-Quest of Unknown Kadath,* is worth a slow, thoughtful reading by the aspiring fantasy writer. Time and again, Lovecraft minutely pinpoints the flavor of his imaginary locale with the telling stroke of corroborative detail. His hero, Randolph Carter, does not just go into Earth's Dreamlands —*zing!*—like that; he goes "down the seven hundred onyx steps and through the Gates of Deeper Slumber." A stone image glimpsed in passing is nailed down with the information that it was "carved on the solid rock of the mountain Ngranek, on the isle of Oriab, in the Southern Sea." The city of Celephaïs is not thrust baldly upon us, but presented with a sketch of surrounding landscape: Celephaïs, "in the land of Ooth-Nargai, beyond the Tanarian Hills."

Another writer who employed "business" brilliantly was E. R. Eddison. In *Mistress of Mistresses,* when the High Admiral Jeronimy is introduced, Eddison notes that he wore about his neck "the kingly order of the hippogriff." In *The Worm Ouroboros* he tosses off the remarkable information that his Mercurians have horns by observing, amidst a summary of the appearance of the Lord Zigg of Demonland, that "his horns were dyed with saffron, and inlaid with filigree work of gold." In that same novel, the seventh chapter, the protagonist, King Gorice of Carcë, makes a dramatic entrance; his costume is described, but the telling bit of unnecessary "business" that specifically characterizes him is the description of his cloak, which was "of the skins of black cobras, *stitched together with gold wire.*" So much can be conveyed through the choice use of selected detail!

Another superb use of "business" can be seen earlier in the same book, in chapter three, after the famous wrestling-scene. Eddison tosses off a completely unnecessary "extra" bit of scenic color following the dance of the Kagu (which would, in itself, have been sufficient "color" to carry the scene for any writer less prodigal in his imaginative invention than Eddison). I refer to the solemn, grave dance of the adorable Catbears, who are "foxy-red above but with black bellies, round furry faces, and innocent amber eyes, and soft great paws, and tails barred alternately with ruddy rings and creamy." The Red Foliot bids the plump, solemn furry creatures "dance the Gigue." At the conclusion of the dance, "standing side by side, paw in furry paw, they bowed shyly to the company, and the Red Foliot called them to him and *kissed them on the mouth.*"

This scene was not needed for mood or color—the dance of the Kagu alone would have sufficed. The scene, therefore, is pure *lagniappe.*

"Business" is almost always pure *lagniappe.* Be advised.

4. The Problem of Flora and Fauna

FURTHER corroborative detail, and a final example of "thinking things through," can be seen in the area of zoölogy, or whatever. When a fantasy world is clearly specified as a non-terrestrial planet, like Barsoom or Xiccarph or my own Zarkandu and Iridar, it should not include familiar earthly birds and beasts. This seems to me such an obvious point that I will not belabor it. Considering how obvious it is, however, it is somewhat surprising how few authors in the genre seem to have thought things through to this realization.

Eddison himself is an example of this. I have already cited his use of "Irish yews" on the planet Mercury—a glaring anamundism. Nor is he alone in this: Leiber's Nehwon, Jake's Para-Terra, Andre Norton's Witch World, and de Camp's world of *The Goblin Tower* and *The Clocks of Iraz* commit similar errors. Why do they do this? Fritz Leiber has people riding around on horses. Now, I grant you, the inhabitants of an imaginary world are likely to employ some local, easily-domesticated beast for the purpose of transportation—but why must they be familiar, everyday *Equus caballus*? Even as klutzy a writer as Jane Gaskell, whose use of the most blatant anachronisms has already met with severe criticism in these pages, has her Atlanteans mounted on huge birds like ostriches or emus.

Fritz Leiber argues the point in a recent article published in the fanzine *Anduril,* the bulletin of the Tolkien Society in Great Britain:[2]

> Futile to ask how there could be men, horses, and yew trees on this world [i.e., Eddison's Mercury] . . . In America, Hal Clement, James Blish, L. Sprague de Camp and others have detailedly stated the proper methods for building up a non-solar imaginary planet . . . it will certainly have a different biology . . . but science fiction is not fantasy, *which must only be self-consistent,* not science-consistent.

Fritz has a logical point here, surely. He goes on, regarding his own Nehwon, to reason: "Most of its inhabitants are men, and so it is equally natural that there should be horses, cats, dogs, pine-trees."

There is much to be said for Leiber's position on this question. And in his defense, as well as John Jakes' and Miss Norton's, I should in all fairness point out that there is considerable internal evidence that Witch World and Nehwon and Para-Terra (de Camp's *Goblin Tower* planet, too) impinge upon our earth at various points of history and geography, as does Katherine Kurtz's world of *Deryni Rising* and its sequels. Such worlds are clearly supposed to be very close to ours in space/time, separated along the time dimension, maybe, but at any rate definitely "parallel worlds," in the parlance of science fiction.

On the other hand, just what is wrong with constructing fantasy worlds according to the Clementine/ Blishian/de Campesque formula of science fiction world-making? That it has seldom, if ever, been done is no argument against its theoretical validity. In my unfinished *Khymyrium,* I am attempting to do exactly that: build a fantasy world through the techniques evolved by modern science fiction.

Another world, quite simply, ought not to have terrestrial birds and beasts. There is no reason why the author cannot simply invent outré analogues of the mundane creatures. Let's look at this theory in practice, citing actual examples, and see if it "works."

HERETOFORE, the method used in most fantasies was to have people riding around on horses, through forests of oak and pine, hunting unicorns with hounds, and so on. (Recall the splendid Unicorn-Hunt scene in Dunsany's *The King of Elfland's Daughter?* Of course, the whole point of Dunsany's work is that he makes unicorns and magic and elves a part of the *human* scene.) But, strictly speaking, it *is* committing an anamundism to do this, and it *can* be avoided, if a writer wishes to bother.

Some writers seem to have recognized the problem of anamundism and avoid it in interesting ways. Burroughs, for example, has created a unique, original biosphere for his imaginary version of Mars. In place of the horse, his characters ride about on eight-legged mammals he calls "thoats"; for heavy draft-animals like oxen, he invents the mastodonic "zitidars." He is to be praised for having carried his solution to its logical conclusions: Barsoom does not even have cats and dogs; in place of these domestic pets Burroughs introduces the "calot" and the "sorak."

In the course of his Martian series, Burroughs added to his Barsoomian bestiary. There is the "apt," a six-limbed, white-furred Arctic beast; the hairless, lion-like "banth"; and yet other creatures—the "darseen," the "orluk," and so on. These are, most of them, well visualized and quite original. Burroughs followed much the same practice in his Venus and Pellucidar books, too.

The admirable thing about Burroughs' use of this technique is that he *designs and invents* new beasts, rather than merely putting ordinary horses on Mars and calling them "thoats." Consider his "calot," for instance. This Martian "hound" was first introduced in *A Princess of Mars* thusly:

In response to her call I obtained my first sight of a new Martian wonder. It waddled in on its ten short legs, and squatted down before the girl like an obedient puppy. The thing was about the size of a Shetland pony, but its head bore a slight resemblance to that of a frog, except that the jaws were equipped with three rows of long, sharp tusks.

The Martian girl assigns the brute to keep watch over Burroughs' Earthman hero, John Carter, who playfully eludes the ferocious-looking beast and is attacked by an ape-like monster. The Martian watchdog, Woola, follows his charge and battles the ape-thing, which all but slays him. Carter watches the conflict and find himself strangely moved with compassion for the loyal, if hideous, watchdog:

Presently I saw the great eyes of my beast bulging completely from their sockets and blood flowing from its nostrils. That he was weakening perceptibly was evident . . . his great eyes fastened upon me in what seemed a pitiful appeal for protection. I could not withstand that look . . .

Carter takes up a weapon and battles the ape-creature himself. Later, his green-skinned Martian captors happen along; they are about to callously dispatch the mangled watchdog, but Carter strikes aside the pistol, saving the life of the faithful calot. The passage concludes:

I had at least two friends on Mars; a young woman who watched over me with motherly solicitude, and a dumb brute which, as I later came to know, held in its poor ugly carcass more love, more loyalty, more gratitude than could have been found in the entire five million green Martians who rove the deserted cities and dead sea bottoms of Mars.

While this passage may, to some, seem overly sentimental, anyone who has owned a dog knows the depth of affection and simple love that such a beast is capable of. What Burroughs has done here, quite cleverly, is to capture the *essence* of "doggishness," and in his skillful sketch of Woola "the faithful Martian hound," he transfers those qualities to a beast of his own invention.

Moreover, he has found the Proper Name. Thipdar, banth, thoat, zitidar—such names have an innate rightness to them that can be sensed and recognized, but never quite explained. In contrast with the aptness of Burroughsian names, even his best contemporary imitator, Otis Adelbert Kline, comes off markedly inferior —in this respect, at least. A glance through one of Kline's novels selected at random, *The Prince of Peril*, demonstrates how feebly Kline tries to coin names. His names for Venusian beasts are clumsy and awkward— "ordzook," for example—and his Venusian nomenclature in general displays little facility for neocognomina. Zovil, Zinlo, scarbo, kova, Urg, Uxpo, Azpok, Ropok, Rogvoz—these names are simply awful. They have a dreary, bisyllabic sameness of sound, and a quality of uncouth ugliness.

In my own Lemurian books, I followed the example of Burroughs in creating a biosphere and attempting to match the look and sound of the invented names to the nature of the beast. "Phondle" seems to me an excellent name for a plump, gazelle-like creature; "kroter" is my name for the Lemurian analogue of the horse, and "zamph" for a lumbering triceratops-like beast of burden. I am also pleased with names like "deodath," the ferocious dragon-cat of the Kovian jungles, "poa," a carnivorous river-serpent, and "vandar," a species of majestic, black-furred Lemurian lion. Sometimes, however, my Lemurian nomenclature fails to satisfy me: "grakk," my name for the pterodactyl, "dwark," an immense jungle dinosaur, and "larth," or some kind of plesiosaur—these names seem to me now as awkward and poorly-conceived as the worst of Kline's coinage.

It cannot but assist a writer in creating and maintaining that "inner consistency of reality" of which Tolkien speaks, if his system of invented nomenclature is continuous throughout the novel. A world which has "kroters" and "zamphs" instead of horses and oxen, ought also to have its own invented flowers, trees, metals, and jewels. It seems to me that you are only doing half your job if, after inventing new analogues for lions, horses, dogs, or cattle, you lapse lamely into mentioning oak trees or rose bushes or emeralds.

And why should you? Burroughs invented new trees for his Barsoom—"sorapus" and "pimalia." Is there anything so difficult about the technique?

Some writers have recognized this and have fleshed out their invented worldscapes with interesting new verbal devices. Lovecraft, with his "Shantak-birds" and "Night-Gaunts" and "Dholes," is a case in point. Dunsany is rich in this kind of invented nomenclature: his story "In Zaccarath" mentions that torches "soaked in rare Bhyrinian oils, burned and gave off a scent of blethany"; another story, "Bethmoora," mentions a wine made of the "syrabub"; new musical instruments appear in his World's Edge stories—"men beat the tambang and the tittibuk, and blew melodiously the zootibar"; new coins, called "piffeks," appear in "Idle Days on the Yann," as do "toomarund" carpets, and a kind of food or drink called "tollub."[3]

It *can* be done, then; and I see no reason why it should not.

In brief, a new world should be new all the way, an imaginative invention from the magma up, so to speak. "Make it new," Ezra Pound advises regarding verse. The maxim makes sense for prose as well, at least in the context of this particular genre.

Fritz Leiber has called attention to an apparent fallacy in this theory of mine. In the course of a review of my anthology *New Worlds for Old* in Ted White's magazine *Fantastic,* he remarked:

> This method has at least one almost unsurmountable drawback: no matter how many strange animals and weird intelligent tribes there be on such a world, its chief inhabitants must, especially in a fantasy, be men, or else very like men.

The observation is a shrewd one, but not one with which I must necessarily agree. Burroughs' oviparous red Martians and giant four-armed green Tharks are sufficiently unlike *Homo sapiens* to suggest that perhaps their creator was hinting at undelineated strangenesses beyond even these. Eddison's Mercurian denizens of Demonland, with their small burnished horns (and, as Leiber asks, do their Witchland adversaries also possess small rudimentary tails?), may be less human than we think, the token variation from the terrene norm suggesting a greater alienness left undescribed.

It should not be impossible to write a Sword and Sorcery novel, set on another planet, whose intelligent dwellers are descended, say, from reptiles rather than mammals. To pull the trick off would require considerable research into the sex-life, dietary habits, and other similar details concerning the smaller Miocene carnivora. But it *could* be done . . .

Something of that nature will come out in my own *Khymyrium*. The inhabitants of Istradorpha, I now think, will have small rudimentary horns like those of Eddison's Mercurians. It may be a faulty bit of reasoning on my part, but I seem to have trapped myself into the idea, for I have already discerned to my own satisfaction that the mammals of Istradorpha all have horns—hence, the people must, as well. This may prove, in the end, a disastrous notion. For one thing, it is bound to cause some readers to criticize me for "imitating Eddison," but I am always accused of being a rank imitator anyway, so it will be nothing new. The point is that my Istradorphans are behorned *for a reason*—because all the mammals in the biosphere of *Khymyrium* have horns.

My Istradorphans will also have an extra sense unknown to those who dwell here in the Fields We Know, and an extra sense organ as well, whose name I have not yet discovered. The sense organ gives them the unique power to perceive the aura of magical force about an ensorcelled artifact, or the emanations of Power from a supernatural personage. This, too, was devised for a reason—in this case, a plot reason, concerning which I will say only (and rather mysteriously, I'm afraid) that it permits them to perceive *the Shaar,* by which is meant "the Glory." But of this I shall speak in another place and another book.

The horns and the new sensory organ should be understood as a sign that however much the dwellers upon Istradorpha may seem to resemble humankind, it is not to be taken for granted that they are like us. They are very different—but more on this some other time.

THE conclusion, then, is that Fritz Leiber may well be wrong in his opinion that the characters in all fantasy novels must, in the end, be "merely human." Not all of Tolkien's characters can so be described, nor the inhabitants of Tormance, nor the shadowy dwellers upon the Night Land, nor the Old Ones who ruled the Witch World before the coming of men, nor Zerd of Atlan, nor the deodands of the Dying Earth, nor the elves and trolls whereof Poul Anderson so eloquently writes, nor the Dragon Kings of my prehistoric Lemuria.

The great fantasy that will be written in the future remains an unpredictable quantity in our calculations. We cannot discuss books yet unwritten, stories yet untold, songs yet unsung. However, we may safely assume that some of the fantasy writers of tomorrow are among those of you who are reading this book today. I hope that this book has made clear to you the splendid and rich tradition of fantasy literature, its origins, its endless variety, its inexhaustible potential, and something of the rules by which it may be, and has been, written.

It is for you to break or augment or circumvent the rules, and to devise new ones. It is for you to experiment with and employ, to discard or evolve yet further, the writing techniques described here. And it is for you to add new masterpieces to the many I have listed and discussed here.

Beckford, Macdonald, Morris, Burroughs, Dunsany, Cabell, Eddison, Merritt, Lovecraft, Smith, Lewis, Pratt,

Bok, Howard, and Kuttner are dead. Their achievements were unique and they themselves are irreplaceable. New writers will continue to enter the ranks of the world-makers and will contribute new works to the canon of fantastic literature, that great and rich body of work which began forming long before our lives began, and which will continue to grow and develop long after we are gone from the Fields We Know to drink peace of the Well and rest under the heights of Pegāna, for—

> *Each age is a dream that is dying,*
> *Or one that is coming to birth.*[*]

THE END

Notes

Introduction

1. The epigraph from Samuel Johnson (1709–1784) is from his poem "Prologue at the Opening of Drury Lane Theatre" (1747). He was thinking of William Shakespeare, but his text may be construed, I think, to refer to fantasy writers in general.

2. These quotations are from the early Dunsanian period of H. P. Lovecraft. The first four are from "Celephais" (1920), as is the general epigraph of this book itself, which you will find on page 17; the fifth is from "The Silver Key" (1926).

3. Quotations are from the novel by Robert E. Howard, *Conan the Conqueror* (New York: 1950), p. 2.

4. Pioneer science fiction pulp magazine publisher Hugo Gernsback was born in Luxembourg in 1884 and emigrated to this country while still in his teens. He became interested in the burgeoning new field of electrical and radio mechanics, and got into publishing in 1905 by issuing a catalog of radio parts, the first such ever printed. His early magazines, such as *The Electrical Experimenter,* occasionally ran light fiction on technical matters when science articles were scarce. Noting that readers' reactions to these stories were unusually enthusiastic, Gernsback tried an all-fiction issue in 1923, and eventually launched a new magazine called *Amazing Stories,* which appeared on the newsstands on April 5, 1926, and is recognized as the first science fiction magazine in the world. Earlier magazines, such as *Thrill Book* and *Weird Tales,* had published science fiction before Gernsback's *Amazing Stories,* but not exclusively, burying it among a potpourri of weird, fantasy, and adventure fiction, Incidentally, Gernsback's original neologism for this new kind of story was "Scientifiction"; he did not coin the term "science fiction" until 1929. See Sam Moskowitz' book, *Explorers of the Infinite* (Cleveland, 1963), pp. 225–242.

5. Fletcher Pratt and L. Sprague de Camp, in their popular series of "Harold Shea" stories for Street & Smith's fantasy magazine *Unknown,* used for settings the worlds of

Irish, Norse and Finnish myth; more recently, Thomas Burnett Swann has written a number of fantasy novels set in the world of Roman mythology. The only fantasy utilizing American Indian folklore for its background, or at least the only one known to me, is Andre Norton's book *Fur Magic*.

Chapter 1.

1. Gilgamesh seems to have been an historical king of Uruk (the Bible calls it "Erech") in the southern part of Babylonia; he built the city wall, which, by the way, still stands—or portions of it, anyway. Scholars believe that various myths, floating around loose in the folk-culture, became attached to his name, and that *c*. 2000 B.C. these myths were woven together into an epic poem by an anonymous hand. The text of the poem, in the form of twelve tablets of baked clay inscribed in cuneiform, each containing a song or canto of about 300 lines on the average, was discovered in the middle of the 19th century when Sir Austen Henry Layard excavated the library of Assurbanipal in Nineveh. It went to the British Museum along with a miscellany of other tablets and fragments of tablets, and its importance was not realized until 1862, when another scholar, George Smith, noticed that one of the tablets in the collection gave an account of the Flood which had amazing parallels with the story of Noah in the Bible. Now, independent corroborative evidence of Old Testament mythology is hard to come by, and as you can imagine, Smith's discovery aroused intense interest, which led in time to the fragmented epic being pieced together and translated. What they had was the Late Babylonian translation of an immeasurably earlier Sumerian original, written down *a thousand years* before the Book of Genesis! (A second copy of the *Gilgamesh epic* was later discovered, and is now in American museums.) The best translation known to me is that of William Ellery Leonard, *Gilgamesh: Epic of Old Babylonia*, (New York, Viking, 1934); concerning its antiquity, Leonard's preface calls the epic "older by many centuries than any other great poem in the world." About nine Sumerian epics have now been unearthed, averaging between 100 and 600 lines, and most of them are as yet incomplete, but the longest of them all, called *Enmerkar and the Lord of Aratta*, runs to

some twenty tablets. See Samuel Noah Kramer's *From the Tablets of Sumer*, first published in 1956, for an excellent introduction to known Sumerian literature. Kramer believes the *Enmerkar* to be the oldest of the epics, pre-dating the *Gilgamesh;* but the last word on the subject has yet to be written, and anyway, the *Enmerkar* is a fantasy, too.

2. We have no really reliable evidence as to the dates of Homer; however, it is thought that an authoritative Athenian text of the *Odyssey* was established by the second half of the 6th century B.C. In India, the classic age of the Vedic hymns began *c.* 1000 B.C. and was over by about 800 B.C. The *Rig-veda*, for example, is usually dated at *c.* 1000 B.C. The *Mahabharata*, an epic of enormous length, with an immense cast of characters and a plot of incredible complexity—but quite readable, for all of that— was composed about the 4th century B.C., runs to some 100,000 stanzas, and is attributed to the mythic sage Vyasa. Akhnaten, or Akhenaton, or Iknaton—take your pick (also known as Amenhotep IV, or Amonhotep IV, or Amenophis IV, but we won't go into *that*)—was a Pharaoh of what historians call the 18th Dynasty and archaeologists refer to as the Amarna period. He is the famous "heretic king" who, at a rough estimate, invented monotheism one hundred and ten years before Moses; he abolished the state religion, closed the temples, and moved the capital to a new city that he had built in honor of his newly-invented solitary divinity, Aton, whose chief symbol was the sun-disc. The priests brought things back to a normal state of utter pantheism as soon as his brief reign ended, and his religion did not long survive him (about twenty minutes, maybe). However, his mighty *Hymn to the Sun* is one of the most glorious religious poems in all of literature. You can find it in any of several anthologies of world poetry, and it's worth looking up. As for the Bible, it is considerably less ancient than is commonly thought. The individual books were *not* written in the order in which they now appear, but were rearranged into the present sequence by the compilers of the Septuagint version during the first three centuries of the Christian era; hence it is not at once obvious which part of the Old Testament is the most ancient, but it was certainly not Genesis. The first rough draft of Genesis was written down in Judah in the 9th or 10th centuries B.C. by an unknown writer with a vivid, picturesque style. Biblical scholars call him "J" from his

characteristic use of the names "Yahweh" or "Jehovah" for God. Sometime after J, a second writer, who lived in the northern kingdom, rewrote this first draft, working in certain legends and traditions common to his part of the country; from his characteristic use of the name "Elohim" for God, scholars refer to him as "E." Not long after the northern kingdom fell in 722 B.C., a third compiler selected what he liked from both the J and E versions, and produced a composite text, called JE. This final redaction was the nucleus around which the Mosaic scriptures accumulated, and is what we know today as Genesis. While the earliest draft of Genesis is of fair antiquity, the oldest single part of the Bible is thought by some to be the fifth chapter of Judges, the so-called "Song of Deborah," which may date from 1100 B.C.

3. The *Popol Vuh* is the oldest book we have that was written in the western hemisphere. It is a rambling jumble of cosmogony, mythological texts, and history, rather like the Bible. In fact it is often referred to as the Bible of the Quiché, a branch of the ancient Mayan empire situated in Guatemala. The kingdom of the Quiché Mayans survived well into the time of Columbus, but they did not for very long survive the coming of those civilized and charming Christian gentlemen, the Spanish Conquistadores, who, in their eagerness to rescue the poor heathens from idolatry, murdered several million of them in the process of converting them to the gentle ways of the True Faith. The *Popol Vuh* is a mythological textbook and not a narrative. It existed from an unknown date in oral tradition and was not written down until the middle of the 16th century, when a literate Indian preserved it for us in the original Quiché language, using the Latin alphabet. One Father Francisco Ximénez, parish priest of the largest of the Indian towns in Guatemala, copied it toward the end of the 17th century from this original manuscript, which has since been lost. (Father Ximénez was something of a rarity among the gentlemen of the cloth in his time; his coreligionists spent most of their time on the job burning entire Pre-Columbian national literatures, believing these works to be inspired by the Devil. One such was Diego de Landa, the jolly Bishop of Yucatán, who consigned the entire literature of the Mayans to the bonfire because it consisted of nothing but "superstition and lies." He was

quite thorough: only five pieces of a vast literature survived, one of them the *Popol Vuh*.)

As for the *Instruction* of Ptah-hotep, which is sometimes called "the oldest book in the world," it is a slender treatise on morals, a collection of precepts, and not a narrative, either. Ptah-hotep was one of several viziers or prime ministers to the Pharaonic court during the period known as the Middle Kingdom, that is, the 11th to 13th Dynasties, according to the present system. Dating the Egyptian reigns is a complicated problem upon which the several schools of thought have yet to come to full agreement. Battiscombe Gunn, who rendered Ptah-hotep into English, used the now-discredited Flinders Petrie chronological system, which puts Ptah-hotep back some four thousand years before the Christian era. More recent writers settle on 2100–1700 B.C., a span of four centuries, for the period of the Middle Kingdom. Unfortunately, we don't know for certain in just which part of those four centuries Ptah-hotep flourished. For a modern chronology of the Middle Kingdom, see Leonard Cottrell's book, *The Lost Pharaohs* (New York, Holt, Rinehart and Winston, 1961).

4. The Siegfried legend occurs in many variant forms in the literatures of Northern Europe. It first appears in the *Elder Edda*, which was written down in Iceland about 1200 A.D., but dates back centuries in oral tradition. In that version the dragon-slaying hero is called "Sigurth" and his sword is called "Gram." After Saemund the Wise compiled the *Elder Edda*, Snorri Sturluson wrote one of his own, called the *Prose Edda*. In his version of the tale, Sigurth becomes "Sigurd" (or Sigurdr) and Gram becomes "Gramr." About 1270 A.D., thirty years after Snorri Sturluson was murdered by his son-in-law, another Icelandic sage, this time an anonymous one, retold stories from the *Elder Edda* in a work called the *Völsunga Saga*. In this one we are back to Sigurd and Gram again. Of course, the story—one of the world's greatest—has a lengthy history outside of Icelandic literature. In *Beowulf*, XIII, at the victory-feast King Hrothgar threw to celebrate the killing of Grendel and his monstrous mother, a *scop* sings to entertain the Geatish princeling: in subtle compliment to Beowulf's deed, the song is about another monster-slaying hero, here called "Sigemund." Gram is mentioned but not named. And, of course, the great German na-

tional epic, *Nibelungenlied,* is entirely built around the story. In this one the dragon-slayer is called "Siegfried" and his sword, acquired in a different way than in the Icelandic versions, "Balmung." When Wagner came along to turn the epic into opera, he attempted to reconcile the plot as given in the *Völsunga Saga* and the plot of the *Nibelungenlied;* in his version, Siegfried remains Siegfried but the sword was renamed "Nothung." So, depending on which version of this oft-told tale you are familiar with, the hero's name is Sigurth, Sigurdr, Sigurd, Sigemund, or Siegfried, and his magic sword either Gram, Balmung, Gramr, or Nothung. You pays your money and you takes your cherce. The development of this legend is explored in far greater detail in my book *Tolkien: A Look Behind "The Lord of the Rings"* (New York, Ballantine, 1965), pp. 152-165.

5. It sounds Shakespearian enough to my ear, anyway. Tennyson is no longer in favor, either with the college-age kids, who haven't read enough and can't be expected to know better, or with most of their professors, who have, and should. However, this is largely due to that deplorable and silly (but virtually universal) tendency of each new generation to find its grandmother's taste in poetry as laughable as her choice of hats. At their best, certain of the *Idylls* have an enchanting music to them, as in this scene: Bedivere's poignant cry of agony and loss to his dying king as the Three Queens take Arthur on board the mystic barge bound for Avalon—

> Ah! my lord Arthur, whither shall I go?
> Where shall I hide my forehead and my eyes?
> For now I see the true old times are dead,
> When every morning brought a noble chance,
> And every chance brought out a noble knight.
> Such times have not been since the light that led
> The holy Elders with the gift of myrrh.
> But now the whole Round Table is dissolved
> Which was an image of the mighty world;
> And I, the last, go forth companionless,
> And the days darken round me, and the years,
> Among new men, strange faces, other minds.

Or this: the strange, haunting vision Tennyson uses to describe the ultramundane isle of Avalon—

Where falls not hail, or rain, or any snow,
Nor ever wind blows loudly; but it lies
Deep-meadow'd, happy, fair with orchard-lawns,
And bowery hollows crown'd with summer sea.

Great stuff!

6. In his famous speech, "The Art and Craft of the Machine," which he gave at Hull-House in the Chicago slums in 1901, and which is regarded as a turning-point in the history of modern architecture, Frank Lloyd Wright said: "All artists love and honor William Morris. That he miscalculated the machine does not matter. He did sublime work for it when he pleaded so well for the process of elimination its abuse had made necessary; when he fought the innate vulgarity of theocratic impulse in art as opposed to democratic; and when he preached the gospel of simplicity." Toulouse-Lautrec is quoted by Henri Nocq in his *Tendances Nouvelles* as saying: "Je crois qu'il n'y a qu'à regarder William Morris, pour avoir une réponse à toutes vos questions."

7. *Waverly* was published in 1814; Morris was born in 1834.

8. Not in 1895, as I erroneously stated in my introduction to the Ballantine edition of *The Wood Beyond the World*. A limited de luxe edition appeared first in 1894, with the larger and less-expensive trade edition coming the following year.

Chapter 2.

1. Or so claims Padraic Colum in his introduction to the Modern Library edition of Dunsany's *A Dreamer's Tales and Other Stories* (New York: no date, but prob. 1917). In fact, Colum says "the domains, the castles and the titles" date from "the thirteenth century," and not from the 12th century, as I have it. However, the Norman Conquest of Ireland took place in the reign of Henry II, the king of Anjou who succeeded to the English throne at the death of Stephen; and Henry, the first of the Plantagenets, reigned from 1154 to 1189, which makes it the 12th century. At any rate, and whenever the first Plunkett arrived in Ireland, the title of Baron Dunsany was not created until 1439, when Christopher Plunkett became

the first baron of the line. He was the second son of
another Christopher Plunkett, the Sir Christopher who had
served his king as deputy Lord Lieutenant of Ireland from
1432 to 1445. A correspondent, John Boardman, Ph.D.,
an English instructor at Brooklyn College, suggests that
the barony was created to curry favor among the British
nobility resident in Ireland during a time when the Duke
of York was attempting to win the active support of the
Anglo-Irish aristocracy in his bid for the crown.

2. Most of the information given here on Dunsany's
life and career is drawn from the first volume of his
autobiography, a book entitled *Patches of Sunlight* (New
York, Reynal & Hitchcock, 1938).

3. For example, the first line of the *Njals Saga* reads:
"There was a man named Mord whose surname was
Fiddle; he was the son of Sigvat the Red, and he dwelt
at the Vale in the Rangrivervales." See *The Story of Burnt
Njal,* the translation by Sir George Dasent (New York,
Baker & Taylor; no date, but first published in England
in 1861).

4. Orville Prescott, from his Introduction to a recent
edition of *The Worm Ouroboros,* published in 1952, by
Doubleday.

5. *Sintram and His Companions* is a novel written by
the German novelist and poet, Friedrich, Baron de La
Motte-Fouqué (1777–1843), whose most famous work is
the verse-play *Undine.*

6. See her charming and informative Introduction to
the 1958 reprint edition of her father's novel.

7. I do not know this for certain, but I strongly suspect
that Saxton's book incorporates some of the unpublished
material from the main body of the Islandia papers. At
least, I would be very surprised to learn that this was not
the case.

Chapter 3.

1. A curiously Merrittesque short story has recently
been discovered in the back files of *The American Weekly.*
Signed with the otherwise completely unknown name of
W. Fennimore, this story, "The Pool of the Stone God,"
has all the earmarks of being an early Merritt story, or a
rough draft of a story. It is the opinion of the leading

Merritt scholar and bibliographer, Walter J. Wentz of Eugene, Oregon, as well as the historian of the pulp magazine era, Sam Moskowitz, and myself, that Merritt certainly had a hand in the writing of "The Pool of the Stone God," to say the least. In a letter to me dated January 22, 1972, Mr. Wentz points out: "It is entirely possible that Merritt published many such short stories during the period of 1910–1925, in any of a score of papers. He was a free-lance writer before he joined *The American Weekly*, and his fancy sketches may have been reprinted in the tabloids for which he once worked."

2. There were also pulps entirely devoted to fiction about aviation, prize-fighting, football, spies, historical adventures, as well as a number of queer hybrids, such as *Ranch Romances*, the unlikely fruit of a liaison between the wild west tale and the love story, and *Spicy Adventure Stories*, which served up swashbucklers crossed with what passed in those days (above the counter, anyway) for pornography. See Tony Goodstone's excellent book, *The Pulps: Fifty Years of American Pop Culture* (New York, Chelsea House, 1970), if only for the gorgeous color reproductions of scores of magazine covers.

3. I am indebted to Sam Moskowitz for much of this information on the early history of *Weird Tales* and its troubles. Moskowitz has interviewed J. C. Henneberger and has been privileged to look through his old correspondence files. Some of this information Moskowitz included in his introduction to an anthology edited by Leo Margulies called *Worlds of Weird* (New York, Pyramid Books, 1965), but some of these facts have never been made public before and were told to me by Moskowitz during a telephone interview. Neither I nor Sam Moskowitz can be certain, of course, that Mr. Henneberger has remembered these long-ago events correctly.

4. Or what would, in his time, have been called madness. Lovecraft's father suffered from a form of paralysis called paresis; by the time Lovecraft was a child of three his father had degenerated to the point at which he was considered no longer competent to manage his affairs and was placed under a legal guardian; his behavior became increasingly abnormal and five years later he died. Lovecraft's mother seems to have been an unstable, neurotic woman, ultraprotective where her son was concerned, the sort of woman who smothers her son with affection to

such an extent that he has little to do with other women throughout the rest of his life, which was largely the case with Lovecraft. August Derleth, Lovecraft's chief disciple, writes that she was obsessed with the threat of bankruptcy, grew "mentally and physically exhausted," and eventually took refuge in the Butler Hospital in Providence, where she remained until her death two years later. My only source for this information is August Derleth's informative monograph, *H. P. L.: A Memoir* (New York, Ben Abramson, 1945).

5. On page 66 of the monograph on Lovecraft mentioned in the above note, August Derleth wrote: "Lovecraft identified his literary influences readily enough. The first was Lord Dunsany . . . 'from whom,' he says, he 'got the idea of the artificial pantheon and myth-background represented by Cthulhu, Yog-Sothoth, Yuggoth;' Dunsany's work 'gave a vast impetus' to his weird writing, and he admits that he 'turned out material in greater volume than ever before or since.' " Derleth seems to be quoting from one of Lovecraft's letters in this passage, but the full text of the letter has not yet been published, to my knowledge.

6. Little has been published on Clark Ashton Smith's life, but I have been privileged to read in manuscript the first two hundred pages of a biographical work currently being written by Mrs. Clark Ashton Smith, the author's widow. My remarks on Smith in this chapter, however, together with the various opinions expressed and information given, are not to be construed as Mrs. Smith's but are entirely my own.

7. So reports the leading authority on Howard's life and career, L. Sprague de Camp, in an article entitled "Memories of R. E. H.," which appeared in *Amra* in 1960 and was included in a book of Howardian studies called *The Conan Reader* (Baltimore, Mirage Press, 1968). I am indebted to the same article for the information, given earlier in this section, about Howard's physical and emotional nature.

8. Although he at least started some two dozen in all. Many of these rough drafts, outlines, notes, or fragments of unwritten stories have been completed by L. Sprague de Camp or myself, including the remnants of an aborted King Kull series that Howard abandoned.

9. There were 5½ Jirel stories, if you want to quibble about it. The "½" was "Quest of the Starstone" in the

November 1937 issue of *Weird Tales;* this story was a sort of tour de force, in which, somehow or other, that fiery gal from the Middle Ages, Jirel of Joiry, shares an adventure with the 21st-century space hero, Northwest Smith, the story thus being half a Jirel and half a Smith. The story was a collaboration with Miss Moore's future husband, Henry Kuttner, by the way.

Chapter 4.

1. And if it hasn't been said by anybody yet, well, it should have been.

2. Both of these Norvell Page novels have been reprinted in recent paperback editions. *Flame Winds* and *Sons of the Bear-God* were published in 1969 by Berkley Medallion Books, and may still be in print, in case you missed them.

3. Ace Books has preserved the entire saga of Fafhrd and the Gray Mouser in paperback in a series of five volumes published between 1968 and 1970. The books are titled *The Swords of Lankhmar, Swords Against Wizardry, Swords in the Mist, Swords Against Death,* and *Swords and Deviltry.* The titling of these books may leave something to be desired in the way of novelty, but the contents are beyond reproach and are thoroughly entertaining.

Chapter 5.

1. The actual writings of Epictetus have not survived to our day for the very good reason that, like Socrates, he never wrote anything. His pupil, Arrian, the biographer of Alexander the Great, preserved an account of his teachings for us in two books, the *Discourses* and the Manual or *Encheiridion;* it is from this second book that the epigraph of this chapter is quoted.

2. This information on the life of William Hope Hodgson is considerably more detailed and more accurate than the data given in the Arkham edition of *The House on the Borderland and Other Novels.* In my introductions to the Ballantine editions of *The Boats of the 'Glen Carrig'* and *The Night Land* I unknowingly perpetuated these Derlethian and Koenigian inaccuracies. I am happy to set

the record straight in this chapter, and to express my gratitude to Mr. R. A. Everts, the scholar who unearthed the new information with the cooperation of the surviving members of the Hodgson family, and who very kindly passed it along to me.

3. Lovecraft's opinions on Hodgson's work are quoted from his long essay, "Supernatural Horror in Literature," the version published by Ben Abramson (New York, 1945), pages 83–84. The remarks by C. S. Lewis in the same passage are from his article "On Science Fiction," which Walter Hooper included in his collection of the Lewisian marginalia, a book called *Of Other Worlds* (London, Geoffrey Bles: 1966); see p. 71.

4. *Surprised by Joy* is the story of Lewis' conversion from atheism to Christianity, and not genuine autobiography at all.

5. C. S. Lewis, *Surprised by Joy* (New York, Harvest edition, 1956); see pp. 163–164.

6. See *Letters of C. S. Lewis,* edited by W. H. Lewis (New York, Harcourt, Brace, 1966).

7. See *Surprised by Joy,* p. 35.

Chapter 6.

1. See *Letters of C. S. Lewis.*

2. From a letter from Lewis to Charles Moorman, dated May 15, 1959, in the *Letters.* The passage continues: "We listened to his work, but could affect it only by encouragement. He has only two reactions to criticism: either he begins the whole work over again from the beginning or else takes no notice at all."

3. It is called *The Lineage of Lichfield* and is of no great length. The most easily available edition is in our recent paperback printing of *The Cream of the Jest* (New York, Ballantine, 1971); see that edition, pp. 225–266. Cabell was a trained genealogist and published two formal works in that field, his *Lichfield* being in the nature of a private joke, but none the less scrupulously professional for that.

4. Again, with the possible exception of Austin Tappan Wright. The quibble here is that while Tolkien's data is all there in print, the major portion of Wright's Islandian notes and documents languish in manuscript and have

been examined by only a few. And another point: Tolkien's epic covers much more ground than does *Islandia,* which confines itself to the southernmost coastline of the imaginary continent.

5. It is just possible that I am overestimating the sort of influence Tolkien will exert on fantasy-writing for the remainder of this century. Of the examples cited, Kendall has ceased writing, and Garner and Alexander have long since moved on to other kinds of books than the Tolkienian. And those fantasy writers who have arisen since, like Ursula K. LeGuin, seem to have absorbed and fully digested their Tolkien, going on to write books completely their own. In the past few years, only Joy Chant's *Red Moon and Black Mountain* appears to be solidly in the Tolkienian stream of influence. The new fiction by unpublished writers that I receive in my capacity as editorial consultant for Ballantine seems either unabashed Sword & Sorcery or more Dunsanian than anything else. Perhaps the spurt of Tolkienian influence has already run its course; on this matter, only time will tell, as usual.

Chapter 7.

1. Like many another fantasy writer, Howard was an accomplished versifier as well as a prose-writer of undeniable gifts. His poems have been collected into three volumes: *Always Comes Evening* (Sauk City, Wisc., Arkham House, 1957), *Singers in the Shadows* (West Kingston, R. I., Donald M. Grant, 1970), and *Echoes from an Iron Harp* (Grant, 1972). "The Singer in the Mist," the poem from which the epigraph for this chapter was selected, appears in *Always Comes Evening,* p. 7.

2. In his article "Pratt's Parallel Worlds," in *The Conan Reader* (Baltimore, Md., The Voyager Series, 1968).

3. *Ibid:* see the article "Conan's Ghost," p. 6.

4. *Ibid,* p. 9.

5. *Ibid,* p. 8.

6. John Boardman, in an article on a later novel of mine called *The Giant of World's End,* in *Science Fiction Review* #38, dated June 1970. A long-time member of the Hyborian Legion and a frequent contributor to *Amra,* Dr. Boardman generally knows what he's talking about when it comes to Sword & Sorcery.

7. Preface to *Brak the Barbarian* (New York, Avon Books, 1968), p. 7.

8. For Barth's use of the word "gnomon" to describe his fiction, see Israel Shenker's article "Complicated Simple Things," in the *New York Times Book Review* for September 24, 1972, p. 36.

9. In all honesty, I've never been able to figure out just who is, and just who isn't, a New Wave writer. My confusion seems to be shared by the New Wave writers themselves, some of whom, like Zelazny and Delany, consistently deny membership in the so-called movement. At times I am almost convinced the movement is a complete hoax, and that *nobody* belongs to it. Alexei Panshin, who wrote the Hugo-Award-winning novel *Rite of Passage,* is generally considered a part of the New Wave.

10. From a letter dated February 20, 1943, in the *Letters of C. S. Lewis.* While in general I agree with Lewis' opinion on this matter, I must in all honesty point out that any number of excellent writers have, in fact, attempted to "imagine a new primary colour"—David Lindsay, for one—as well as "a third sex" and the rest of the things Lewis lists. While genuine imaginative creation, in the sense in which Lewis employs the term, is of course the rarest of human gifts, that doesn't mean we shouldn't strive for it.

11. From a review quoted in the front matter of Moorcock's novel *Stormbringer* (London, Herbert Jenkins, 1965).

12. The Hyborian Legion is one of those organizations which do not really exist, if you know what I mean. That is, the club has no dues or officers, and exists only by a tacit agreement among those of us who claim to belong to it. *Amra* certainly does exist, however, and is to my taste the most interesting fanzine around these days. If you are interested in subscribing to *Amra,* you will find the necessary information in Bibliography I: General References, under "Howard, Robert E." The only way to tell members of the Hyborian Legion from non-members, since no roster exists, is that members may purchase a handsome bronze medallion with the Aquilonian coat of arms thereon in high relief. The medallions are handcrafted by a Philadelphia jeweler. There is, or used to be, a membership scroll available which was printed on parchment paper in Egyptian hieroglyphics with facing English text, but

whether these are still available or not I cannot say. Like S. A. G. A., the Legion bestows honorary titles on certain members as reward for a meritorious service to the field of heroic fantasy, such award usually given by acclamation. I, for example, was declared Royal Necromancer of Aquilonia some years ago.

13. A book of the nature of *Imaginary Worlds* will probably bring me in three or four hundred pieces of fan-mail during its first year of life. From my earlier books, *Tolkien* and *Lovecraft,* I have learned that the readership of such books runs the gamut from college professors, publishing people, and colleagues all the way to inexperienced teenaged fantasy buffs, in general an intelligent and very enthusiastic group of people, some of whom, however, display a lamentable tendency to assume that my time for answering questions is unlimited. The spirit may be willing, but neither time nor flesh permit! Now, *Imaginary Worlds* discusses scores if not hundreds of books, and it is obviously impractical for me to list relevant publishing data on each. If I have anywhere in these pages mentioned or discussed a book that sounds interesting, a book that you would like to hunt up and read, and, moreover, if it is a book whose mention here is not accompanied with publishing data—please, *please* do not write and ask me where you can find it. It's not that I don't enjoy hearing from my readers; I do. But answer questions I cannot. If there's a book you'd like to read, go to your public library and look it up in the card catalogue. If you can't find it there, ask the librarian to show you a standard publishing-trade reference book called *Books in Print;* if it's a paperback, there's another such reference book called *Paperback Books in Print.* If you find the book in question listed in one of these, but it is published by a publishing house you've never heard of and don't know how to get in contact with, look *them* up in yet another standard reference called *Literary Market Place. Ask your library.*

Chapter 8.

1. The epigraph is a quotation from an undated letter C. S. Lewis wrote to Arthur Greeves. You will find it on p. 28 of the *Letters.*

2. I strongly recommend the fairy tales of James Thurber to any reader interested in charming fantasy, and regret that their nature places them, strictly speaking, beyond the range of *Imaginary Worlds*, for I love them muchly and would enjoy discussing them.

Chapter 9.

1. In the case of "The Fortress Unvanquishable, Save for Sacnoth," however, it should be noticed that Dunsany made things easy for himself by adopting a style and theme comfortably familiar to his reader: that of the fairy-tale or dragon-slayer legend. A superior example of how this problem has been solved without reliance on the fairy-tale flavor would perhaps be "Idle Days on the Yann." Since that story in no way resembles the traditional tale, Dunsany has to lick the problem by an adroit use of the several techniques of world-making discussed here in Chapters 9, 10, and 11.

2. What Coleridge actually wrote is this: "It was agreed that my endeavors [in the planning of the book *Lyrical Ballads*] should be directed to persons and characters supernatural, or at least romantic; yet so as to transfer from our inward nature a human interest and a semblance of truth sufficient to procure for these shadows of imagination that willing suspension of disbelief for the moment which constitutes poetic faith." The passage appears in the fourteenth chapter of his *Biographia Literaria* (1817).

3. It is not particularly surprising that, of all the various legendary or prehistoric civilizations, Atlantis is the one most frequently chosen by writers of fantasy fiction for their setting. Smith, Howard, Kuttner, de Camp, Gaskell, Anderson, Norton, and myself are among the more-or-less contemporary writers who have done so, but the field of Atlantis-in-fiction constitutes an immense library in its own right. Quite often the occultist will select Atlantis for the scene of his pseudo-fiction, as did Daphne Vigers in her *Atlantis Rising*, or Clara von Raven in her *Selestor's Men of Atlantis*, or *A Dweller on Two Planets*, which Frederick Spencer Oliver wrote under the silly pseudonym of "Phylos the Tibetan." The literary pretensions of such books are often absurd, as are their authors' pretensions to secret sources of arcane information about the Lost Continent,

zealously guarded from the rest of us boobs and unbelievers. Miss von Raven, for example, informs us that her book was dictated by an Egyptian spirit-control with the remarkably *un*Egyptian name of "Selestor," while Miss Vigers goes her one better, claiming to have actually visited Atlantis herself via astral travel. As for Mr. Oliver, his private source of Atlantean data was a Chinese super-sage named Quong who lives inside Mount Shasta in California. Silly and ignorant as these books usually are, however, the occult novelists are at times capable of excellent imaginative invention. Oliver, for example, wrote a quite readable book which, although rare and hard to find, is indeed worth searching for. I was particularly struck with his gift for coining names, such as that of his Atlantean protagonist, "Zailm Numinos," and one of his Atlantean cities, "Caiphul."

The preeminence of Atlantis as the favorite setting for a considerable amount of fantasy fiction is certainly understandable: the legend of the Lost Continent is one of the greatest inventions of the human imagination, and an enduringly fascinating one. I could wish, however, for a little more variety and originality in site-selection from the next generation of fantasy writers. How about the prehistoric lost continent of "Gondwanaland" in the Indian Ocean, or "Shamballah," the imaginary super-civilization in the Gobi desert, or the almost completely untouched (and totally imaginary) pre-Columbian North American civilizations called "Saguenay" and "Norumbega"? (For a concise account of all available data on these last, see Samuel Eliot Morison's splendid recent book, *The European Discovery of America: The Northern Voyages,* New York, Oxford University Press, 1971.) I have read most of the better-known Atlantis novels, and the best of them all is still C. J. Cutcliffe Hyne's *The Lost Continent.* As for employing new and novel settings, far be it from me to commend my own works to the Trusting Reader, but my new series of stories set in the fabulous Seven Isles of Antillia—of which the first story, "The Twelve Wizards of Ong," may be in print by the time you read this—is pretty much the sort of thing I suggest new writers attempt.

Chapter 10.

1. Lear, however, was a gifted coiner of names, as a glance through his marvelous nonsense verses will prove. He had a good ear for the "shape" and "flavor" of invented words: *viz.*, "runcible," an all-purpose adjective, or the "Bong-tree," or "the Yonghy-Bonghy-Bò," or—*mirabile dictu*—"the great Gromboolian plain" in a poem called "The Dong with the Luminous Nose." Such words and names mean absolutely nothing, yet somehow strike us as *just right*. This is the kind of magic involved in cognominal coinage, the "Proper Name." Most authorities would concede Lewis Carroll to be Lear's superior in nonsense verse. Not me: Lear has a delicious quality of infectious good humor that is lacking in the more solemn and also more sentimental Carrollian verse (although I certainly cannot deny the irresistible genius of the poem "Jabberwocky").

2. Regrettably, in the latter-day Conan pastiches that L. Sprague de Camp and I have been adding to the Howardian canon, we have had to follow even Howard's bad habits, since we are engaged in a deliberate and knowing imitation of his style. Hence we have striven to resist the temptation to coin reasonably good names all our own, and have turned to the more accessible histories and atlases for our new names, as Howard would have done. I hope John Jakes reads this note: since I have been taking him to task somewhat in the passage to which this comment applies, he deserves to take satisfaction in my shamefaced admission to the same fault.

3. As does "Khymyrium," the title of my unfinished prose epic (mentioned elsewhere). The name was evolved from the same premise as "Palmyrium," I'm afraid, but I doubt that readers will be confused.

4. It is probably not news to my readers to hear that entire non-fiction books have been written based on the internal data of these and similar series—formal and scholarly biographies of Sherlock Holmes, for example, and whole volumes about the geography of Barsoom. I myself have for some years been puttering away at compiling information gleaned from the forty-odd Oz books, gathering notes towards an eventual history of the Marvelous Land of Oz.

5. In the afterword to my recent collection of Dunsanyana, *Beyond the Fields We Know*. The afterword is a brief monograph entitled "The Naming of Names: Notes on Lord Dunsany's Influence on Modern Fantasy Writers." In it I demonstrate his influence or his alleged influence, on several contemporaries through their obvious imitation of his style of coinage.

Chapter 11.

1. I strongly recommend a careful reading of *An Experiment in Criticism* to anyone seriously interested in a professional career as a fantasy writer. The insights and shrewd observations into storytelling, scenic reality, plot, and characterization, are invaluable. The book was published by the Cambridge University Press in 1961, and the passage quoted can be found on page 57.

2. Next to *Amra, Anduril* is the most interesting and thought-provoking fanzine in the field of heroic fantasy currently being published. If you're at all interested, you might write to the editor, John Martin, 27 Highland Drive, Bushey, Herts., England.

3. An interesting and thoughtful look at the coining of the "Proper Name" in imaginative writing can be found in an article by George Brandon Saul, "Strange Gods and Far Places: The Short Stories of Lord Dunsany," which appeared in the *Arizona Quarterly*, 19, #3, dated Autumn, 1963. Saul points out that "to many readers the names in themselves seem magically evocative," and coins a useful term for this quality—"ideational onomatopeia." He illustrates this by noting that "Hish," for example, seems precisely right as a name for God of Silence, as does "Slith" for a sly, cunning thief.

4. The quotation at the end of this chapter is from Arthur O'Shaughnessy's "Ode," quoted also in the epigraph to Chapter 2.

Bibliography I: General References

Any comprehensive work of literary history and criticism, such as this book, draws from a broad variety of research sources. These sources range from standard reference works such as the *Encyclopedia Britannica, Readers Guide to Periodical Literature, Books in Print,* and *Twentieth Century Authors*—which may be found in larger libraries—to articles and reviews in specialized or general periodicals, which themselves range from fanzines like *Amra* to *The Saturday Review of Literature.*

It would seem a futile exercise to list here *all* the various sources of information I have consulted during my research for this book; it would also be a pointless waste of space.

However, since no general or comprehensive history of fantasy in modern literature seems to have been published prior to the writing of *Imaginary Worlds,* it may be of interest to my readers, and of some value to future critics or historians of fantasy, to have a summary of my basic research sources on the major writers or schools of writing discussed in this book. Many of these sources consist of privately-printed brochures now long out of print and unavailable; these remain unlisted in the major references and are thus unknown to academic scholars. A concise bibliography follows, therefore, arranged alphabetically by subject-author; the listings are given chronologically in order of publication. The listings under each author, by the way, are *not* to be considered complete and exhaustive, but consist of those publications I have found most useful and informative. Wherever a club, society, or individual magazine(s) exists which is devoted to a particular author, I have included data on it, together with an address wherever possible, so that those readers interested in further information may pursue the matter themselves, rather than loading my mailbox with personal queries.

Bok, Hannes:

1. *Luna,* #4, 1965. Special commemorative issue devoted to Bok, consisting of letters, anecdotes, memorabilia, etc., by those who knew Bok well. A fan periodical published by Frank Dietz, 655 Orchard Street, Oradell, N.J. 07649.
2. *And Flights of Angels: the Life and Legend of Hannes Bok,* by Emil Petaja and others. San Francisco, 1970. Informal biographical sketch, with tributes and reminiscences.

Note: An organization known as The Bokanalia Foundation exists for the purpose of reprinting the graphic work of this author, and several portfolios of his work have thus far appeared under this imprint, as well as a volume of Bok's verse. Write to Box 14126, San Francisco, Calif. 94114.

Burroughs, Edgar Rice:

1. *The Dream Weaver: An Edgar Rice Burroughs Chapbook,* by Alvin Fick. Fort Johnson, N.Y., 1962. Includes a map of Barsoom.
2. *Edgar Rice Burroughs: A Bibliography,* by Bradford M. Day. Woodhaven, N.Y., 1962.
3. *A Golden Anniversary Bibliography of Edgar Rice Burroughs,* by Henry Hardy Heins. Albany, N.Y., 1962. A revised, updated edition was subsequently published in hardcover.
4. *A Reader's Guide to Barsoom and Amtor,* by David G. Van Arnam and others. New York, N.Y., 1963. Limited edition of 200 copies. Includes foldout map of Barsoom, glossaries of the Martian and Venusian languages, as well as a superb essay on Barsoomian geography. Published by Richard A. Lupoff.
5. *The Big Swingers,* by Robert W. Fenton. Englewood Cliffs, N.J., Prentice-Hall, 1963. A formal biography of the author.
6. *Edgar Rice Burroughs: Master of Adventure,* by Richard A. Lupoff. New York, Canaveral Press, 1965. Anecdotal biography and critical study of the

Burroughsian *oeuvre*. A revised and updated version was published in paperback by Ace Books in 1968.

Note: There are a number of fanzines devoted to Burroughs, of which the most recent I have received are *ERB-dom*, published by Camille Cazedessus, Jr., at Box 550, Evergreen, Cal. 80439; and *The Jassomian*, published by William Dutcher, Box 1305, Yuba City, Calif. 95991. A club called The Burroughs Bibliophiles is devoted to the work of this writer and publishes a magazine called *The Burroughs Bulletin:* write to Vernell Coriell, 6657 Locust St., Kansas City, Missouri 64131 for information.

Cabell, James Branch:

1. *The Art of James Branch Cabell,* by Hugh Walpole. New York, Robert M. McBride Company, 1920. Monograph.

2. *James Branch Cabell*, by H. L. Mencken. New York, McBride, 1927. Monograph.

3. *Cabellian Harmonics*, by Warren A. McNeill. New York, Random House, 1928. Technical study of Cabell's prose style, published in an edition of 1500 copies.

4. *James Branch Cabell*, by Carl Van Doren. New York, McBride, 1928. Booklength monograph, #1 in McBride's "Modern American Writers" series.

5. *Notes on "Jurgen,"* by James P. Cover. New York, McBride, 1928. Booklength exegesis of the novel, published in an edition limited to 850 copies.

6. *Notes on "Figures of Earth,"* by John Philips Cranwell and James P. Cover. New York, McBride, 1929. Booklength exegesis of the novel, published in an edition limited to 865 copies.

7. *As I Remember It: Some Epilogues in Recollection,* by James Branch Cabell. New York, McBride, 19. 5. Partial, episodic, and anecdotal autobiography.

8. *Between Friends: The Letters of James Branch Cabell and Others,* edited by Padraic Colum and Margaret Freeman Cabell. New York, Harcourt, Brace and World, 1962. Huge compilation of letters exchanged among members of the "Cabell circle": fascinating and revealing literary history of the times.

9. *James Branch Cabell,* by Joe Lee Davis. New York, Twayne Publishers, 1962. Booklength critical study; volume 21 in Twayne's "United States Authors" series.

10. *Jesting Moses: A Study in Cabellian Comedy,* by Arvin R. Wells. Gainesville, Fla., University of Florida Press, 1962. Literary critique and stylistic study; highly professional.

11. *James Branch Cabell: The Dream and the Reality,* by Desmond Tarrant. Norman, Okla., University of Oklahoma Press, 1967. Literary critique in depth, with study of style and symbolism.

Note: An organization called The James Branch Cabell Society exists to promote the publication and appreciation of this author. The Society publishes an excellent, highly informative, and entertaining journal of Cabellian studies called *Kalki.* Those interested should write to Mr. Paul Spencer, 665 Lotus Avenue, Oradell, N.J. 07649.

Lord Dunsany:

1. *Dunsany the Dramatist,* by Edward Hale Bierstadt. Boston, Little, Brown, 1917. History and critique of this author's playwriting career only.

2. *Patches of Sunlight: An Autobiography,* by Lord Dunsany. New York, Reynal & Hitchcock, 1938. Casual memoirs covering the author's life through the end of 1918. Completely invaluable source of information on the locale and inspiration behind many of his most important stories.

3. *While the Sirens Slept,* by Lord Dunsany. London, Jarrolds, 1944. Further memoirs.

4. *The Sirens Wake,* by Lord Dunsany. London, Jarrolds, 1946. Final volume of the memoirs, carrying the author's life through about 1943.

5. *Lord Dunsany: King of Dreams,* by Hazel Littlefield. New York, Exposition Press, 1959. Anecdotal personal portrait of Lord Dunsany by an American admirer who was his host during his several visits to this country.

6. *Journeys to the World's Edge: A Dunsany Bibliography,* by Lin Carter. New York, Carcosa Press,

1974. Complete, annotated bibliography of this author's books, including pamphlets and brochures.

Haggard, H. Rider:

1. *The Days of My Life,* by H. Rider Haggard (edited by C. J. Longman). 2 vols. London, Longmans, Green & Co., 1926. The autobiography.
2. *Rider Haggard: His Life and Works,* by Morton N. Cohen. New York, Walker & Company, 1960. Superb recent biography which conveys a genuine sense of the writer's personality and his period; highly recommended to anyone interested in knowing more about Haggard.
3. *Rudyard Kipling to Rider Haggard: The Record of a Friendship,* edited by Morton N. Cohen. London, Hutchinson, 1965. Selections from the correspondence between these writers, skillfully bridged and annotated by Haggard's biographer.

Howard, Robert E.:

1. *The Hyborian Age,* by Robert E. Howard. Los Angeles, Calif., 1938. Privately-printed brochure, including an introductory letter by H. P. Lovecraft and the essay "A Probable Outline of Conan's Career," by P. Schuyler Miller and John D. Clark, Ph.D.
2. "An Informal Biography of Conan the Cimmerian," by P. Schuyler Miller, John D. Clark, and L. Sprague de Camp. In *Amra,* vol. II, no. 4 (June, 1959). Expansion and updating of the above essay.
3. "An Exegesis of Howard's Hyborian Tales," by L. Sprague de Camp. 2 parts, serialized in *Amra,* vol. II, nos. 5 and 6 (1959).
4. *The Robert E. Howard Fantasy Biblio,* by Robert Weinberg. Newark, N.J. (no date, but about 1969).

Note: An organization named The Hyborian Legion was founded in New York City on November 12, 1955, to "give honor to Conan and his creator," as George R. Heap, one of the founding members, phrased it. The province of Legion activities was quickly broadened to include the works of all Sword & Sorcery writers and heroic fantasy in general, and from an original nucleus of twelve members from New York and Philadelphia, the Legion has grown to include many hundreds of fantasy buffs the world over. The magazine *Amra* was established in 1956 to serve as the informal bulletin of the Legion. It is still going strong today, seventeen years later, and has twice garnered the Hugo Award given annually to the best fan publication of the year. For information on membership in the Legion or subscription rates to *Amra*, write to Box 8243, Philadelphia, Pa. 19101. Another publication, *The Howard Collector*, is devoted to this writer exclusively. The publisher is Glenn Lord, literary agent for the Howard estate; for information write to Mr. Lord at Box 775, Pasadena, Texas 77501.

Lewis, C. S.:

1. *Surprised by Joy,: The Shape of My Early Life*, by C. S. Lewis. New York, Harcourt, Brace & World, 1956. As noted elsewhere in this book, not so much a formal autobiography as an account of this writer's conversion.
2. *The Letters of C. S. Lewis*, edited by W. H. Lewis. New York, Harcourt, Brace & World, 1966.

Note: An organization called The Mythopoeic Society was established some years ago to study and discuss the mythic elements in fantastic literature in general and, in particular, the works of C. S. Lewis, Charles Williams, and J. R. R. Tolkien. The Society by now has some twenty-one chapters or study-groups listed, ranging from Texas to Illinois to California, and publishes a number of periodicals, among which is *Mythprint*, a monthly bulletin. Those interested should write to the Society at Box 24150, Los Angeles, Calif. 90024. More recently, a club has been organized known as The New York C. S. Lewis Society, which meets regularly to discuss this author's work and thought. The New York group publishes a monthly *Bulletin*, and those interested should contact its editor, Mr. Eugene McGovern, at 9 Bradshaw

Drive, Ossining, N.Y. 10562. I should also mention that a Walck monograph on C. S. Lewis by Roger Lancelyn Green has been published; I have not seen this monograph, and hence do not list it above, mentioning it here for the sake of completeness.

Lindsay, David:

1. *The Strange Genius of David Lindsay*, by J. B. Pick and others. London, John Baker, 1972. A compilation containing valuable information on this obscure but hardly minor fantasy master. Includes Pick's biographical sketch and material on the unpublished manuscripts of Lindsay, an article by Colin Wilson on Lindsay's mysticism, and memorabilia by E. H. Visiak about his meetings with the author.

Lovecraft, H. P.:

1. *H. P. L.*, by Corwin Stickney. Privately printed, 1937. Memorial brochure published in a limited edition of 25 copies.
2. *The Notes and Commonplace Book of H. P. Lovecraft*, edited by Robert H. Barlow. Lakeport, Calif., Futile Press, 1938. Printed in an edition limited to 75 copies.
3. *In Memoriam: Howard Phillips Lovecraft*, by W. Paul Cook. North Montpelier, Vermont, Driftwind Press, 1941. Printed in an edition limited to 94 copies.
4. "Autobiography: Some Notes on a Nonentity," by H. P. Lovecraft, in *Beyond The Wall of Sleep*, edited by August Derleth and Donald Wandrei. Sauk City, Wisc., Arkham House, 1943.
5. *Lovecraft and Benefit Street*, by Dorothy Charlotte Walters. North Montpelier, Vermont, Driftwind Press, 1943. Less than 100 copies are believed to have been printed.
6. *Marginalia*, by H. P. Lovecraft (and others), edited by August Derleth and Donald Wandrei. Sauk City, Wisc., Arkham House, 1944. Early fiction, verse, amateur press articles, etc., by Lovecraft, together with articles, appreciations, memoirs, and tributes to

him by other writers. The first of four such volumes of miscellany to be published.

7. *H. P. L.: A Memoir,* by August Derleth. New York, Ben Abramson, 1945. Extended biographical sketch, together with detailed critique of this writer's work.

8. *Rhode Island on Lovecraft,* edited by Donald M. Grant and Thomas P. Hadley. Providence, R. I., 1945. Articles and memoirs; includes text of the Walters brochure (#5 above).

9. *H. P. Lovecraft: A Bibliography,* by Joseph Payne Brennan. Washington, D.C., 1952. Incomplete and not accurate in all entries.

10. *The Lovecraft Collector's Library,* edited by George Wetzell. North Tonawanda, N.Y., SSR Publications, 1955. See in particular Vol. VI, "Commentaries," and Vol. VII, "Bibliographies," the latter containing an excellent listing of this author's amateur press work (compiled by George Wetzell) and of his professional appearances (compiled by Robert E. Briney). A subsequent addenda volume, un-numbered but entitled *H.P.L.: Memoirs, Critiques, and Bibliographies,* is also useful.

11. *H. P. L.: An Evaluation,* by Joseph Payne Brennan. New Haven, Conn., Macabre House, 1955. Literary critique, released in an edition limited to 75 copies.

12. *The Howard Phillips Lovecraft Memorial Symposium,* edited by Steven Eisner. Detroit, Mich., 1958. Articles and commentaries by Derleth, Brennan, Leiber, Keller, etc.

13. "H. P. Lovecraft: The Books," and "H. P. Lovecraft: The Gods," by Lin Carter, in *The Shuttered Room and Other Pieces,* edited by August Derleth. Sauk City, Wisc., Arkham House, 1959. Exhaustive summaries of then-extant information on the imaginary books and gods of the Cthulhu Mythos.

14. *Some Notes on H. P. Lovecraft,* by August Derleth. Sauk City, Wisc., Arkham House, 1959. Brochure limited to 1000 copies.

15. *The Gentleman from Angell Street,* by Muriel E. Eddy. Privately printed, Providence, R. I., 1961. Personal memoir printed in a limited edition of 100 copies.

16. *Lovecraft: A Symposium,* edited by Leland Sapiro. Los Angeles, Calif., 1964. Transcription of a round-

table discussion, recorded in 1963, between Leiber, Bloch, and others; later annotated by Derleth.

17. *Selected Letters,* Vol. I, edited by August Derleth and Donald Wandrei. Sauk City, Wisc., Arkham House, 1965. Covers the period from 1911 to 1924.

18. *Mirage on Lovecraft,* edited by Jack L. Chalker. The Anthem Series. Baltimore, Md., 1965. Includes the text of #4 above, plus other articles. Printed in an edition limited to 497 copies.

19. *H. P. Lovecraft, A Portrait,* by W. Paul Cook. The Anthem Series. Baltimore, Md., 1968. Personal memoir; does not seem to be the same as #3 above.

20. *Selected Letters,* Vol. II, edited by August Derleth and Donald Wandrei. Sauk City, Wisc., Arkham House, 1968. Covers the period from 1925 to 1929.

21. *The Howard Phillips Lovecraft We Knew* and *H. P. Lovecraft, Esquire, Gentleman,* by Muriel E. Eddy. Two brief, personal memoirs privately printed in brochure form, perhaps in Providence, R. I., *c.* 1970–1971.

22. *Selected Letters,* Vol. III, edited by August Derleth and Donald Wandrei. Sauk City, Wisc., Arkham House, 1971. Covers the period from 1929 to 1931.

23. *Lovecraft: A Look Behind the "Cthulhu Mythos,"* by Lin Carter. New York, Ballantine Books, 1972. The first booklength study of this writer's life, work, relationships with other authors, and influence on macabre literature.

Note: Insofar as I have been able to discover, the earliest magazine devoted entirely to Lovecraft studies was *The Lovecraft Collector,* published by Ray H. Zorn, with its first issue dated January, 1949. The periodical apparently did not survive its first year, and copies are now exceedingly rare. The relatively enormous critical literature on Lovecraft suggests the enthusiasm of his great following. In regard to this, it is odd that no serious attempt seems to have been made to organize a society devoted to Lovecraftiana until the recent founding of The Dark Brotherhood a year or two ago by George H. Record. This society publishes a monthly newsletter and an occasional *Journal* of articles, poems, and stories concerning the Cthulhu Mythos. Those interested should write to Mr. Record at Box 426, Denver, Colo. 80201.

As the above bibliography suggests, Lovecraftian scholarship has been an actively growing field for more than thirty years, and the end is nowhere in sight. At the time of this writing, L. Sprague de Camp is at work on a full-scale biography to be entitled *Eldritch Yankee Gentleman*, which will be published by Doubleday; and I am puttering away on a revision and updating of my glossaries (see #13 above), which will be published in The Anthem Series under the title, *Notes on the Cthulhu Mythos*.

Macdonald, George:

1. *George Macdonald and His Wife*, by Greville MacDonald. London, George Allen & Unwin, 1924. The best biography, written by the author's eldest son. An earlier biography by Joseph Johnson, *George Macdonald* (London, 1905), is quite useless.
2. "A Bibliography of George Macdonald," by J. M. Bullock. In *The Aberdeen University Library Bulletin*, 5, 30 (February, 1925).
3. *The Golden Key*, by Robert Lee Wolff. New Haven, Conn., Yale University Press, 1961. Exhaustive study of Macdonald's fiction, perhaps too deeply concerned with the Freudian implications in his use of symbols.

Merritt, A.:

1. *A Merritt Bibliography*, by Walter J. Wentz. Privately-printed brochure, Roseville, Calif., 1965. Excellent and exhaustive publishing history of the short stories and novels, together with data on the film versions of *Burn, Witch, Burn* and *The Seven Footprints to Satan*.

Morris, William:

1. *William Morris: Selected Writings and Designs*, edited by Asa Briggs. Baltimore, Md., Penguin Books, 1962. Contains speeches, articles, verse, and fiction by this writer, with a detailed outline of his life and career.

2. *William Morris, His Life, Work and Friends,* by Philip Henderson. New York, McGraw-Hill Book Company, 1967. Superb, exhaustive, authoritative modern biography of this writer, neglecting only his contribution to modern fantasy.

Note: An organization called The William Morris Society was founded on September 13, 1955, in London; today it has members throughout the United Kingdom and in the United States as well. It sponsors exhibitions of Morris' work in graphics and design, and encourages the modern manufacture of his textile and wallpaper designs. The Society publishes a journal of activities twice yearly, and those interested may write to the Honorary Secretary, 260 Sandycombe Road, Kew, Surrey, England.

Smith, Clark Ashton:

1. *The Tales of Clark Ashton Smith: A Bibliography,* by Thomas G. L. Cockroft. Lower Hutt, New Zealand, 1951. Authoritative listing of this writer's appearances in print through 1951; generally quite accurate, but lacking mention of at least nine published stories.

2. *Addenda* to *The Tales of Clark Ashton Smith: A Bibliography,* by Thomas G. L. Cockroft. Lower Hutt, New Zealand, 1959. Additions and corrections to #1 above; still not completely comprehensive, however.

3. *In Memoriam: Clark Ashton Smith,* edited by Jack L. Chalker. The Anthem Series. Baltimore, Md., 1963. Tributes, memoirs, and articles contributed by Ray Bradbury, Theodore Sturgeon, Leiber, de Camp, and others; also includes the first appearance in print of Smith's Zothiquian verse-play, "The Dead Will Cuckold You." This brochure is currently out of print but an expanded second printing is scheduled.

4. *Ivory and Orichalc and Jade: The Tales of Clark Ashton Smith,* by Lin Carter. New York, Carcosa Press, 1973. A chronological bibliography of the known tales of this author, including all appearances of each story.

Note: To my knowledge, no organization has yet been

founded for the purpose of Klarkashtonian studies, but Mr. Roy Squires of 1745 Kenneth Road, Glendale, Calif., has for several years now been privately publishing exquisite limited editions of previously uncollected verse by this writer, and circulates a list of Smith manuscripts and memorabilia for sale to collectors several times a year. The Anthem Series (see #3 above) has currently in the compilation stage and will soon publish an illustrated brochure on Smith's outré sculptures, which will constitute a valuable document on this little-known phase of Smith's varied and interesting artistic career. There exists as well an unfinished biography of Smith, written by his widow, a copy of which is currently in my possession. Doubtless this work will eventually be published, either by Arkham House or by The Anthem Series, or perhaps by the Smith estate itself. The letters of Clark Ashton Smith have yet to be collected, and should eventually appear in book-form.

Sword & Sorcery:

1. *The Conan Reader*, edited by L. Sprague de Camp. The Voyager Series. Baltimore, Md., 1968. A varied selection of articles and pieces which appeared originally in the fanzine *Amra* and which discuss such writers in the genre as Howard, Dunsany, Vance, Pratt, Hubbard, and others. The book also includes a revised and updated version of de Camp's significant "Exegesis of Howard's Hyborian Tales," in which the coined names in the Conan saga are traced to their original sources in myth, history, geography, and legend.

2. *The Conan Swordbook*, edited by L. Sprague de Camp and George H. Scithers. The Voyager Series. Baltimore, Md., 1969. Like #1 above, a second gleaning from the pages of *Amra* of various articles, reviews, and tributes by de Camp, Leiber, Anderson, Brackett, and others, including the revised and updated third appearance of the "Informal Biography of Conan the Cimmerian."

3. *The Conan Grimoire*, edited by L. Sprague de Camp

and George H. Scithers. The Voyager Series. Baltimore, Md., 1972. More of the same by most of the above, plus Lin Carter, Bjorn Nyberg, Avram Davidson, and E. Hoffmann Price.

Note: De Camp is currently in the process of writing a formal history of heroic fantasy in general and Sword & Sorcery in particular, which will soon be published under the title, *Masters of Heroic Fantasy*. Those interested in books listed above in either The Anthem Series or The Voyager Series should write to Mr. Jack L. Chalker, 5111 Liberty Heights Avenue, Baltimore, Md. 21207.

Tolkien, J. R. R.:

1. *The Tolkien Relation,* by William Ready. Chicago, Henry Regnery Co., 1968. Inept, confused, rambling dissertation on this writer's work. Reissued in paperback under the title, *Understanding Tolkien and "The Lord of the Rings"* by Paperback Library in 1969.
2. *Tolkien and the Critics,* edited by Neil D. Isaacs and Rose A. Simbardo. University of Notre Dame Press, 1968. Collected reviews of the trilogy and criticisms, etc.
3. *J. R. R. Tolkien,* by Catharine R. Stimpson. New York, Columbia University Press, 1969. She can't understand what all the shouting is about.
4. *Tolkien: A Look Behind "The Lord of the Rings,"* by Lin Carter. New York, Ballantine Books, 1969. Biographical sketch, plot outlines, and history-in-brief of the imaginary world tradition, together with studies tracing Tolkien's plot sources to the Icelandic sagas and many of his names to the Anglo-Saxon language.
5. *Tolkien Criticism: An Annotated Checklist,* by Richard C. West. Kent, Ohio, Kent State University Press, 1970. A bibliography of reviews and criticisms, including unpublished theses and dissertations.
6. *Good News from Tolkien's Middle Earth,* by Gracia Fay Elwood. Grand Rapids, Mich., Eerdmans, 1970. An inexplicable tome that ventures to interpret

Tolkien in the light of psychical research and the "psychic photography" of Ted Serios. I confess myself unable to complete reading this one.

7. *A Guide to Middle-Earth,* by Robert Foster. Baltimore, Md., Voyager/Anthem, 1971. Superb, exhaustive, authoritative glossary of the place- and personal-names in this writer's works, together with all pertinent information on each entry. A model of brilliant scholarship and a labor of love.

Note: The Tolkien Society of America has been in existence for some years, with local chapters (called "smials") scattered about the country. The official newsletter of the Society is *The Tolkien Journal,* founded by Richard D. Plotz and most recently under the editorship of Edmund R. Meskys. Due to Mr. Meskys' health, the Society has recently merged with The Mythopoeic Society, and all inquiries should be directed to Box 24150, Los Angeles, Calif. 90024. There are numerous other fanzines in the field of Tolkien studies, most recent of them being *Anduril,* a publication of the British Tolkien Society, edited by John Martin, 27 Highland Drive, Bushey, Herts, England.

Weird Tales Magazine:

1. *Index to the Weird Fiction Magazines* (by Title), by Thomas G. L. Cockroft. Lower Hutt, New Zealand, 1962. Complete and authoritative indexing of the contents of such publications as *Weird Tales, Strange Stories, Strange Tales, Thrill Book, Oriental Stories, Magic Carpet, Golden Fleece,* and so on.

2. *Index to the Weird Fiction Magazines* (by Author), by Thomas G. L. Cockroft. Lower Hutt, New Zealand, 1964. A companion volume to #1 above. Includes special listings of stories in series, etc., as well as data on the pen-names employed by various writers. These twin volumes form an invaluable reference source, scrupulously edited.

3. *Weird Tales in the Thirties,* by Reginald Smith. Santa Ana, Calif., 1966. An affectionate, nostalgic tribute to the greatest of all the fantasy-oriented pulps; the

monograph has twice been reprinted, most recently in 1967.

White, T. H.:

1. *T. H. White*, by Sylvia Townsend Warner. New York, The Viking Press, 1967. A formal, full-scale biography of the writer, which beautifully captures the essence of his character and personality and the tragedy of his life. Highly recommended.
2. *The White/Garnett Letters*, edited by David Garnett. New York, The Viking Press, 1968. Extensive selections from the correspondence between the writer and his closest friend ranging from 1936 to 1962, the year before his death. Very interesting and most revealing. Would that someone would perform the same service for the letters of Merritt or Dunsany!

Addendum:

One final reference source deserves citation here, and that is Roger Lancelyn Green's priceless little book *Tellers of Tales*, first published by Edmund Ward in Leicester, England, in 1946, and most recently reissued in 1953. Theoretically, this book is an informal history and appreciation of children's fantasy in England from its beginnings to date; actually, I discovered it to be a goldmine of information and anecdota on Haggard, Morris, Macdonald, and to a somewhat lesser degree, Lewis and Tolkien. Deliciously readable, the book is filled with useful information difficult to locate elsewhere.

Bibliography II: The Adult Fantasy Series

Ballantine Books' interest in adult fantasy developed out of the phenomenal success of their authorized editions of Professor Tolkien's *The Hobbit* and *The Lord of the Rings*. In the interval between their first printings of these books and my own arrival on the scene as consultant, Betty Ballantine pursued the more celebrated fantasy classics, which Ballantine Books put into print in paperback for the first time in this country. Although none of these fantasies bears the Unicorn's Head colophon, I list them below, in sequence of publication, as a sort of preface to the Series proper: they are all books I would certainly have urged Ballantine to publish.

1. *The Hobbit*, by J. R. R. Tolkien. August, 1965.
2. *The Fellowship of the Ring*, by J. R. R. Tolkien. October, 1965.
3. *The Two Towers*, by J. R. R. Tolkien. October, 1965.
4. *The Return of the King*, by J. R. R. Tolkien. December, 1965.
5. *The Tolkien Reader*, by J. R. R. Tolkien. September, 1966.
6. *The Worm Ouroboros*, by E. R. Eddison. April, 1967.
7. *Mistress of Mistresses*, by E. R. Eddison. August, 1967.
8. *A Fish Dinner in Memison*, by E. R. Eddison. February, 1968.
9. *The Road Goes Ever On*, by J. R. R. Tolkien & Donald Swann. October, 1968.
10. *Titus Groan*, by Mervyn Peake. October, 1968.
11. *Gormenghast*, by Mervyn Peake. October, 1968.
12. *Titus Alone*, by Mervyn Peake. October, 1968.
13. *A Voyage to Arcturus*, by David Lindsay. November, 1968.
14. *The Last Unicorn*, by Peter S. Beagle. February, 1969.
15. *Smith of Wootton Major & Farmer Giles of Ham*, by J. R. R. Tolkien. March, 1969.
16. *The Mezentian Gate*, by E. R. Eddison. August, 1969.

Early in 1967 I conceived of the idea of writing a book about the Professor and his famous trilogy. My agent agreed that the notion had considerable potential and took the outline to Ballantine Books, the publisher most likely to be interested in the project. Mr. Ballantine was indeed interested, and we signed a contract on June 13, 1967. The book was six or eight months in the writing, and was delivered early in 1968. Mr. and Mrs. Ballantine were delighted with it and called me into the offices the next day for a conference.

You see, one of the motives which had impelled me to write *Tolkien: A Look Behind "The Lord of the Rings"* in the first place was my annoyance at some of the younger, less-well-read and more vociferous of the Tolkien-enthusiasts; they seemed to regard the trilogy as a masterpiece without precedent in literature—something wholly original and new. Well, *The Lord of the Rings* was certainly a masterpiece, but not an unprecedented one. The trilogy was simply an imaginary-world romance, and part of a long and rich tradition. The Tolkien fans had it all mixed up and the other way around, thinking the tradition had, like the trilogy, sprung full-panoplied from the brow of the Professor. In my book I traced the history of the imaginary-world romance, and described and quoted from some of the more celebrated examples of the tradition which had appeared in print long before Professor Tolkien came on the scene.

It was this part of the book in particular that the Ballantines had found exciting. I love these books, and some of my own gusto for this sort of writing had seeped over into my pages. Even before signing a contract for *Tolkien*, we had discussed the idea of my compiling twin anthologies of "ancient" and "modern" writers in the imaginary-world genre; and now it occurred to Mrs. Ballantine that the firm should retain my services as a consultant to recommend such books for a reprint series. Such a series would comprise the category that she was already calling "adult fantasy." We signed a memorandum of agreement on the Adult Fantasy Series on November 22, 1968. My book, *Tolkien*, was published in March of the following year; so far it has gone through five printings and has been reviewed in everything from *Luna* to the *Saturday Review of Literature*.

I have compiled the following *complete* list of books

published thus far in the Adult Fantasy Series for two reasons: first, to save myself the trouble of scattering footnotes throughout the text of *Imaginary Worlds* informing my readers which of the titles under discussion have been revived by Ballantine; and second, because I have received so many letters from readers asking for just such a list. Ballantine does not maintain such a list for distribution because any such list would soon be out of date. All titles are reprints unless designated as "originals," and of course the anthologies I have edited, although consisting of reprinted material, are, in the tradition of publishing, considered originals and are protected by copyright as such.

THE BALLANTINE ADULT FANTASY SERIES

1969

1. *The Blue Star,* by Fletcher Pratt. May.
2. *The King of Elfland's Daughter,* by Lord Dunsany. June.
3. *The Wood Beyond the World,* by William Morris. July.
4. *The Silver Stallion,* by James Branch Cabell. August.
5. *Lilith,* by George Macdonald. September.
6. *Dragons, Elves, and Heroes,* edited by Lin Carter. October.
7. *The Young Magicians,* edited by Lin Carter. October.
8. *Figures of Earth,* by James Branch Cabell. November.
9. *The Sorcerer's Ship,* by Hannes Bok. December.

1970

10. *Land of Unreason,* by Fletcher Pratt & L. Sprague de Camp. January.
11. *The High Place,* by James Branch Cabell. February.
12. *Lud-in-the-Mist,* by Hope Mirrlees. March.
13. *At the Edge of the World,* by Lord Dunsany, edited by Lin Carter. March.
14. *Phantastes,* by George Macdonald. April.
15. *The Dream-Quest of Unknown Kadath,* by H. P. Lovecraft, edited by Lin Carter. May.
16. *Zothique,* by Clark Ashton Smith, edited by Lin Carter. June.
17. *The Shaving of Shagpat,* by George Meredith. July.

18. *The Island of the Mighty*, by Evangeline Walton. July.
19. *Deryni Rising*, by Katherine Kurtz. August. (Original)
20. *The Well at the World's End*, Vol. 1, by William Morris. August.
21. *The Well at the World's End*, Vol. II, by William Morris. September.
22. *Golden Cities, Far*, edited by Lin Carter. October.
23. *Beyond the Golden Stair*, by Hannes Bok. November.

1971

24. *The Broken Sword*, by Poul Anderson. January.
25. *The Boats of the 'Glen Carrig,'* by William Hope Hodgson. February.
26. *The Doom That Came to Sarnath*, by H. P. Lovecraft, edited by Lin Carter. February.
27. *Something About Eve*, by James Branch Cabell. March.
28. *Red Moon and Black Mountain*, by Joy Chant. March. (Original)
29. *Hyperborea*, by Clark Ashton Smith, edited by Lin Carter. April.
30. *Don Rodriguez: Chronicles of Shadow Valley*, by Lord Dunsany. May.
31. *Vathek*, by William Beckford. June.
32. *The Man Who Was Thursday*, by G. K. Chesterton. July.
33. *The Children of Llyr*, by Evangeline Walton. August. (Original)
34. *The Cream of the Jest*, by James Branch Cabell. September.
35. *New Worlds for Old*, edited by Lin Carter. September.
36. *The Spawn of Cthulhu*, edited by Lin Carter. October.
37. *Double Phoenix*, by Edmund Cooper & Roger Lancelyn Green. November. (Original)
38. *The Water of the Wondrous Isles*, by William Morris. November.
39. *Khaled*, by F. Marion Crawford. December.

1972

40. *The World's Desire*, by H. Rider Haggard & Andrew Lang. January.
41. *Xiccarph*, by Clark Ashton Smith, edited by Lin Carter. February.

42. *The Lost Continent,* by C. J. Cutcliffe Hyne. February.
43. *Discoveries in Fantasy,* edited by Lin Carter. March.
44. *Domnei,* by James Branch Cabell. March.
45. *Kai Lung's Golden Hours,* by Ernest Bramah. April.
46. *Deryni Checkmate,* by Katherine Kurtz. May. (Original)
47. *Beyond the Fields We Know,* by Lord Dunsany, edited by Lin Carter. May.
48. *The Three Impostors,* by Arthur Machen. June.
49. *The Night Land,* Vol. I, by William Hope Hodgson. July.
50. *The Night Land,* Vol. II, by William Hope Hodgson. July.
51. *The Song of Rhiannon,* by Evangeline Walton. August. (Original)
52. *Great Short Novels of Adult Fantasy* #1, edited by Lin Carter. September.
53. *Evenor,* by George Macdonald, edited by Lin Carter. November.

1973

54. *Orlando Furioso:* The Ring of Angelica, Volume I, Translation by Richard Hodgens. January. (Original)
55. *The Charwoman's Shadow,* by Lord Dunsany. February.
56. *Great Short Novels of Adult Fantasy* #2, edited by Lin Carter. March.
57. *The Sundering Flood,* by William Morris. May.

INDEX

"Abominations of Yondo, The," 179

Ace Books: Vance in, 112; edition of *LOTR*, 118–19; Norton in, 140; Carter in, 142; Leiber series in, 143; Davidson in, 154; Brunner in, 156; Swann in, 168

"Adept's Gambit," 75

Aeneid, The, 14, 17, 177

Alexander, Lloyd, 128–30, 166. *See also* Prydain

Alice in Wonderland, 17, 19

All Story, 49, 51–52

Amadis of Gaul, 4, 15n, 189

Amazing Stories, 70, 81

Amra, 66, 74, 153, 188, 196

Anderson, Poul: obsessed by "the Northern Thing," 20; in *Astounding*, 71; in S.A.G.A., 149–153 *passim*; Chaos vs. Creation theme in, 157; and LeGuin, 164; saga redaction, 178; use of realism, 221; use of nonhumans, 231

Arabian Nights, The, 15n, 17n, 18–19, 56, 72, 182

Arkham House, 76, 188

Arthur (king of Britain), 17, 41, 96, 199

Arthurian legend and literature, 7, 173, 177

Asimov, Isaac, 71, 207

Astounding Science Fiction, 71, 77, 132

Atlantis (continent): in Smith, 61; in Kull series, 64; in Kuttner, 67; in de Camp, 136–37; and Thule, 155; as setting, 178; in Carter, 190–91

Atlan Trilogy, the, 123, 178, 205, 224. *See also* Gaskell, Jane

Auden, W. H., 102, 148, 192

Avon Books, 144, 155

Baird, Edwin, 53–55, 60

Ball, Clifford, 66, 146

Barsoom (planet), 179, 210, 224, 229. *See also* Burroughs, E. R.

Baudelaire, Charles, 59, 62

Beagle, Peter S., 160–62

Beckford, William, 18–19, 60

Bellairs, John, 165–67

Beowulf, 15, 16n, 65, 109, 111, 217

"Bethmoora," 219

Big Planet, 151, 202

Biography of Manuel, The (series), 43, 120. *See also* Cabell, James B.

Black Star, The, 190

Black Wheel, The, 85

Blavatsky, Helena Petrovna, 61, 136

Blish, James, 93, 225

Blue Star, The, 10, 81, 122

Boats of the 'Glen Carrig' The, 88–89

Bok, Hannes, 52, 83–84, 122–23

Book of Ptath, The, 85, 202

Book of Wonder, The, 32

Brackett, Leigh, 197, 201, 218

Brak the Barbarian (series), 123, 143, 179, 196–97. *See also* Jakes, John

Broken Sword, The, 153

The World's Best Adult Fantasy Ballantine Books Spring — 1973

ORLANDO FURIOSO: The Ring of Angelica, Volume I, translated by Richard Hodgens

THE CHARWOMAN'S SHADOW
Lord Dunsany

GREAT SHORT NOVELS OF ADULT FANTASY, Volume II, edited by Lin Carter

A VOYAGE TO ARCTURUS
David Lindsay

THE SUNDERING FLOOD
William Morris

IMAGINARY WORLDS
Lin Carter

To order by mail, send $1.25 per book plus 10¢ for handling to Dept. CS, Ballantine Books, 36 West 20th Street, New York, N.Y. 10003.

The World's Best Adult Fantasy
Ballantine Books
1972

To order by mail, send $1.25 per book plus
10¢ for handling to Dept. CS, Ballantine Books,
36 West 20th Street, New York, N.Y. 10003.